CW01239123

NI

Building the Future of Innovation
on millions of years of Natural Intelligence

Leen Gorissen

Copyright © 2020 by Leen Gorissen

All rights reserved. No part of this publication may be reproduced or transmitted by any means, except for the use of quotations in reviews or other non-commercial uses, without prior permission of the publisher.

ISBN: 978-94-6400-757-2

Cover picture by Raf Gorissen
Book design by Wordzworth

Published by Studio Transitio
www.studiotransitio.com

Studio Transitio does not have any control over, or any responsibility for, any author, company or third party websites referred to in or on this book.

More info:
www.naturalintelligence.info

This book is published through print-on-demand, meaning that it is only printed after each purchase which preserves resources and energy and reduces supply chain waste.

All paper for the publication of this book is sourced from SFI and/or FSC certified mills.

Logo design by GenesisDesign

For my grandparents,
who passed on their love for nature

And for Santiago,
the most beautiful spirit

Disclaimer

Nature always builds on what came before and this work is no different. Many pioneers have inspired me with their revolutionary insight, and I have tried to give tribute to these mentors wherever possible. The way I have interpreted their work however, rests solely with me. Of course, these pioneers also have been inspired by the work of those that came before them. It is therefore impossible to give credit to everyone who contributed to the scientific insights, the ideas, concepts and examples described in this book. Yet their work was as vital as the work of the ones mentioned. The pioneering companies that are described are a selection of companies that popped up during my research and the product information shared is all part of the public domain. I do not in any way profit from describing these products and companies in this book, nor have they asked me for their public endorsements. Although the author and publisher have made every effort to ensure that the information in this book was correct at press time, the author and publisher do not assume and hereby disclaim any liability to any party for any loss, damage, or disruption caused by errors or omissions, whether such errors or omissions result from negligence, accident, or any other cause.

Table of Contents

PREFACE   XIII

Aha! A revelatory sneeze   xiii

Of words and mindsets
   —and why they matter   xv

CHAPTER 1 – INTRODUCTION   1

We are not as good engineers, designers, and managers as we think we are   2

Towards a new paradigm for innovation   3

CHAPTER 2 – NEW INSIGHTS IN BIOLOGY CHANGE THE WAY WE LOOK AT THINGS   11

Life is the network
   —you are a society   12

It is not mutations that invent new things
   —it is learning at the genetic level that drives evolution   14

Forget the struggle
   —long term evolutionary success depends more on the snuggle for survival   15

The proof is in the patterns
   —macro level patterns are mirrored on the micro level and vice versa   19

Humans did not domesticate wolves, wolves domesticated themselves
   —it is the friendliest that have the survival advantage   24

Squid, Octopi and Boquila lianas hack and reprogram their own genes
    —*nature can shortcut the process of slow evolutionary change*   31

CHAPTER 3 – WELCOME TO THE AGE OF BIO-LOGICS   35

Bio-sphere
    —*mushrooms make rain, arctic foxes green the tundra,*
    whales cool the climate and wolves change rivers   36

Bio-logic
    —*life creates conditions pro life*   45

Bio-diverse
    —*biodiversity inoculates against extinction*   47

Towards business that is pro instead of anti-life   50

CHAPTER 4 – BIOLOGY IS THE TECHNOLOGY OF THE FUTURE   55

Bio-inspired
    —*building the future on millions of years of field tests*   56

Bio-logical
    —*it is only an investment if it leaves the world better off*   59

Bio-chemical
    —*nature's chemistry is biocompatible and biodegradable*   60

Bio-fabrication
    —*infrastructure is grown, not manufactured*   63

Bio-data
    —*nature's information systems advance collective intelligence*   66

Bio-hacking
    —*a fast track to evolutionary change*   67

Bio-philia
    —*nature not only makes us healthier;*
    she makes us happier and smarter too   70

CHAPTER 5 – IMPROVING BUSINESS AND THE WORLD THROUGH NI   75

Health Care	76
Energy	81
Agriculture	85
Buildings and Cities	93
Green Chemistry and Manufacturing	99
Human Resources and Organizational Development	105

CHAPTER 6 – CHANGING THE LOGIC OF VALUE CREATION   115

The nature of innovation and innovation in nature	116
From status quo thinking to regenerative thinking —*What can you do?*	123
From reducing negative impact to creating positive impact —*What can your company do?*	131
From degenerative to regenerative value creation —*What can the business world do?*	137

CHAPTER 7 – CONCLUSION   141

EPILOGUE   145

NOTES   147

PHOTOGRAPH CREDITS   169

ACKNOWLEDGEMENTS   171

GLOSSARY   173

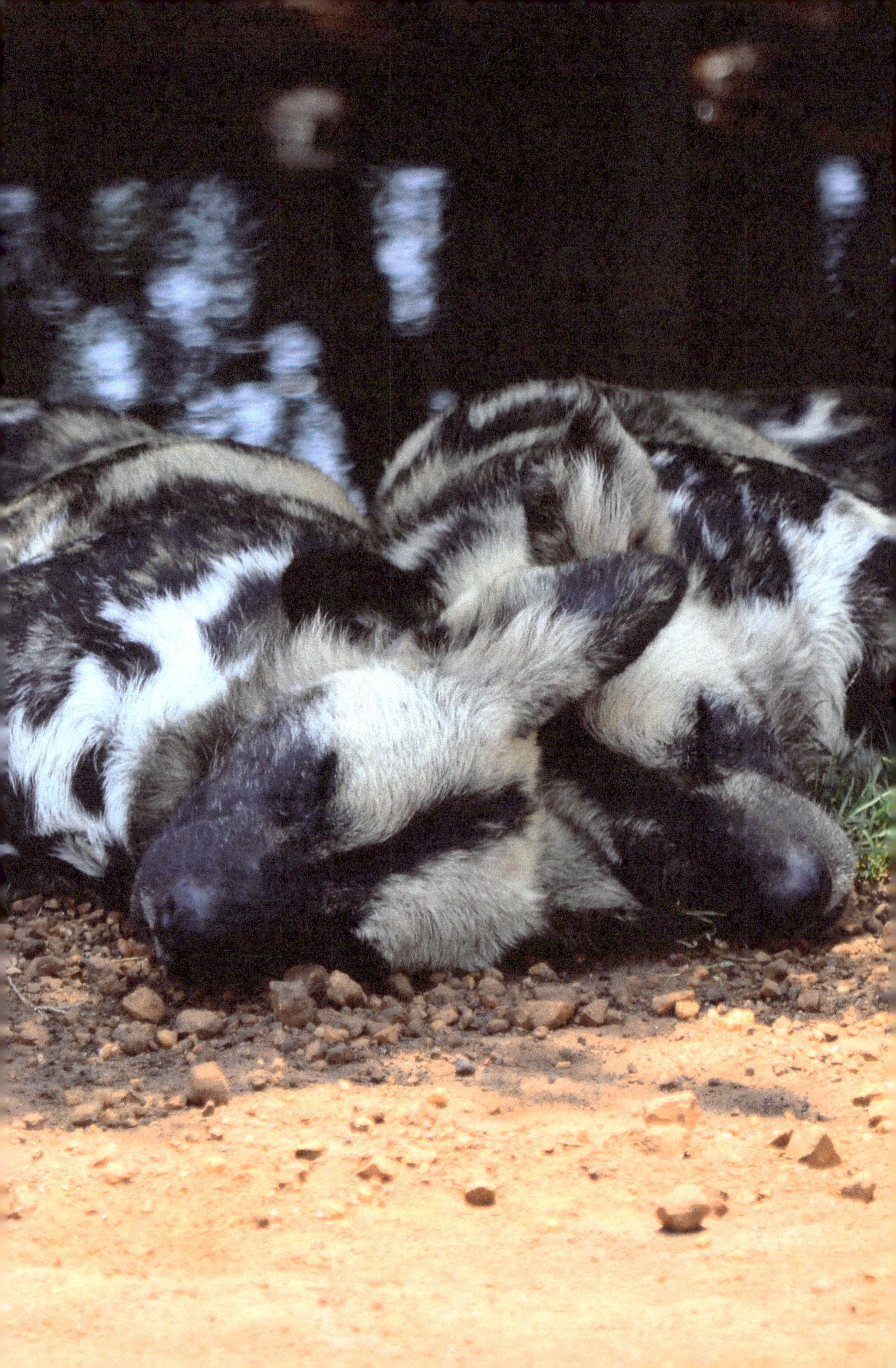

Preface

Aha! A revelatory sneeze

I learned an important lesson in humility from our dogs. Ours is a multispecies household, and like all good households, we learn together, by trial and error, how to make our cohabitation happy and efficient. For years I had been puzzled by our dogs' sneezing. At first, I thought that maybe our two adopted shelter dogs were allergic to something in the house, because we humans tend to associate sneezing with sickness or allergies. Yet that did not make any sense since we try to use eco-friendly and non-toxic detergents, paints, and products as much as possible. The rush of everyday life, juggling demanding jobs with a social life and a household kept me from a deeper exploration of this peculiar behavior, until one day I came across an article that showed how African wild dogs vote over pack decisions by sneezing.

The study showcased that sneezing is an important communication signal in collective decision-making processes of the pack. It is used to initiate a hunt by acting as a voting system or quorum. If a certain threshold was achieved, the group changed activity. Interestingly, if the dominant male and female sneezed, less sneezes were needed to start the hunt, but when they kept quiet, the group vote overruled the preferences of the dominant couple when the consensus between other pack members was sufficient.

Both my face and brain smiled with this new insight from biology, and the revelation still generates the same effect every time I think back to this Aha! moment. It was a truly humbling experience for me. As a trained biologist with a doctoral dissertation on bird communication, I am regarded as an expert in our human world. So how did this so-called expert miss such an important communication signal from two very close companions? I'll tell you how.

Our human advances in language and technology have disconnected us from the natural world, and our innovations have made us believe that we are better than and separate from nature. But this separateness and false sense of superiority are illusions. Bees, ants, and foxes use mathematics in a way that is far more sophisticated than we ever imagined. Slime mold, gelatinous aggregations of individual cells that swarm together, remember the shortest routes to food without a brain. Moisture-loving fungi make rain. Plankton create clouds when the sun burns too hot. Squid and octopus edit their own brain genes. And wild dogs use sneezing as a collective decision-making process to organize activities.

The natural world is far more clever than we humans realize, and the real question we should ask ourselves is posed by the title of Frans de Waal's book, *Are We Smart Enough to Know How Smart Animals Are?* Even though I acquired all the necessary credentials to be considered "smart" in the human world, my dogs proved how subjective our human take on "smart" really is.

What is more, their faithful sneezing to questions (or intentions—I am not sure just what part of human behavior they respond to exactly) also shows that they are more than just pets. Our dogs are active participants in the decision-making processes in our home. When my gaze has been glued too long to the computer screen, they come over and start sneezing, telling me it is time to exchange the virtual world for the natural one, that it is time for our daily hike in nature.

And that brings me to the focus of this book. While exponential technologies and radical disruption have gained a lot of airplay in the world of innovation, a tsunami of profound, new insights uncovered in the life sciences, many of which are real game changers for the ways we think about change, innovation and evolution, has largely gone unnoticed.

That is what this book is about. By combining knowledge from the world of research & development, innovation, and entrepreneurship with a background of and passion for understanding the natural world, I hope to inspire you *to rethink the nature of innovation.*

PREFACE

Of words and mindsets
—and why they matter

Before I take you on a journey to discover the ingenious ways in which nature works, I need to share a note on ways of thinking, language, and the conception and arrangement of this book. As a biologist trained in avian communication, I have learned that successful transfer of information requires the *sender* to tailor the signal to the antennae of the *receiver*. Or, put differently, if you want to be heard, you had better learn to speak the language of those you want to listen. This sums up the most challenging task of writing this book: to convey insights from biology into a language that is accessible to readers from the business spectrum, without disrespecting the integrity of the science.

It is not an easy task. Like any other discipline, biology has a very specialized jargon with specified definitions that aren't always easy to understand for non-specialists. To make things even more complicated, how information is processed within the receiver depends, to a large extent, on the glasses through which they interpret the world. There are two great minds that I would like to refer to here, because they coined the complications associated with mental models so articulately. The first is Robin Wall Kimmerer, enrolled member of the Citizen Potawatomi Nation and professor at the State University of New York. She writes, "We are all the product of our worldviews, even the scientists that claim pure objectivity." The second is Dee Hock, founder and emeritus CEO of VISA and the mastermind behind what is probably the most successful bio-inspired business model to date. He asserts, "Deep in most of us, below our awareness, indelibly implanted there by three centuries of the industrial age, is the mechanistic, separatist, cause-and-effect, command-and-control, machine model of reality."

I have learned that it is this deeply ingrained, yet unconscious way of thinking that forms the biggest barrier to the transformations our world urgently needs. We might have more information now than ever in history, yet we don't act in accordance to that information. The ever-increasing amount of data and knowledge isn't being processed into understanding, let alone wisdom. What is happening here? Again, Hock pinpoints it eloquently when he writes, "Native societies, which endured for centuries with little increase in the capacity to receive, utilize, store, transform, and transmit information, had time to develop a very high ratio of understanding and wisdom to data and information. They may not have known a great deal by today's standards, but they understood a very great deal about what they did know. They were enormously wise in relation to the extent to which they were informed, and their information was conditioned by a high ratio of social, economic, and spiritual value. In contrast, our society understands very little about what it knows. It has ever less understanding of the information at its command. It has ever less wisdom about the knowledge it develops. The immensity of data and information that assaults our lives is conditioned by an ever-declining ratio of social, economic, and spiritual value. Vast scientific, technological, and economic power is thus unleashed with inadequate understanding of its systemic propensity for destruction, or sufficient wisdom to creatively, constructively guide its evolution."

So, while you are reading this book, I invite you to think about your thinking and how your mental models might affect the way the information that is shared is processed in your brain.

It is not only mindsets that shape how we view the world. Language also plays an important role, and one we often fail to recognize. With Native American roots and an education in science, Kimmerer skillfully illustrates how our mechanistic model of reality has promoted a language that separates us from the natural world, a language that has led to objectification of nature. All living things are nowadays referred to as *it*, which means that we do not differentiate between living entities and nonliving products. In English, they are all *its*. By using *it*, Kimmerer explains, we distance ourselves and set others outside our circle of moral consideration.

It is no surprise then that the English language, the predominant language in scientific literature, reinforces the worldview of human exceptionalism and creates hierarchies of difference that justify our actions. Many indigenous languages, however, recognize other beings as our relatives, and grant personhood to other life forms beyond humans. They do not refer to living entities as *it*. These points on mindsets and language highlight how disconnected we have become from all other species that share the planet with us, which in turn, offers (part of) the explanation as to why we understand so little about the ways in which life works.

PREFACE

There is another tricky challenge which matters for innovation, which is that our language often lacks truthfulness. How is it that centuries of human development have led to…

> governments that can't govern
> economies that can't economize
> corporations that can't incorporate
> schools that don't get the essence of learning
> investments that don't leave the world better off
> consumer goods that don't do good
> healthcare systems that don't care
> tax systems that are unfair

Yet, words build worlds. Even using the word *nature* reinforces the disconnect between humans and the rest of life. That's why the focus of this book—to bridge the world of biology with the world of business through language—is a slippery endeavor. And if I slip up, the error is mine, because, of course, my world view also determines what I see. As my understanding is a continuous work in progress, so is the thinking shared in this book.

Before you read on, it is important to highlight that I will be mingling words from biology and words from the business world. But when I describe biological processes, I use many words with their definitions that originate in biology. This means that these words might have a different meaning than what is generally understood in terms of our current innovation culture. For instance, when I talk about *design* in nature, I am referring to the total of all adaptations that allows an organism to appropriately respond to the dynamics of change that it has been exposed to since it originated. When I use the word *degenerative*, I am referring to a process that leads to decline and deterioration.

Another tricky word is *natural,* as we often assume the cultural connotation behind it. In his book *Sapiens*, Yuval Noah Harari writes, "Culture tends to argue that it forbids only that which is unnatural. But from a biological perspective, nothing is unnatural. Whatever is possible is by definition also natural… In truth, our concepts 'natural' and 'unnatural' are not taken from biology, but from Christian theology." He argues that a good rule of thumb to distinguish between what nature does and what people merely try to justify through biological myth is the phrase, "biology enables, culture forbids." More definitions are provided in the glossary at the back of the book.

Finally, a word on the structure of the book. If you like to be surprised, then you might want to skip this paragraph and see where the story takes you. But if you are reading this book a few pages at a time, then it might help to understand the logic behind the structure of the book. **Chapter one** starts off with a short rationale on why we need to transform the way we innovate. **Chapter two** discloses new insights from the life sciences and why they may radically change the way we look at change and innovation in businesses, organizations, and society at large. **Chapter three** subsequently zooms in on the way life works, and the chapter ends with what these learnings may mean for the future of business. **Chapter four** sums up and describes core features of innovation based on Natural Intelligence. **Chapter five** highlights a selection of pioneers from the business world who, in one way or another, already adopted this NI-inspired innovation and the novelties and inventions that they have developed. **Chapter six** then digs deeper into how nature might inform the nature of innovation, introducing a new way of looking at innovation paradigms through the perspective of Natural Intelligence, and ending with more demonstrative examples on the individual, organizational and network level. **Chapter seven** finally offers a concluding reflection and a few ideas on how to transform the nature of our innovation.

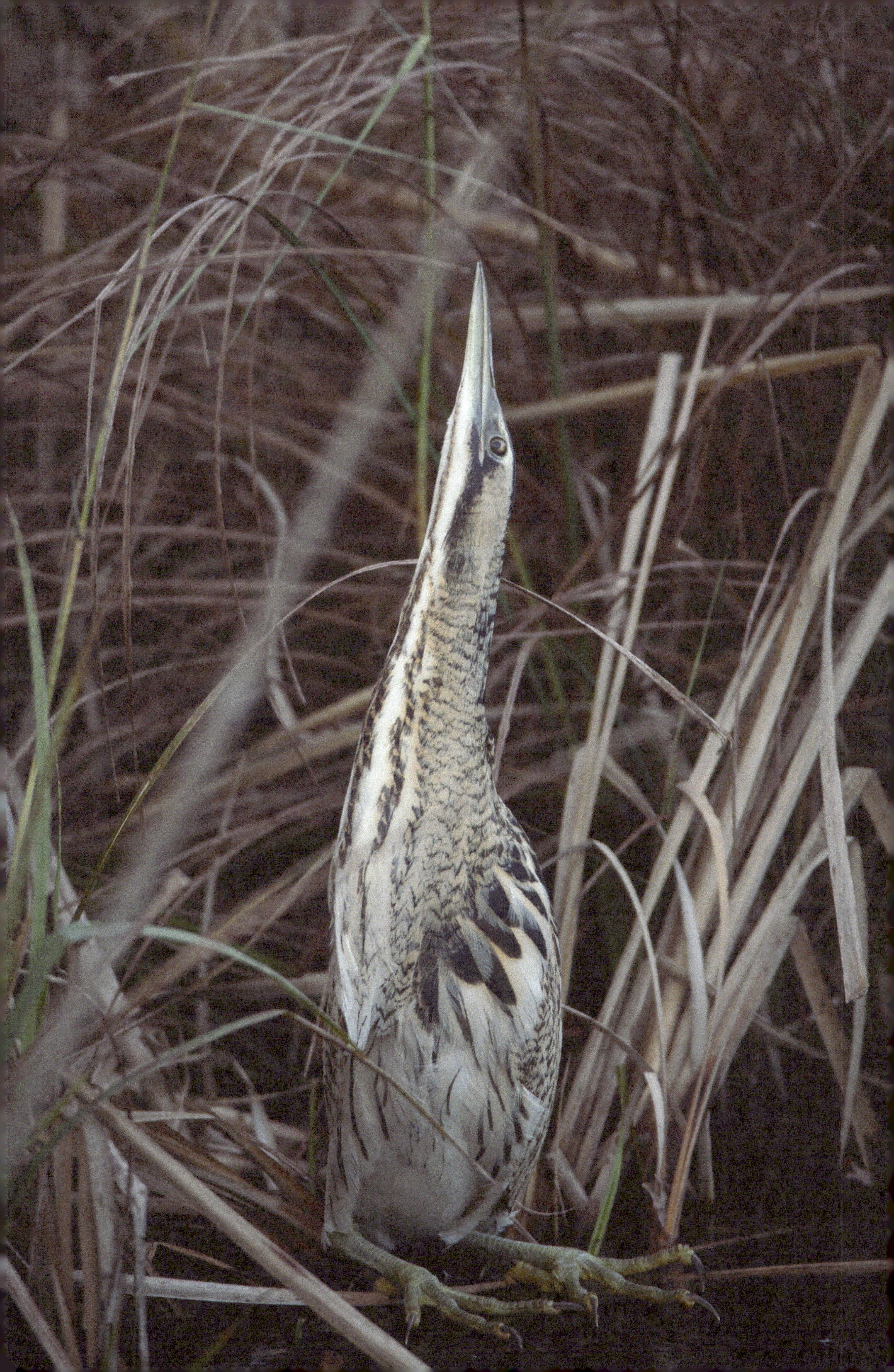

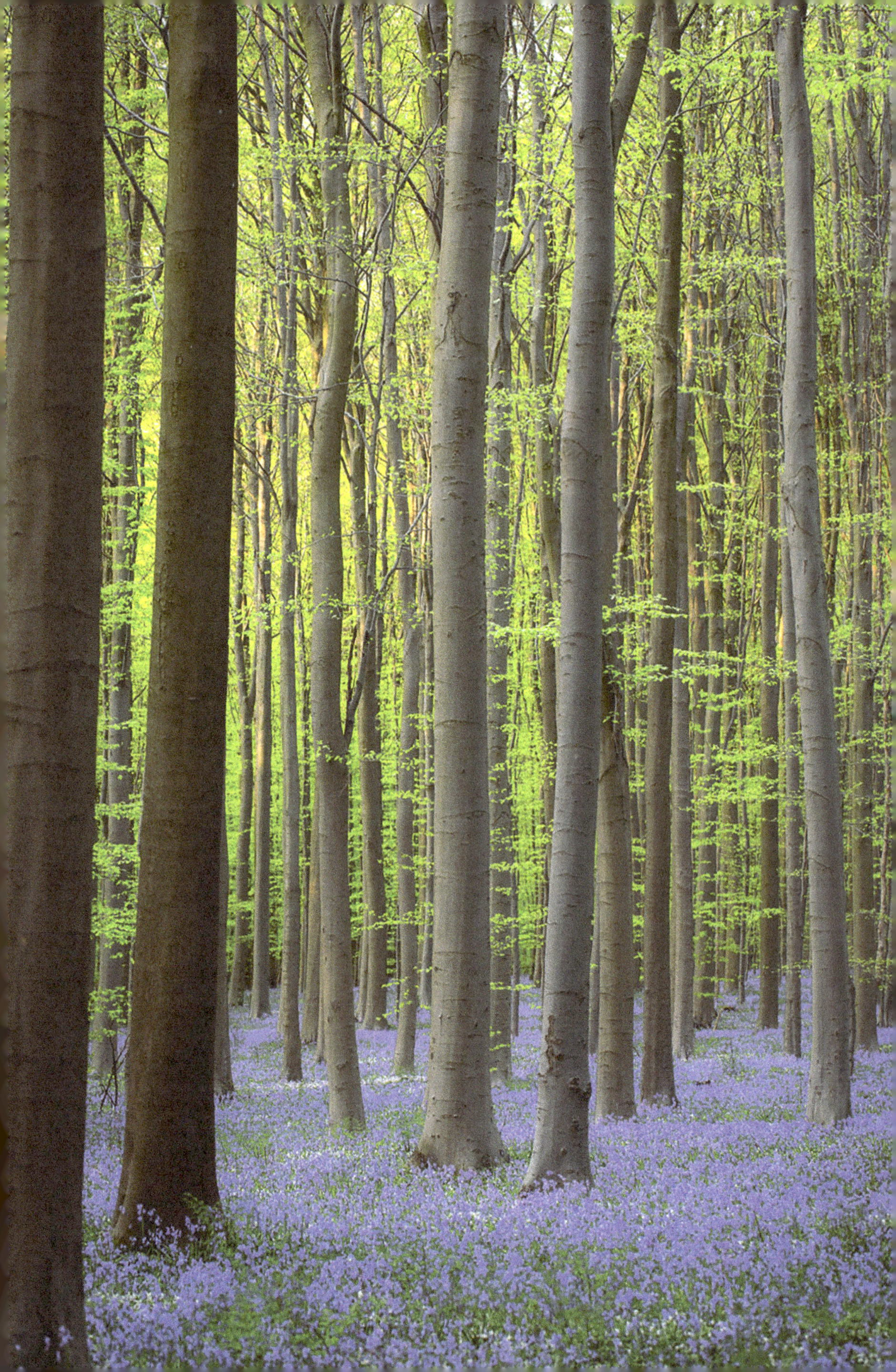

CHAPTER 1

INTRODUCTION

We are not as good engineers, designers, and managers as we think we are

As humans, we have created and achieved incredible things. We have conquered every piece of land and mobilized an astonishing amount of resources for human expansion. We have overcome the harshest conditions, from mining the deep sea to flying into space. Yet, our progress has come with serious side effects, which not only erode our environmental life-support system, but erode our human nature too. On a planetary scale, we face challenges such as climate change, resource depletion, biodiversity loss, ecotoxicity, and ecosystem collapse, to name but a few. On a human scale, exhaustion, attention disorders, allergies, cancer, burn-out, and depression are on the rise at an alarming pace.

Instead of getting smarter, innovation is actually making us more obtuse. Recent scientific evidence shows that ecotoxicity, like air pollution, impedes cognitive ability and while techno-economic progress has significantly extended both human wealth and life span, the number of healthy years is actually declining. As a citizen of the so-called developed world, I wonder, have we developed the wrong things? Have we forgotten to develop ourselves?

We have created powerful agents that trick and cheat to defend the status quo. The income gap between rich and poor keeps growing, while trust in public authorities is dwindling. We pay intelligent minds to develop strategies of planned obsolescence (artificially limiting the useful life of products) and to direct our attention to social media platforms that take away our time, focus and energy from real human interaction. All of which comes from the mindset of *how to generate more profit*. But are we really profiting or are we entertaining and enterprising ourselves into extinction?

Mass production makes our products cheaper; however, what we do not pay in money, we end up paying in health, viability, and quality of life. More than 80% of tap water worldwide is polluted with microscopic plastic particles that disrupt hormones and other vital, physical processes. Infants are born with hundreds of harmful chemicals in their bodies. Skyrocketing glyphosate use in gardens, on golf courses, and in agriculture has entered the air we breathe, the water we drink, the soil we live on, and even our own bodies. The chemical cocktail we expose ourselves to is aggravated by air pollution, linked to cancer, asthma, stroke and heart disease, diabetes, obesity, dementia and other neuropsychiatric complications. In the UK alone, around 40,000 deaths each year are attributed to exposure to outdoor air pollution, costing health care and business more than £20 billion every year. These man-made particles and chemicals are not life-friendly, and every habitat on Earth is affected by them. They are wiping out life at a frightening pace. Yet the rush of our rat-race world prevents us from noticing insectageddon, the dramatic coral reef die off, the explosion of mental and physical health problems, and the paradox of our way of life: sacrificing nature and our health to make money, only to spend that money again to restore nature and our health.

And while we make some pretty cool gadgets, like smart phones and robots, we are still highly inefficient in our manufacturing processes. According to the recent circularity gap report, our entire industrial system operates at only 9% efficiency. That means that more than 90% of resources end up as waste. In North America, only 1% of materials is still in use after six months. No wonder that only 25% of employees worldwide are motivated in their job. Who takes pride in making a product that ends up as waste within months?

Rogier De Langhe, a Belgian economic philosopher, says that the current burn-out epidemic is not a crisis of work overload, but one of meaning: people lack meaningfulness in their jobs. Even though humans tend to forget, we share the same purpose as the rest of life. Life wants to live. Evolutionary Biologist Tamsin Woolley-Barker said it best, "Life wants to create the next generation and ensure its success." Therefore, meaningless jobs that trash the planet are eroding human nature too.

While there are many more examples that illustrate the dark side of innovation-as-usual, I hope you get the gist of the rationale: We are not as good engineers, designers, and managers as we think we are. The majority of the solutions society devised during the industrial revolution are now creating more problems instead of solutions. Pesticides create super pests. Antibiotics create super bugs. Chemotherapy creates super cancer cells. We are in an arms race which innovation-as-usual cannot win.

Towards a new paradigm for innovation

It is clear that we need a new paradigm for innovation. So where to look for inspiration? We can scan the cosmos for intelligent, extra-terrestrial life, or we can bet on artificial intelligence and hope that ET and AI will spare us, which many great minds think is unlikely given the magnitude of human induced deterioration. And while AI is still in diapers, NI (Natural Intelligence) has been around for 3.8 billion years, surviving and thriving despite change, shocks, and disruption.

Biomimicry3.8, the first organization worldwide to translate nature's pre-tested strategies into design principles for human innovation challenges, illustrates brilliantly what 3.8 billion years of life on Earth means by summarizing the history of the Earth into one calendar year. From this time perspective, all of human history takes place in the last half hour of December 31. The industrial revolution takes place in the last two seconds before New Year's Eve. As relative novices on Earth, the biggest challenge for humans is therefore to avoid joining the 99.9% of species that once inhabited our planet but are now extinct.

This viewpoint eloquently illustrates that it is not the world that needs saving. We do. That may sound dramatic but consider the facts. We have filled nearly every inhabitable place on Earth, we are exploiting resources at a pace greater than the planet can replenish, and we have no planet B. Spaceship Earth is it. Maybe it is time, to quote Jonathon Porritt's words, "to consider living on the earth as if we intend to stay here." Evolution is not just about quantitative growth. It is also about qualitative growth and about learning to become self-renewing right where we are. Because in nature, those that resist evolution become extinct. If we cannot evolve ourselves, our businesses, and our institutions, we will end up like the dinosaurs. And we cannot transform our systems unless we transform our mindsets.

To shift our innovation paradigm, we need to become aware of the mechanistic, reductionist goggles through which we have interpreted the world since the industrial revolution. We have created academic ivory towers, business monopolies and governmental silos, and divided disciplines, policies and responsibilities. We have compartmentalized the things we do for money from the things we do for love. Look how many of us escape the sterile cemented cities in the weekend for a dose of nature while supporting business models that devour, pollute or degrade the natural environment during the week. Or how many of us take pills to restore gut microbiota but still use detergents and pesticides that wipe out beneficial microbiota in and around the house. How many of us invest in the quality of life for our family pet, yet buy meat that is mass-produced at facilities that have no regard for the quality of life of the animals they keep? If we want to stay around for the long run and maintain our health, viability, and quality of life, we need to revise our ways of degenerative thinking and doing.

INTRODUCTION

It is time to *think outside* and tap into the Natural Intelligence that surrounds us. While we are a relatively young species on this planet, there are some organisms that have been around for millions of years, withstanding generations of change and disruption, and colonizing all parts of the world. Or in the words of Janine Benyus, natural science writer and co-founder of the Biomimicry3.8 institute, "After 3.8 billion years of evolution, nature has learned what works, what is appropriate, what lasts." Natural Intelligence, consequently, is far more sophisticated than human intelligence. Nature designs, nurses, communicates, heals, experiments, calculates, reprograms, and advances. Ecological economist and Professor Robert Costanza describes it like this, "Evolution is in a very real sense intelligent. It can learn from experience and improve." Currently, we are learning the hard way that deeply ingrained rational, analytic, and reductionist ways of thinking fall short when addressing complex, real world characteristics, such as non-linearity, uncertainty, volatility, and randomness. In an increasingly unpredictable world, we will have to learn to develop and rely more on inter-relational, whole living systems thinking—something a bit closer aligned to intuition rather than ratio.

Learning from the natural world is becoming increasingly popular, and several established businesses like Google, Nike, Patagonia, Boeing, Kohler, Natura, Ford, Procter & Gamble, General Electric, HOK Architects and Kraft are tapping into the powers of Natural Intelligence. What is more, pioneering business enterprises, like Interface, Pax Scientific, Sharklet Technologies, Columbia Forest Products, Warner Babcock Institute for Green Chemistry, Biomatrica, Blue Planet, Turbulent, Veryan Medical, Waggl, and New Forest Farm, are not only showcasing that bio-inspired innovation makes business sense, but they are changing the rules of the game in the process. More on this in Chapter 5.

And it is not only the business world that is discovering NI. Topics like swarm logic, self-organization, circular economy, nature-based, and regenerative design are entering the public and civic domain as well. When the U.S. Green Building Council realized that a hierarchical, top-down approach was not supporting their mission nor boosting their relevance and performance, the organization adopted a different reorganization strategy inspired by the symbiotic interdependence between fungi and trees. This networked system is largely self-organized and works with keystone species instead of hierarchies. Mimicking this interdependent system allows the USGBC to develop an interlaced system of shared information across the entire network, organized around important nodes (like keystone species) rather than hierarchical elements.

In 2019, the European Commission announced the European Green Deal, which aims to make Europe the first climate-neutral continent by 2050, boosting the economy, improving people's health and quality of life, caring for nature, and leaving no one behind. To finance the transition, the European Commission pledged to dedicate at least 25% of the EU's long-term budget to climate action, and the European Investment Bank will provide further support.

Another example of nature inspired design entering the civic realm is permaculture. Permaculture is a design philosophy and framework that draws inspiration from natural ecosystems to develop more ecologically sound and regenerative ways of living and feeding the world. In place of controlling and fighting nature, as conventional agricultural practices, permaculture practitioners set out to collaborate with nature. They develop the land in harmony with the dynamics of living systems (working with nature and promoting biodiversity) and not only produce healthier food but support a wide variety of ecosystem services, such as carbon sequestration, oxygen production, nutrient cycling, pollination, and water purification. Because permaculture is a design approach that considers the relationships between organisms within and across all kingdoms of life, it explores how humans can positively contribute to their environment and the rest of life on our planet.

In 2016, three million permaculture practitioners in 140 countries produced food in a life-friendly, regenerative way. What is more, the practice of permaculture is multiplying at an incredible speed across the globe, so by the time you're reading this, that number is probably much higher. While these are just a few examples, they illustrate the fact that more and more, we are looking to nature for guidance to come up with more sustainable, more well-adapted and more resilient answers for the future. Finally, bio-inspired innovation is taking root.

Even though the practice of nature-inspired innovation is not new—as many indigenous cultures have been practicing this for centuries—the discipline of intentionally emulating NI to improve contemporary organizational, manufacturing, agrarian, and design logic is. After spending nearly a decade in sustainability research and development, I have come to conclude that the most promising fields for future-proofing innovation are *biomimicry, permaculture, regenerative design and development, biophilic design* and *living systems thinking*.

INTRODUCTION

These fields work to shift innovation from degradation to regeneration and from short-term profit to long-term benefit. And each improves efficiency, adaptability, and resilience. They go further than mere bio-utilization which is the focus of most nature-based solutions (using nature for beneficial purposes such as, integrating green roofs in buildings to promote energy efficiency, air quality, and water retention) because they tap into the intelligence of the natural world. Regenerative design and development, biomimicry and permaculture particularly, use the design and organizational logic deeply embedded in natural systems and perfected through millions of years of field tests to inform product design, production and manufacturing, human development, organizational development, and building and landscape design.

Their focus is bio-inspired innovation—innovating like nature, which is not merely copying and pasting nature's solutions. It is about changing our mindsets, our businesses, and our institutions to incorporate a capacity for evolution. It is about ending up on the 0.1% of the equation.

Nature's prevailing systems are incredibly creative, diverse, and complex, and we have only started to uncover just how interrelated everything in nature is. If you think of a car, you can have all the parts of a car, but the parts alone will not take you anywhere. You need all the parts to function in their proper relationship, fulfilling their proper role, before the car becomes a means of transport. The whole is a lot more than the sum of the parts. The difference between a mechanical system like a car and a living ecosystem is that in the latter both the parts and the relationships evolve.

We do not live in a mechanical world but in a living one, which is why it is vital to increase our understanding of living systems, and also why I cluster the fields mentioned above. Even though they have different foci, they all fit under the umbrella of Natural Intelligence (NI), because they are all based on an understanding of living systems.

Before we go on, I want to articulate exactly what I mean when I use the word *intelligence* in this book. I use a slightly different definition of intelligence than the one we humans generally use, a definition that focuses on human intellectual capacities such as logic, understanding, and reasoning. When I use intelligence, I am referring to life's intelligence, which is based on a big history perspective and remains present in all species that have managed to stay alive for eons.

Natural Intelligence then, is the combination of all success factors that have allowed life to endure despite millions of years of change, disruption and major upheaval. It refers to the intelligence deeply embedded in all life forms, the kind of intelligence that has stood the test of time. That is why the infinity symbol is fitting as an icon for NI. Because at its core, the life that endures always creates conditions pro-life.

This is the opposite of what we have been doing up until now. Luckily, the tide is turning. Breakthrough innovations in science and technology have spurred our understanding and appreciation of the living world and as our knowledge of NI grows, it is overturning the ways in which we think about innovation, change, and sustainability. Because once you understand how life works, you will see that sustainability is the by-product of regenerative value creation. Only those that add value to their environment, that invest in the biosphere, will last over the long haul.

If *you* want to be part of a business that is fit for the future, I invite you to keep reading. In this book, I will share some of the most incredible recent discoveries in biology and show you *how they can drastically change the way we look at and do business*. Tapping into the oldest form of intelligence can help us (re)design products, manufacturing processes, business models, buildings, factories, cities, and landscapes to be supportive to life. I will also feature some of the most ground-breaking companies that apply this kind of thinking and how the natural world has inspired them to come up with game-changing innovations that may well become huge disruptors of business-as-usual.

Michelle Holiday captures our current predicament lucidly, "Humanity is at a fork in the road. In one direction: struggle, division and despair. In the other: wisdom, compassion and thriving." Building the future of innovation on millions of years of NI is not only possible and feasible, it points away from a future of depletion, crises and misery towards the "Age of Thrivability".

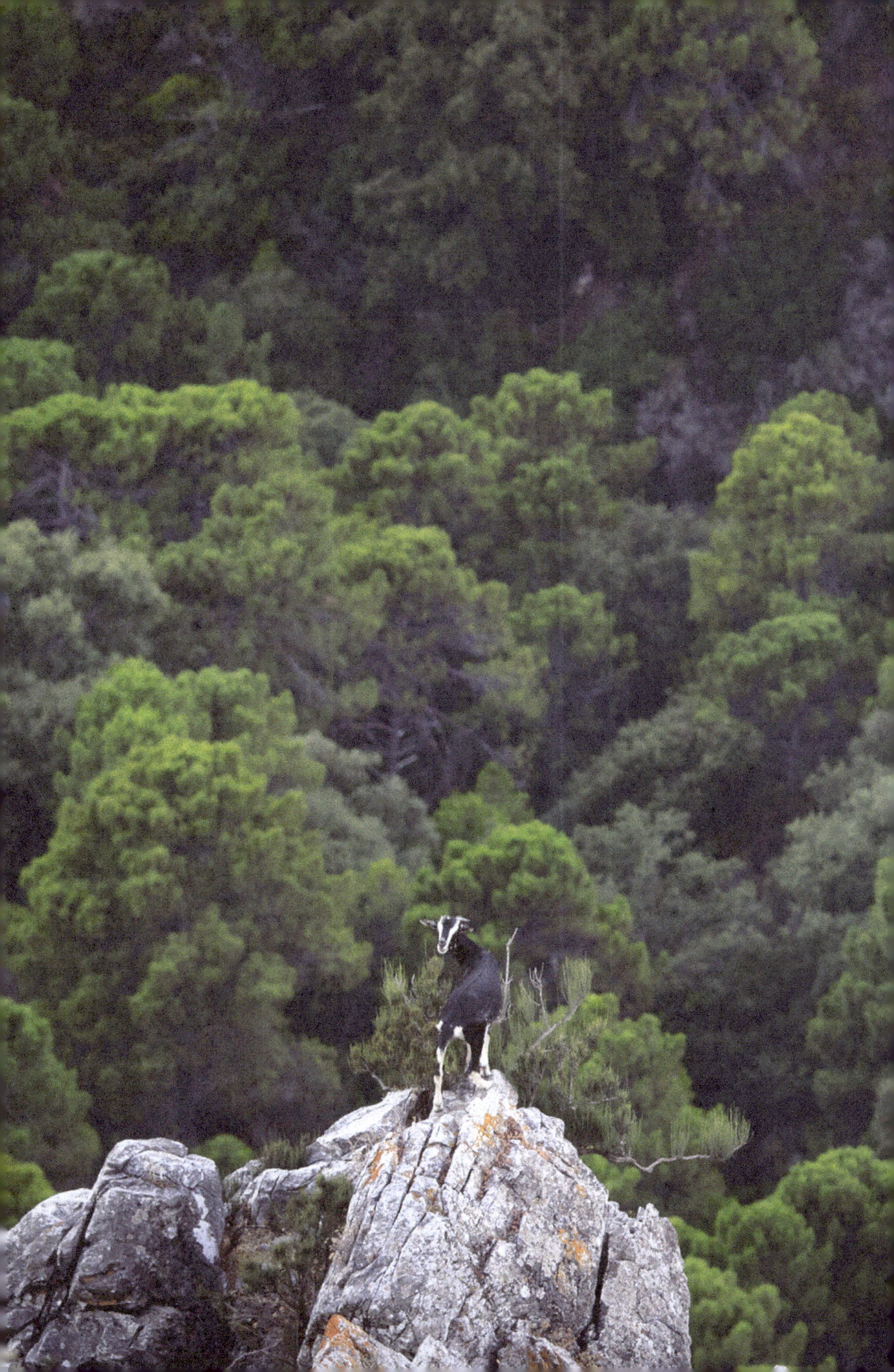

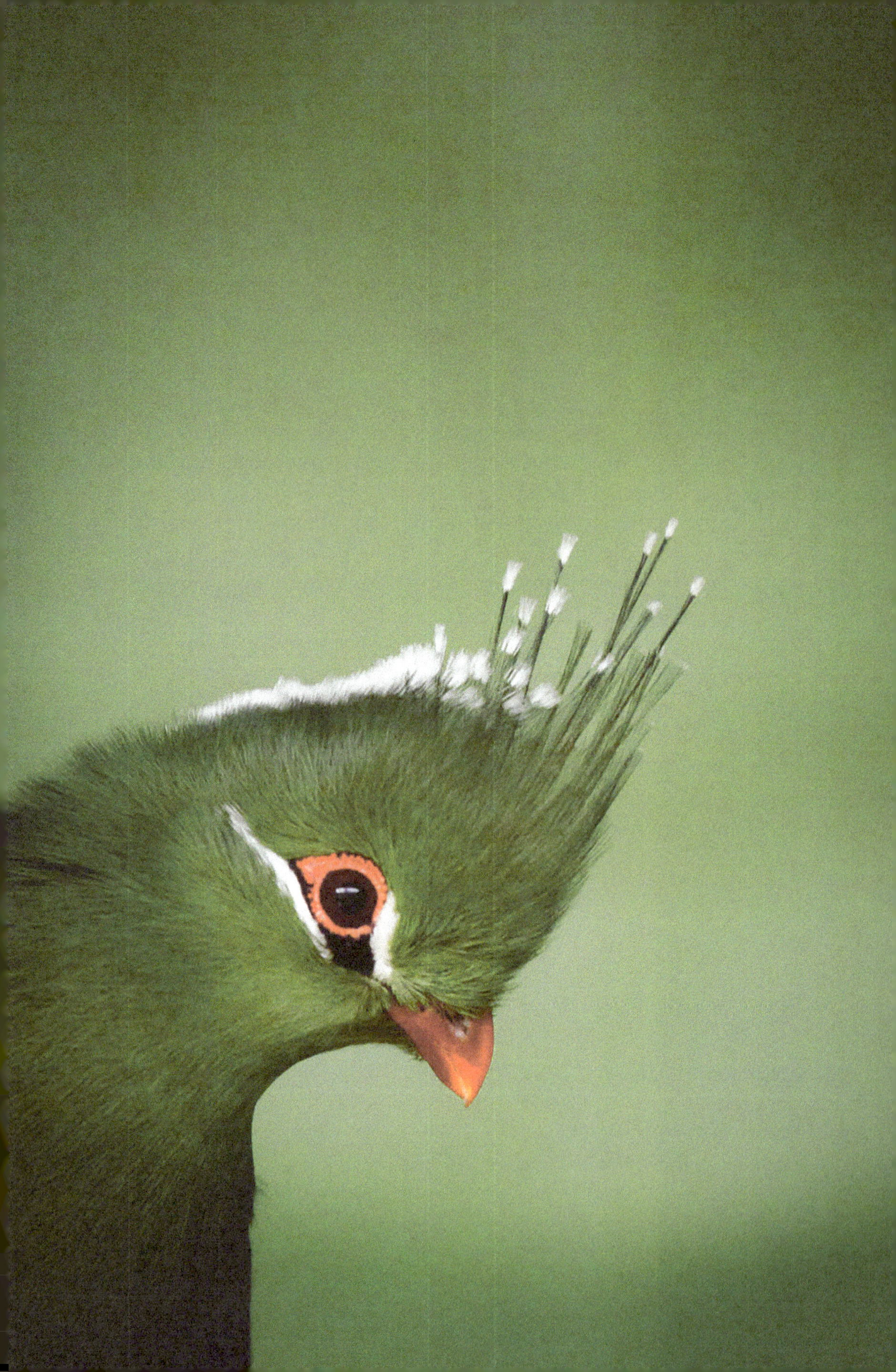

CHAPTER 2

NEW INSIGHTS IN BIOLOGY CHANGE THE WAY WE LOOK AT THINGS

Life is the network
—you are a society

More and more, we are learning that the fundamental unit of nature is not the self, but the network. Pulitzer Prize finalist and Biology Professor David George Haskell states that individuality is nothing more than the temporary manifestation of relationship. The self in itself, is a society.

These statements do not come out of thin air. They are backed up by breakthroughs in science. Professor Haskell illustrates his theory through the example of a leaf: a leaf of a tree is made up of more than plant cells. In fact, one leaf comprises millions of non-plant cells from many domains and kingdoms of life, all working together to turn sunlight into sugar. It is a community of algae, fungi, bacteria, protists, nematodes, and plant cells. Studies of DNA reveal hundreds of species in every leaf. A leaf is thus a multispecies community: it is made of relationships. And so is the human body.

According to recent estimates, in our body non-human cells outnumber human cells by approximately 8 trillion. The human body is a community too, like the leaf. We ourselves are the perfect examples to show how networked relationships are vital to life, that networks work. The beneficial associations between human and microbial cells inside our body (often referred to as the human microbiome when wholesome) help us digest a wide variety of food and keep us healthy and energetic. The same logic applies to large ecosystems. For example, beneficial associations between fungi and trees allow forests to produce food for an entire ecosystem of organisms in the process. In fact, before humans started massive deforestation activities, forest ecosystems were one of the most successful ecosystems on land, colonizing not just the temperate, Mediterranean, subtropical, and tropical climates but the boreal and subarctic regions too. They even moved into the coastal areas by evolving specific features to grow in saltwater environments. We know such forests as mangroves. But that is not all that we can learn from forest ecosystems.

The networked configuration of forests allows them to interact with and even alter the chemical and physical features of the environment in which they live. Few people know that fungi mine rocks. As a matter of fact, fungi are probably the largest mining cooperative on Earth. This networked alliance between fungi and trees is what biologists call mycorrhiza or the Wood Wide Web. This subsoil internet was invented more than 400 million years ago. It is probably also one of the earliest trade associations between different partners with access to different resources.

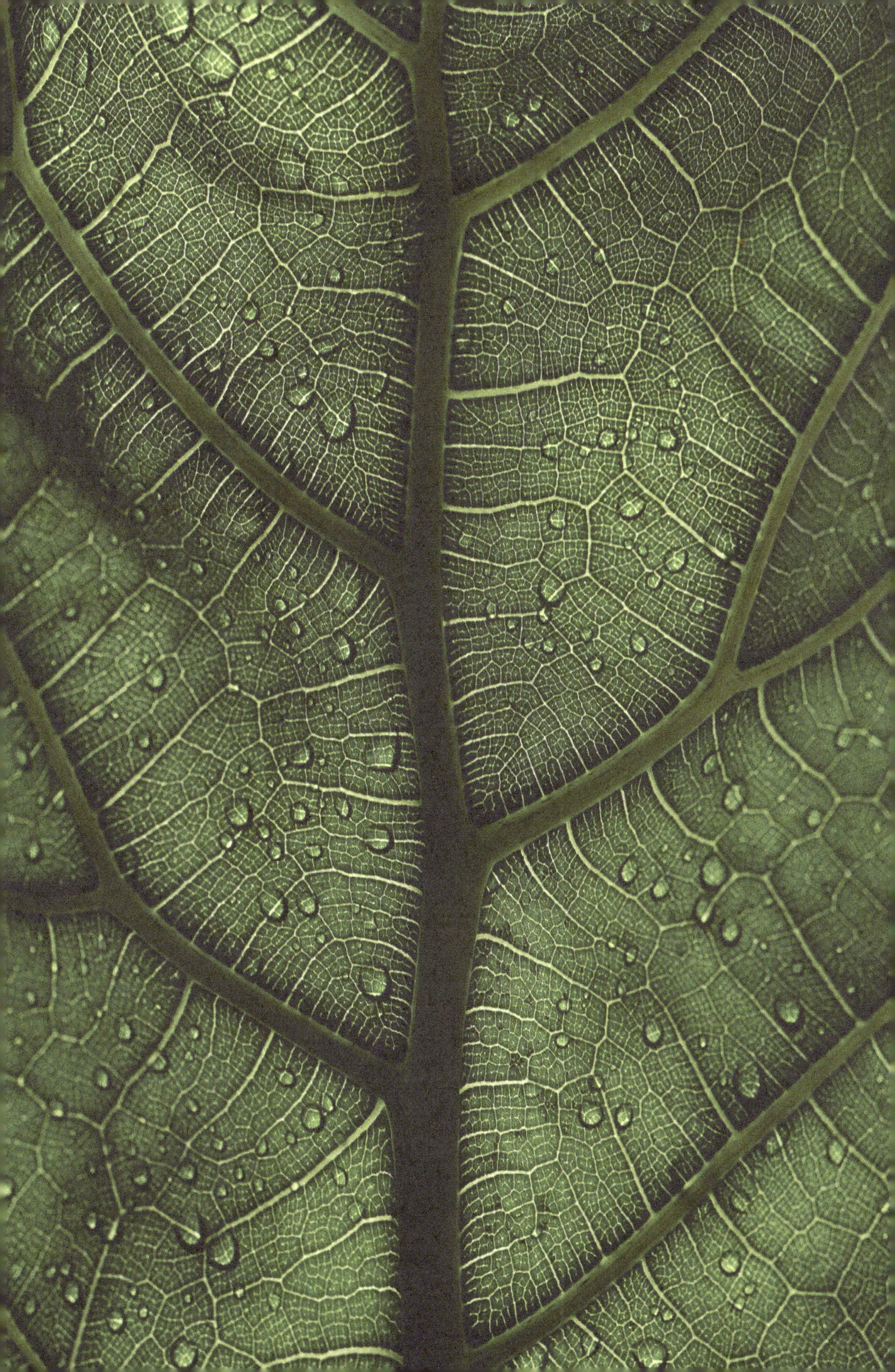

Put simply, the trees function as sugar daddies. They turn carbon, sunlight, and water into sugars, and produce oxygen as a byproduct. Sugars are hard to come by for soil dwelling creatures, like fungi. Fungi, on the other hand, have access to a wide variety of soil-bound nutrients and minerals like phosphorus, nitrogen, copper, iron, and magnesium, which are essential for plant growth. The fungal mineral mamas trade these precious dirt-derived resources with the trees and produce nutritious mushrooms in the process. This alliance between fungi and trees means that together they can access far more resources than they could on their own. What is more, their symbiosis leaves the entire ecosystem better off and better equipped to grow and expand into new territories. These insights also highlight that the emergence of byproducts, like oxygen and mushrooms, where traits that evolved for one purpose have come to serve other purposes, is not a side-issue but absolutely fundamental to evolution. It reveals that the networked way of life is an ancient one.

More importantly, these lessons show us that the world is made of more than just transactions. It is the byproducts generated and the reciprocal relationships that create a cascade of positive impacts producing more life with life. Life *is* the network and evolves *through* the network. Everything is connected to everything. No organism can survive on its own. The web of life is the glue that holds life on Earth together. Through networks of interdependence species create habitats for one another, upgrade their environments, and thrive as a result.

It is not mutations that invent new things —it is learning at the genetic level that drives evolution

Evolution isn't quite the random process as previously thought. Traditionally, biologists have thought that new genetic information is created as the result of mutations, which are considered accidents, disconnected from the living network. However, Adi Livnat from the University of Haifa's Institute of Evolution illustrates that instead of such haphazard pointwise mutations, novelty arises from network-level change that is neither random nor accidental. He states that the inherent ability of elements to come together into novel and relevant higher-level interactions is the source of innovation throughout evolution, and he defines this new framework as "interaction-based evolution." What is even more mind-boggling, building on empirical observations, Livnat compellingly demonstrates that evolution is driven by learning at the genetic level, which is a total upending of the traditional view in biology that mutation is the result of a random accident.

Through a process of learning, a physical and behavioral identity called phenotype can become hardwired into a genetic identity or genotype. This means that the context of an organism and how it fits in its environment is translated into its genetic code, a process which can induce novel qualities or behaviors and give rise to innate features. For example, pointing in pointer dogs—freezing to show the location of the prey instead of hunting it down—did not occur suddenly and haphazardly. It arose through learning processes that were gradually hardwired into their genomes until it became innate. Nowadays, some pointer dogs can point without any learning, because the behavior comes to them naturally. In his paper, Livnat argues that there are no genes dedicated to pointing per se, but rather that pointing is the result of network-level change. That is, it is not mutations that invent new things, it's the network-level learning which absorbs meaning from context that sparks evolution.

Livnat's insights show that the traditional mutation-based view of evolutionary change might no longer hold into the 21st century. Instead, a network-based view of evolutionary change might help us better understand the nature of innovation and can even eradicate the theory of the origin of life in an instant. In short, evolution learns, and it does so through an ever-evolving genetic network and database. Its drivers are not random. According to interaction-based evolution, innovation starts from networks that translate learnings derived from context into novel capabilities and adaptations. Put differently, learning and evolution are linked, and the network is core to the evolution of innovation.

Forget the struggle
—long term evolutionary success depends more on the snuggle for survival

There are endless lessons to be learned from the forested way of life. Over millions of years, forests have been able to survive ice ages, hurricanes, wildfires, avalanches, and meteorite impacts, and not because it is "every tree for itself." Trees in forests often entangle their roots. That way they can spread the pressure of fierce winds across a large surface, making individual trees less prone to be

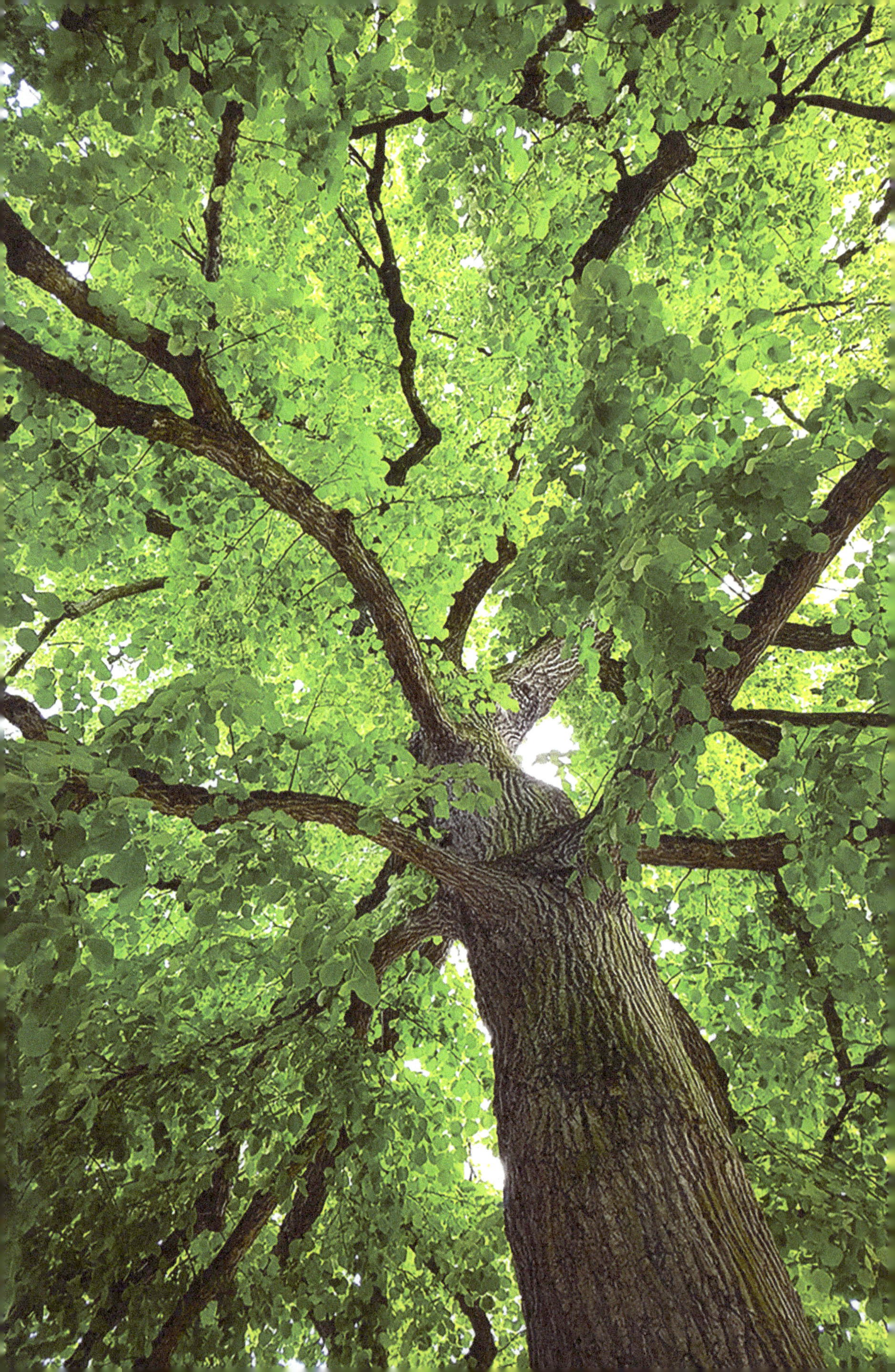

blown to bits. They share food too, not only with their own offspring and root fungi, but with many other non-related tree species.

A recent study in Science showed that up to 40% of the carbon absorbed by a 40-meter-tall spruce was traded over to a neighboring beech, larch, and pine tree. You see, neighboring trees of different species do more than compete for space, nutrients, and water. They share. They support each other. Because the best way for a tree to ensure its health is to invest in the health of others. Not only do they share food, they share health care services as well. That is, if one tree gets attacked by a specific bug species, it shares this information through the Wood Wide Web, and in a response, the surrounding trees raise their defenses. By doing so, the tree neighborhood releases a specific chemical signal that attracts the predator of this specific bug. With more of them waving this signal, the chance of attracting the enemy of their enemy is much higher.

So, why are trees mostly good neighbors to each other? "Because it doesn't make evolutionary sense for trees to behave like competitive resource-grabbing individualists," said Suzanne Simard, a Professor of Forest Ecology and expert on the Wood Wide Web at the University of British Columbia in Vancouver. "Trees live longer and reproduce more in a healthy stable forest." In a way, these findings show that forests are sophisticated social systems, governed by more than the struggle for survival. To care for community is therefore not exclusively human. As many permaculturists know, plants do not only invest in themselves and their offspring, they invest in their communities too. And while there are plenty of examples of predation and competition in nature, we now know that the prevailing relationships in nature are cooperative. Long-term evolutionary success is much more about the snuggle for survival. You have my back and I have yours.

Wait, isn't the dominant theory of evolutionary success based on Charles Darwin's notion of "survival of the fittest", which in economic terms has been popularized as the smartest, strongest, or meanest having the evolutionary advantage over the others? And which in popular culture still holds sway in the conviction that competition is the driving force of innovation. Yes, unfortunately, this has been the dominant theory for a long time. Regrettably, because what Darwin actually meant was "the fitting-est," the one best fitted (or adapted) to his or her environment.

Darwin also wrote that the most important cause of evolutionary change is the way organisms relate to one another, which can be either "by the improvement or the extermination of others." Society has given a lot of airplay to the struggles, fights and battles, which are about competition, and very little attention to the improvement of others, which is about cooperation. Fortunately, as described in the previous section, biologists are learning that competition plays a far less significant role than previously thought.

According to Dayna Baumeister, Professor and Co-director of the Biomimicry Center of Arizona State University and co-founder of the Biomimicry3.8 consultancy, competition in nature is actually rare and for a good reason. Just ask any nature filmmaker how many hours of footage they need to shoot to catch that thirty-second glimpse of two animals fighting. More often than not, it takes days, if not weeks, instead of hours. She explains that, for the most part, disputes in terms of access to food or partners in the wild are settled by less aggressive behaviors, simply by sizing each other up through a stare or growl. Because direct aggressive competition is both costly and risky, living organisms tend to avoid it altogether.

Baumeister further explains that we might witness short bouts of conflict as an interaction, but not as a relationship that exists over time. In fact, she argues, life evolves toward alternative strategies to competition. This certainly corroborates the experience of filmmakers. It usually takes dozens of hours of peaceful footage before the occasional competitive outburst is registered, which often lasts less than a minute. Spectacle sells, but the popular conviction that it is a dog-eat-dog world out there does not correspond with what we find in the natural world. The natural world banks on cooperation and other strategies to avoid competition. It is the avoidance of competition which drives evolution, not competition itself.

According to Martin Nowak, Professor of Biology & Mathematics and Director of the Program for Evolutionary Dynamics at Harvard University, it is cooperation, and not competition, that underpins innovation. Nowak postulates that cooperation is the driving force of creativity throughout evolution, "because without it there can be neither construction nor complexity." Cooperation is central to constructing new levels of organization, and Nowak highlights the human body as an example: genes collaborate in chromosomes, chromosomes collaborate in genomes, genomes collaborate in cells, cells collaborate in tissues like muscles, which collaborate in bodies. Leave out collaboration, and you will cease to exist. Leave out cooperation, and your community will break apart. Leave out mutualisms, the biological term for win-win relationships, and ecosystems fall apart.

This new insight in the role of competition and cooperation has serious repercussions for the way we do business. In the short term, competition might decide who is successful and who is not. Because competition is always costly, biologists refer to it as a double negative (-/-) relationship, one that lowers the fitness of both parties in terms of time and energy lost for more generative activities. Predation and parasitism on the other hand, are (+/-) because one wins and the other loses. But here we might have to reconsider our view as well, given that researchers are beginning to uncover that parasites like parasitic worms also have benefits for human health. These parasites have been shown to induce potent immunomodulatory effects that can cure a variety of inflammatory diseases including asthma, rhinitis, intestinal inflammation disease, type 1 diabetes and several other immune dysregulation disorders. So, our take on parasitism as a (+/-) relationship needs to be revisited as well as our take on competition.

In the long run, relationships that are mutually beneficial (+/+), where the fitness of both increases, have a much better chance to last. That is because in cooperative relationships, one can rely on the other for certain tasks, freeing up energy which can be spent in another way, like in finding new resources or expanding into new territories. In fact, when the going gets tough, life collaborates more and competes less.[1] The harsher the conditions, the more organisms will try to cooperate. Baumeister and colleagues conclude that, "competition really is not sustainable in the long run. Competition doesn't make you stronger; it just makes you need an alternative strategy more urgently." Businesses should therefore not ask how they can become better competitors, but rather ask which alternatives can be created beyond competition. And this brings me to the next point, the role of patterns in nature.

The proof is in the patterns
—macro level patterns are mirrored on the micro level and vice versa

There is something really fascinating about patterns: They are really *persistent*. Think of how difficult it is to break an unhealthy pattern like smoking, drinking, or that well-paid job that makes you miserable. Patterns are everywhere. There are *symmetries*. Most of the animals that we know have a left and right side that is symmetrical. There are *spirals* found in spiraling galaxies, hurricanes, waves, plants, flowers, shells, horns, tendrils, tongues, and tails. Just think of the budding

---

[1] While often used in this book, the word 'nature' is not completely neutral. Using the word 'life' instead does not reinforce the often unconscious idea that nature is something external, outside of the human species. We are nature too.

leaves of a fern, or the spirals inside the sunflower's center. Or of the way the water whirls when you pull out the plug in the bathtub. Patterns get even more intriguing when we zoom in and notice that they are repeated across scales. We call such never-ending patterns fractals. Picture Romanesco broccoli, a beautiful and edible cauliflower. From its tiniest part to the vegetable as a whole, the Romanesco broccoli is built according to the exact same pattern. Such endless patterns are actually quite common in nature. Snowflakes, clouds, river systems, lightning bolts, trees… they all consist of endless patterns. The chromatin in our DNA is a fractal which keeps our DNA from getting entangled. And while it is easy to identify a pattern when you have the technology to zoom in and out, it is much harder to discern a pattern if you yourself are part of it.

Let's look at the human body again. What is cancer, really? It is not something external that enters the body and creates havoc. Cancer is what happens when the natural system that governs our body is disturbed. When cells inside our body forget that they are part of something bigger, that they have a specific role to play, and instead start operating on their own agenda, they turn into cancer cells. Such cells engage in activities with no regard for the other cells and tissues around them. They become uncooperative and no longer recognize that they are part of the body. Cancer is a growth inside the body that is outside of the body's control. It is a degenerative condition, and without intervention, cancer will deteriorate the body, sometimes slowly, sometimes faster, until the body can no longer sustain itself, and dies.

What many people do not know is that defective cells appear in our body every day, without having the opportunity to turn into cancer. This is because evolution has equipped the human body with a smart system of defense: We call it the immune system. This system detects and neutralizes faulty cells, not only pathogens like viruses, but also defective human cells. Our immune system thus not only prevents pathogens from infecting our body, it also prevents our own human cells from turning against us. Only when our immune system is weakened or tricked, and defective cells can no longer be neutralized, do these cells develop into cancer.

This brings me to another crucial aspect of living systems, which is the importance of *nestedness* as a pattern. In nature, everything is nested into something bigger. Let's revisit what makes defective cells different from normal cells. What does it mean when defective cells start to operate on their own agenda, as if they are no longer part of the body? It means that these cells have lost the ability to recognize their role as a nested subsystem of a larger system, such as a tissue or an organ, which is also a subsystem of a larger system such as a body, to which they need to add value for the whole to remain healthy.

In nature, interdependence and nestedness are the codes to life. Think of it like this: a lung cell is nested in the lungs. The cell is an essential building block of the lung tissue in which it is embedded. The lung tissue, nested inside the lungs, adds value to the functioning of the lungs. The lungs in turn are nested in the respiratory system. They add value to this system because they regulate a process of gas exchange by extracting oxygen from the atmosphere and transferring it into the bloodstream, while at the same time releasing carbon dioxide from the bloodstream back into the atmosphere. Therefore, the respiratory system, nested inside the body, adds value to the body, because it allows the body to breathe. It also interconnects the body with the atmosphere. And the story of nestedness goes on: The body is nested in a family, where it contributes to the functioning of a family, which is nested in a community, that is nested in a landscape, that is nested in a biome, etc.

Nestedness is a pattern that is ingrained in nature's designs, and the *interdependence* of nested systems is based upon the principle of value adding. The lung cell on its own needs the higher order systems it is nested in to be healthy for it to function properly. If there is a problem with the respiratory system and not enough fresh air is transported to the lungs, the lung cell cannot transport enough oxygen to organs and tissues. The lung cell also needs to add value to those higher systems for them to remain healthy. For instance, lung cells in the lungs of a jogger will be healthier than those nested in the lungs of a smoker, and the lungs of a jogger living in a pristine environment will be healthier than those of a jogger living in a city with high air pollution. The health of any body or system is therefore dependent on the health of its subsystems and on the health of the environment it is nested in.

And the concepts of interdependence and nestedness extend even further. In car infested cities, choked by toxic smog, tiny pollutants travel with the air into the lungs where they can cause numerous health issues like asthma, to name one. But not only the respiratory system is affected. Recently, researchers have discovered that living in areas with high air pollution during pregnancy increases the risk of Autism spectrum disorders. This proves that different systems within the body, like the respiratory system with its lungs and the nervous system with the brain, are also interconnected. The respiratory system transfers not only the oxygen but also the toxins that come in via polluted air into the bloodstream, which ultimately leads the toxins to the brain where they disrupt the regular order of things and kick-start *disorders*. We can argue that the pattern of disorder in the air in our cities (the pattern of air pollution) is mirrored in the brains of its inhabitants. Smoggy air leads to clogged brains. And it doesn't stop there. There is another striking pattern that is gradually coming to light. *Degradation* of our natural environment is mirrored in a degraded human microbiome (the multispecies ecosystem on and within our body, which we depend on to stay healthy and energetic). In other words, declining species richness in our environment leads to decay of our inner ecosystem, spiraling dis-ease, and disease in human populations.

This again shows us the limits of reductionist scientific thinking that viewed the human body as isolated from nature, which led to the development and application of an arsenal of antibiotics, pesticides and detergents to keep our bodies, food, and houses free from "bugs." Yet in doing so, we not only destroyed a few harmful micro-organisms, but many beneficial ones too. For example, evidence is surfacing that indicates that allergy, human microbiota, and environmental biodiversity are interrelated. Researchers found that people with an allergic disposition had lower biological diversity (biodiversity) in the surroundings of their homes than healthy individuals. The researchers concluded that dwindling biodiversity may be a contributing factor to the global phenomenon of escalating allergies and other chronic inflammatory diseases among urban populations worldwide.

As interaction-based evolution points out, we have co-evolved with our environment and are thus closely linked to that environment. This means that we should not only be worried about the toxins entering our body, but also about the decimating effect humans are having on the biodiverse, networked communities in our environment on which we depend to stay healthy. Our inner and outer nature are connected. So, if we take our health and well-being seriously, we need to change the nature of innovation and development, and shift from degenerative patterns such as pollution, exploitation, and degradation to regenerative ones that support and promote health, vitality, and viability. This might sound utopian, but it has been done before, successfully, by creatures with much smaller brains than ours.

Knowing that our inner and outer nature are connected, exemplifies the need for changing innovation-as-usual. We can now see that global macro-patterns of degeneration, like the massive decline of biodiversity, are mirrored across scales. The poorer the health of the environment, the poorer our own health. Our nature shapes the nature of the environment, and our environment shapes our nature.

NEW INSIGHTS IN BIOLOGY CHANGE THE WAY WE LOOK AT THINGS

Still, there is another pattern that regularly occurs in nature: the fact that intelligence is *distributed*. Just watch floating islands of fire ants after a flood. There is no ant in charge, giving orders to the others. Each and every ant knows what to do: how to trap air, how to stay afloat, and when to change positions with those submerged under water, until they reach new land where they can establish their new colony.

Even in our body, intelligence is distributed. Ever had a gut-wrenching feeling that forewarns you something is up, something that the brain does not grasp yet? Well, science is backing up the saying, "Listen to your gut instinct," because researchers have discovered an information superhighway between our gut and brain called the brain-gut axis, which is an extensive network of neurons, chemical neurotransmitters, and hormones that enables constant communication between the two. Scientists have uncovered that the gut has its own nervous system, called the enteric nervous system, that is not only interconnected with our central nervous system, but is also structurally and chemically similar. That is why the gut is also referred to as the body's second brain. It interconnects the gut microbiome with its trillions of non-human microbiota directly to the human brain. So, while we like to think we are in charge of our thoughts, trillions of non-human bacteria might actually be co-governing our opinions, feelings, and actions. The research is clear that gut microbiota play a vital role in our overall health, from regulating digestion to inflammation, immunity, and even our mental states.

While more and more scientists are uncovering that a biodiverse microbiome is important for health, research is also increasingly showing that the western way of life decreases diversity in gut microbiota. Poor gut health has been linked to a number of disorders like multiple sclerosis, autism spectrum disorders, and Parkinson's disease. Alas, the pattern of degeneration perpetuates itself. Degradation of the environment is mirrored in a degraded human microbiome, and a degraded human microbiome becomes mirrored in a degraded brain system. Makes me wonder whether poor land leads to poor guts, and whether poor guts lead to poor thoughts. Because nature's default innovation leads primarily to increased richness in the land, and increased complexity and sophistication in the living. So, we might assume that degradation of the land leads to the opposite, poor lands leading to poor thoughts.

The above also reminds me of a quote that stuck with me after reading William McDonough and Michael Braungart's book Cradle to Cradle, "Once you understand the destruction taking place, even if you have never intended to cause such destruction, you become involved in a strategy of tragedy. Unless you can design and implement a strategy of change." We have known about the detrimental effects of business on the living environment for decades. Yet despite all the knowledge and evidence provided by science, we have failed to do anything about it. We are still stuck in a strategy of tragedy. It is not lack of knowledge or technology that is preventing us from changing this pattern of tragedy. It is lack of will. And, as the saying goes, "No guts, no glory." We will have to grow the courage to change business-as-usual.

Understanding that the land we live on also shapes us, sheds another perspective on the urgency for biodiversity protection and ecosystem restoration. By regenerating the land on which we live, we not only increase its viability and vitality, we enhance ours as well. And while each and every one of us has a stake in the macro pattern of degradation, we also have a stake in its regeneration. The problem can become the solution. As illustrated above, the tiniest part of any system can become an actualizer of greater overall health, wellness, and vitality of the whole. No one person, organization, or business is too small to matter. In nature, every big thing, from your brain to your body to an ecosystem, is the result of many small things working together. The belief that we cannot turn looming catastrophe into opportunity is based on the illusion that individually, we are too small to matter. By shifting the tangibles on which we have direct impact—like our gardens, our decision-making processes, the way we spend our time and our business model logic—from degenerative to regenerative value creation, we can shift intangibles like the economy. While the global economic pattern of degeneration has reverberated on the individual level, the global pattern can only be changed on the individual level. Life always builds from the bottom up.

Humans did not domesticate wolves, wolves domesticated themselves
—it is the friendliest that have the survival advantage

It is estimated that there are close to one billion dogs in the world today. That would make dogs one of the most successful carnivores of our time. In comparison, while wolves were once one of the most widespread and abundant predators roaming the Earth, scientists now approximate that worldwide, there are less than 300,000 wild wolves remaining. So, if dogs are descended from wolf ancestors,

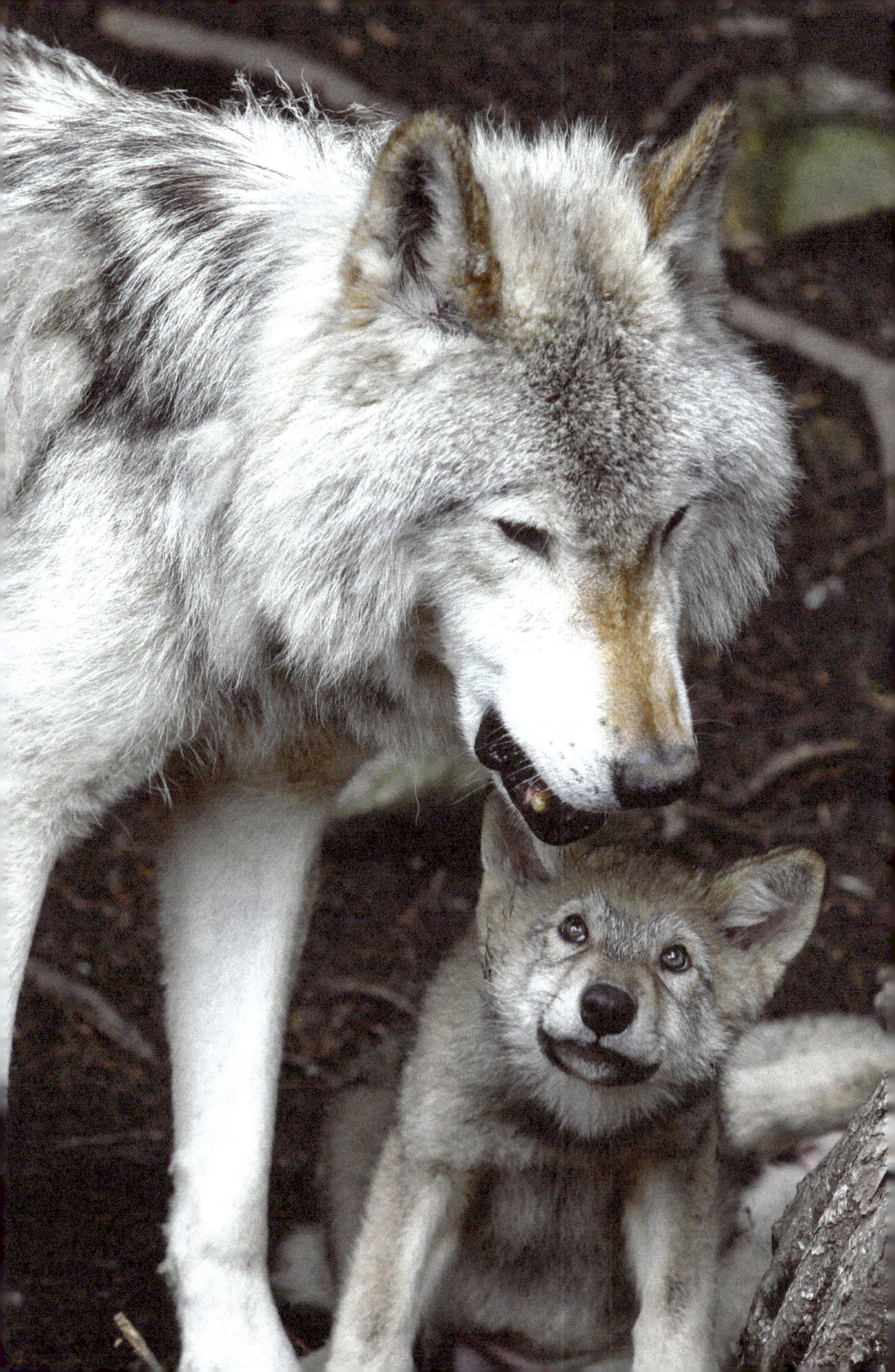

then why did the domesticated version of the wolf become so widely successful, while the wild one was almost driven to extinction?

The answer might be just as obvious as it is unexpected. Ever wondered why we often refer to dogs as "man's best friend?" Well, consider the characteristics that you would assign to your best friend. Most of us would come up with friendliness, loyalty, understanding, and guess what, these are exactly the characteristics that led to the evolutionary success of dogs.

There is an interesting twist to this as well, one that might make us reconsider how we assess and value tolerance and friendliness in the human world. For a long time, scientists have assumed that humans domesticated wolves, thereby intentionally creating dogs. The theory was that somewhere in our past, humans deliberately adopted wolf puppies to tame, and over time, these canines were trained and selected to serve specific purposes like protection or to hoard livestock. But recent evidence paints a different picture.

Brian Hare, a professor in Evolutionary Anthropology at Duke University, stumbled onto evidence that caused him to develop a whole new theory, one that is backed by experimental evidence and shows that humans did not domesticate wolves, wolves domesticated themselves.

Inspired by the research of the Russian geneticist Dmitri Belyaev, Hare uncovered that the first dog breed was not created by human breeding, but by natural selection. That is, it was nature that created the first dogs, not us. According to Hare, natural selection favored the more curious, friendly, and least anxious wolves that lived close to human settlements, so that they could rely on an extra supply of leftover food. This gave these wolves an evolutionary advantage over the wolves that were more fearful or aggressive. While fearful wolves were scared away and aggressive ones killed, friendlier wolves were able to develop new skills to take advantage of this new human species, giving them a better chance to survive and reproduce when their territories overlapped with human settlements. It was the new skills and abilities—tolerance, friendliness, and curiosity—that allowed the friendly wolves to turn a foe into a friend and change the competitive relationship with humans into a collaborative one. Together, man and wolf became better at hunting and safeguarding their joint settlements from intruders, thus improving the survival chances of both.

But here is where it gets even more interesting. Based on Hare's work on how dogs evolved, he also discovered that friendlier animals not only had a better chance at survival, they became more clever too. Learning to understand and respond to human gestures and communication signals allowed the animals to move from the fringes of the territory to the heart of the human homes. The wolves domesticated themselves and evolved from an apex predator into man's best friend.

This process of co-evolution between humans and friendly wolves went on for tens of thousands of years and has led to the unparalleled canine abilities we know today, such as performing complex tasks and identifying objects. Some dogs know more than a thousand words and can assist people in many different ways, guiding the blind, sniffing out explosives and certain types of cancer, aiding in therapy sessions and helping to find human survivors after an earthquake.

Dog intelligence is in every aspect remarkable, as is the insight of Hare and Woods. Their book, *The Genius of Dogs*, provides a convincing, scientifically supported case that turns the popular hypothesis, that in order to get a cleverer generation of animals, one has to breed the cleverest creatures, on its head. Instead, they highlight ground-breaking genetic experiments on foxes that show that selecting the *friendliest* foxes for breeding caused cognitive evolution, leading to a cleverer generation of foxes. In the words of Hare & Woods, "Belyaev had bred the friendliest foxes, who became cleverer by accident." Their findings suggest that intelligence is a by-product of friendliness, which makes a compelling case for "survival of the friendliest."

Dogs became the most successful carnivores on the planet by befriending and teaming up with humans, while wolves were, not so long ago, on the verge of extinction, which illustrates that cooperation is a major driving force for long term evolutionary success, and Hare and Woods pinpoint tolerance as a prerequisite for cooperation. Friendly animals are more tolerant and curious than fearful, aggressive ones. Therefore, only after organisms become more tolerant, will they start to develop more sophisticated forms of cooperative cognition.

Hare and Woods go on to hypothesize that this might have happened in human evolution too. While we have assumed that human cognition became increasingly sophisticated because more intelligent people had better survival and reproduction rates, maybe it was the friendlier humans that had the survival advantage.[2] Friendliness encouraged the development of social skills, and socially savvy humans became better in innovation and collaboration than those who were less socially skilled. These social aptitudes may have allowed the friendly humans to take on more complex tasks, like building mammoth traps,

---

[2] I use the definition used by Belyaev & Hare here: friendliness is the absence of fear and aggression and the presence of tolerance, interest and curiosity.

which contributed to their survival and reproduction. And maybe, as with foxes and wolves, selection of the friendliest humans led to more intelligent humans too. Or, to quote Hare and Woods's hypothesis, "friendliness allowed humans to get cleverer."

If this new perspective rings true, it will have strong repercussions on how we view our economy and how we promote employees. For too long, a dog-eat-dog world view has dominated our economic reasoning and created an environment that is unfavorable for promoting friendliness. Too much emphasis on competition, fuels fearfulness in human beings and leads to territorial and belligerent behavior, as witnessed in intellectual property rights battles and hostile takeovers. Now, I am not saying that our economy is void of friendliness, but in general, amicability is not what gets you ahead. Just consider how often the friendliest colleague gets promoted.

Better yet, consider the mess we are in today. It is not very *sapiens* (which means wise in Latin) of any species to expect that we can grow indefinitely, in both numbers and consumption, on a finite planet. Have we impeded our own cognitive evolution by favoring the least friendly specimens? Controversial as this theory on survival of the friendliest may seem, it is a promising avenue for further exploration. Especially considering the fact that the developed world has never been wealthier, yet from 1988 to 2008, antidepressant use in the United States has increased by nearly 400% among all ages, making them the third most commonly prescribed drug.

Most of us in the Western world have everything to be happy: a family, a house, a comfortable income, friends, hobbies—all that is needed to live a happy life. Still, stress, burn-out and depression are spiraling out of control. Is it because somewhere deep down we feel that the system we have devised is hindering meaningful evolution on a personal, organizational and societal level? Are outdated management styles preventing meaningful development and cognitive evolution? Are we constraining the potential and creativity of individuals by running organizations like machines instead of living and evolving entities?

It certainly looks that way, since more and more people are leaving well-paid jobs in rigid companies to join start-ups or to become self-employed. These people exchange financial security for freedom to pursue their purpose, to develop their own potential and often, to contribute to a greater good. They realize that in a world where change is accelerating, security is the first to go out the window. It is meaningfulness, agility and creativity that build adaptiveness and resilience when the dynamics of change are intensifying, and it is exactly on this front that many large businesses fall short.

So why is the finding that dogs were created by natural selection, and that friendliness might be a more important portal to cognitive evolution than intelligence, important for businesses? Based on the findings of Belyaev & Hare, promoting curiosity, tolerance and friendliness in your organization, can get you ahead, because it is the best way to promote the collective intelligence of your workforce. Instead of fishing for the most intelligent employees, long-term corporate success may actually be promoted by installing an internal culture that promotes and rewards friendliness instead of brilliance. Not convinced? Here is an example of what happens when you do the opposite.

Enter Enron, an interesting case of a corporate scandal that was inspired by Richard Dawkins' book *The Selfish Gene*. The philosophy laid out in the book struck a chord with Enron's CEO Jeffrey Skilling, who believed that people are innately selfish and motivated by fear and greed only. He installed a management system based on intense internal competition, called the "Rank and Yank" appraisal system, which ranked employees openly on their website. Not only were the bottom 10% sacked each year, first their under achievements were publicly shared. This overemphasis on competition created an internal culture of distrust, unethical behavior, and corruption, which led to one of the biggest energy frauds of our time. Investigations, based on tapes and memorandums, show that Enron was creating artificial energy shortages to manipulate market prices, inducing energy black outs affecting up to half a million consumers, and forcing the State of California to call out a power emergency. Enron made more than a billion dollars from these fraudulent black-outs, but eventually went under in 2001, resulting in its shareholders losing tens of billions of dollars, while many of its employees lost their life savings. And the top executives of the company, including Skilling, ended up in prison. Enron's internal competition rose so high that it ate the company from the inside out.

Many companies in the world still operate according to this paradigm, though they probably do not take it to the extreme like Enron. And while competition does fuel motivation to stretch our abilities and creativity to some degree, collaboration is far more effective for long-term success. If one would look at an organization as a living entity, like a human body for instance, then the entity

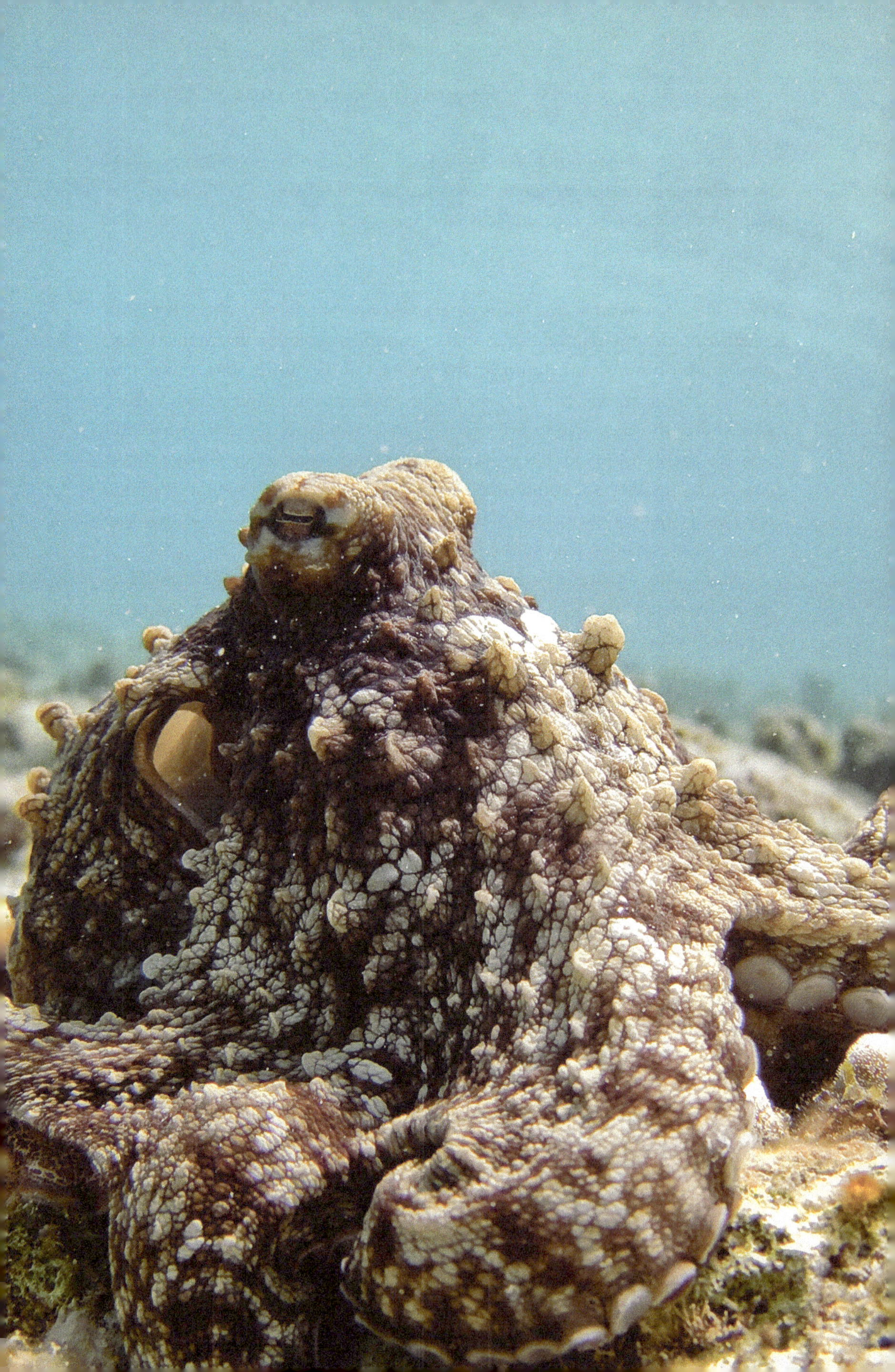

exists only because of intense collaboration between all the different parts that each add value to the larger system they are nested in.

The Enron example also illustrates two other learnings that are important in terms of the topic of this book. First, care is needed when mixing up the jargon from different disciplines.[3] From a biological viewpoint, genes are not "selfish," but are self-promoting. Self-promoting is completely different from the psychological definition of selfish motivation, meaning "wanting or striving to benefit the self without regard for the well-being of others." In fact, Richard Dawkins has been reported to say that his book also could have been titled "The Altruistic Individual." For marketing reasons, they chose *The Selfish Gene,* and a whole generation of people grew up thinking selfishness is ingrained in our DNA.

Second, it highlights a tendency we have of which we are not always aware. Namely, when we focus on one aspect, we often become blind to other aspects. The struggle for survival has received significantly more attention in the past than its counterpart, leading to an overestimation of the importance of competition and an underestimation of the importance of collaboration.

Squid, Octopi and Boquila lianas hack and reprogram their own genes
—nature can shortcut the process of slow evolutionary change

The octopus has long puzzled biologists. Its capabilities are unparalleled by any other species in the animal kingdom. Octopi can solve puzzles, taste, and think with their tentacles, squeeze a body the size of a dog through an egg-sized hole, shift shape, change color, and, of course, squirt ink. And while Australian biologists recently discovered that octopi build underwater cities, illustrating that their social life in Octopolis and Octlantis is far more complex than previously

---

[3] This was and still is a great challenge in communicating about bio-inspired innovation. On the one hand, we need to stay close to the biological terminology to avoid misinterpretations. But on the other hand, to bring this kind of thinking into the world of innovation, we need to make the knowledge accessible and relevant for the business world. Inevitably, this means mixing up jargon and that will always be risky in a way. Ideally, we would implement knowledge about how life works in the curriculum of all disciplines, including engineering departments and business schools.

thought, one six-month-old octopus called Otto in Germany's Sea Star Aquarium kept a highly educated staff in the dark, literally, for days. Otto had learned to balance on the edge of his tank and shoot out the annoying, 2,000-watt spotlight above, with a carefully directed jet of water. It took the staff three days to figure out that Otto was the one responsible for the repeated blackouts.

Marine biologist Mark Nolan, a leading scientist in the field, pointedly stated, "that most of the tests on octopus intelligence actually demonstrate the lack of intelligence in the researchers." Indeed, to survive the predatory marine environment, octopi have evolved very unique skills. They can camouflage into their environment by adopting its color, use clouds of ink to create safe escape routes, or mimic their predator's predator. This latter strategy shows just how smart they really are. So how is it that these creatures, who are so different from us, can rival our cognition? According to a recent study, these cephalopods have developed the uncanny ability to edit and redirect their own brain genes.

While DNA (deoxyribonucleic acid) is the blueprint of genetic instructions laid out at conception, RNA (ribonucleic acid) translates these instructions into manufacturing orders, which turns information into proteins. But squid and octopus have learned to hack this system by editing their own RNA to produce different proteins than the ones called for by the DNA. Research has demonstrated that octopuses use RNA-editing to adapt to changing temperatures, which may indicate that this process of hacking their own genes might make this species incredibly flexible and quick to respond to changing circumstances. In fact, it is not unlikely that this RNA-editing might be a trick to overcome one of the greatest challenges of life: to circumvent the slow process of genome evolution by rapid recoding. By hacking their own RNA, octopi do not depend on the slow process of genetic evolution, requiring many generations, to adapt to changing circumstances. Instead they reprogram their own genetic brain software to upgrade their survival skills.

But octopi are not the only species with this uncanny ability. In Chili and Argentina there lives the Boquila, a ground-rooted, fruit bearing vine plant, or liana, with an astonishing capability[4]. As a climber, the liana often associates itself with a host plant around which it can grow. While this plant has been studied extensively by botanists, its mimetic ingenuity has only recently been discovered. That is, the liana is able to imitate the leaves of its host plant in shape, size, and color, but

---

[4] The Latin name of this plant is *Boquila trifoliolata*.

how the liana knows what to imitate is a mystery, because plants do not have eyes like we do. Yet, Boquila have a highly sophisticated capacity for perceiving all the details of the leaves of the host plant, as botanist Ernesto Gianoli revealed through a set of convincing research tests. He not only showed that the liana is able to imitate the many different host species it climbs, but that it is also able to make these adaptive changes several times during its life time, such as when its surrounding plant community changes.

Because the Boquila appears to always mimic the plant that grows the closest to it, scientists speculate that this capacity helps the plant to blend in, thereby reducing the chances of being eaten by harmful insects. This remarkable ability inspired the world's leading authority in the field of plant neurobiology, Stefano Mancuso, to offer the hypothesis that the plant has some sort of visual capacity. Even more mind-blowing, is the fact that the plant is able to modulate the expression of its genes in real-time so that it can change its look according to a change in its direct environment. The Boquila practices what is probably the most sophisticated form of shapeshifting known in the plant world today.

Like the squid and octopus, the Boquila vine is able to reprogram its genetic information during its lifetime, in order to better adapt to changing circumstances. Still, you might be wondering why these insights are relevant for the business world. Any executive will agree that inducing change into longstanding, established organizations is a slow and challenging process and most change management approaches fail to achieve the required outcomes. That is because conventional change management approaches usually attempt to evoke change from the outside in. In other words, corporate change processes are typically initiated from the top down, which fails to address the intrinsic motivation of the employees that is needed for effective transformation.

However, both the Boquila and octopus show us that real change starts from the inside out and originates in the elemental parts. It is from the rewiring of the software on the gene level that they are able to achieve incredible system change, which allows them to become better adapted to a changing context. While we humans have been focusing mainly on eco-efficiency measures and technological fixes to address the grand challenges of our time, nature shows us that reprogramming our brain is the requisite for real change. What if we could change the hardwired degenerative logic of *take, make, dispose* into a regenerative one? What if we could reprogram our thinking so that we can design and develop business models that add value to the living world rather than extract from it? If we are really serious about the future, then we need to start by regenerating our thinking.

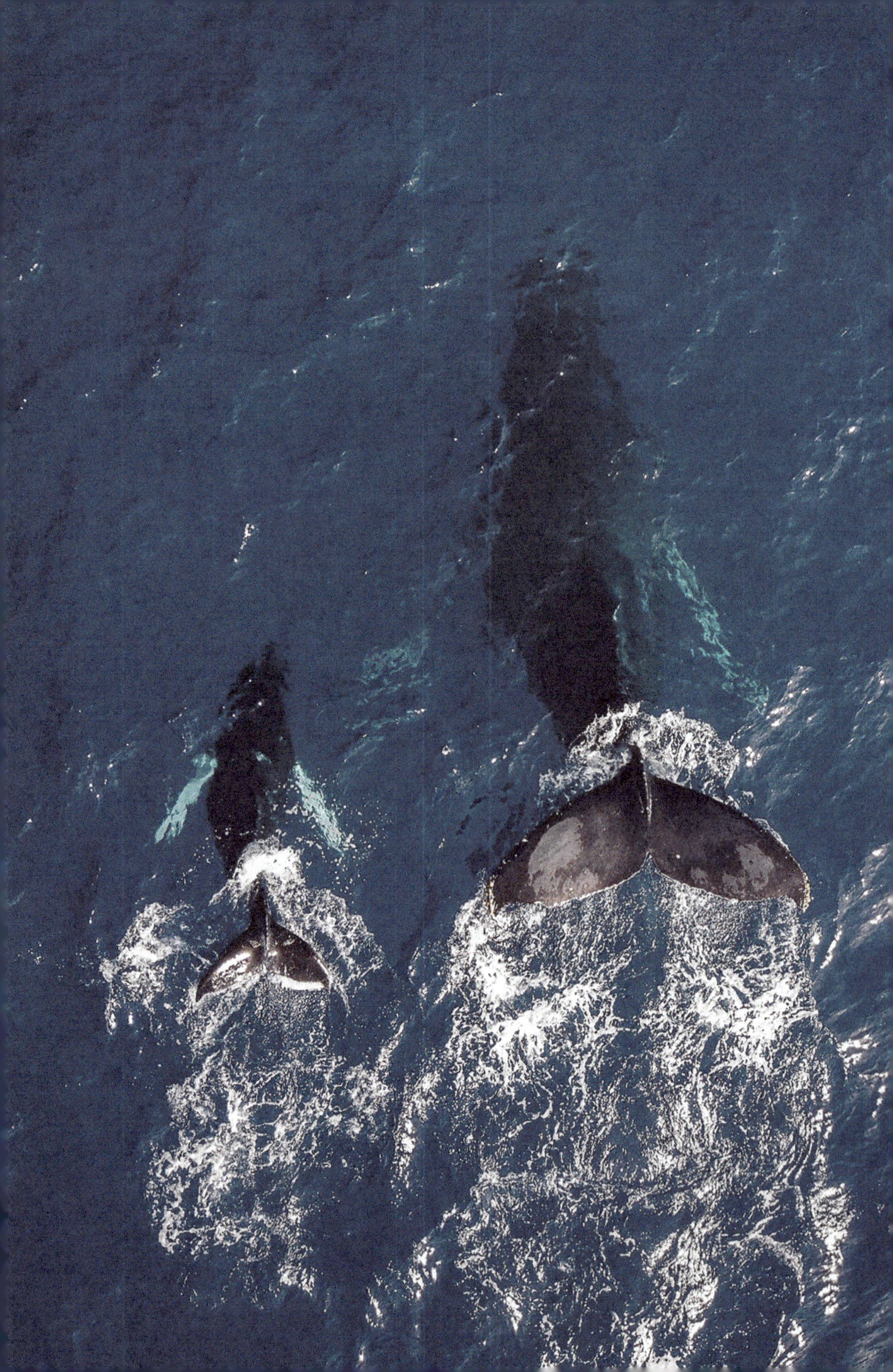

CHAPTER 3

―――

WELCOME TO THE AGE OF BIO-LOGICS

Bio-sphere
—mushrooms make rain, arctic foxes green the tundra, whales cool the climate and wolves change rivers

So how do living entities generate conditions that are beneficial to life? Science is finally catching up and gradually uncovering the sophisticated ways in which life regenerates the biosphere[5]. Let me start with a personal experience. After a hard day's work in the autumn of 2016, we took our dogs out for a hike in a nearby nature reserve. It was evening and close to sunset, and the air was becoming cooler and more humid. At one point, we passed a dead birch tree, which housed a few polypore mushrooms a couple of meters above the ground and it looked like the mushrooms were on fire. We could see a thick smoke rising from them. As a trained biologist, I knew that they weren't on fire but were firing off spores, the fungal equivalent of seeds, to reproduce the next generation of mushrooms. Still, I thought there was something quite counterintuitive about it. The spores travelled upward, like smoke in the air, and this is what puzzled me.

A Story of Mushrooms

So, when I got home, I did a little bit of research and learned that these fungi, which depend on humid conditions for their survival and reproduction, have evolved a pretty smart, moisture-induced launching system to set the spores free when climate conditions are ideal. It works like this: The fungal spores act as a nucleus for condensation. They attract water vapor from the air, which gradually forms a droplet of water on their surface. When the droplet reaches a critical size, it slides across the spore's surface, changing its center of gravity and thereby generating enough force to displace the spore from its seat so that it is released into the air. During this process, many such spores catch a current of rising air and travel all the way up into the sky. Researchers estimate that as much as 50 million tons of spores make it to Earth's atmosphere every year. In a recent study, scientists have discovered that fungal spores in the atmosphere do

---

[5] Please note that the examples illustrated here are still simplifications as science is only at the very beginning of understanding how it all works. In reality, the interrelations of the living world are more complex.

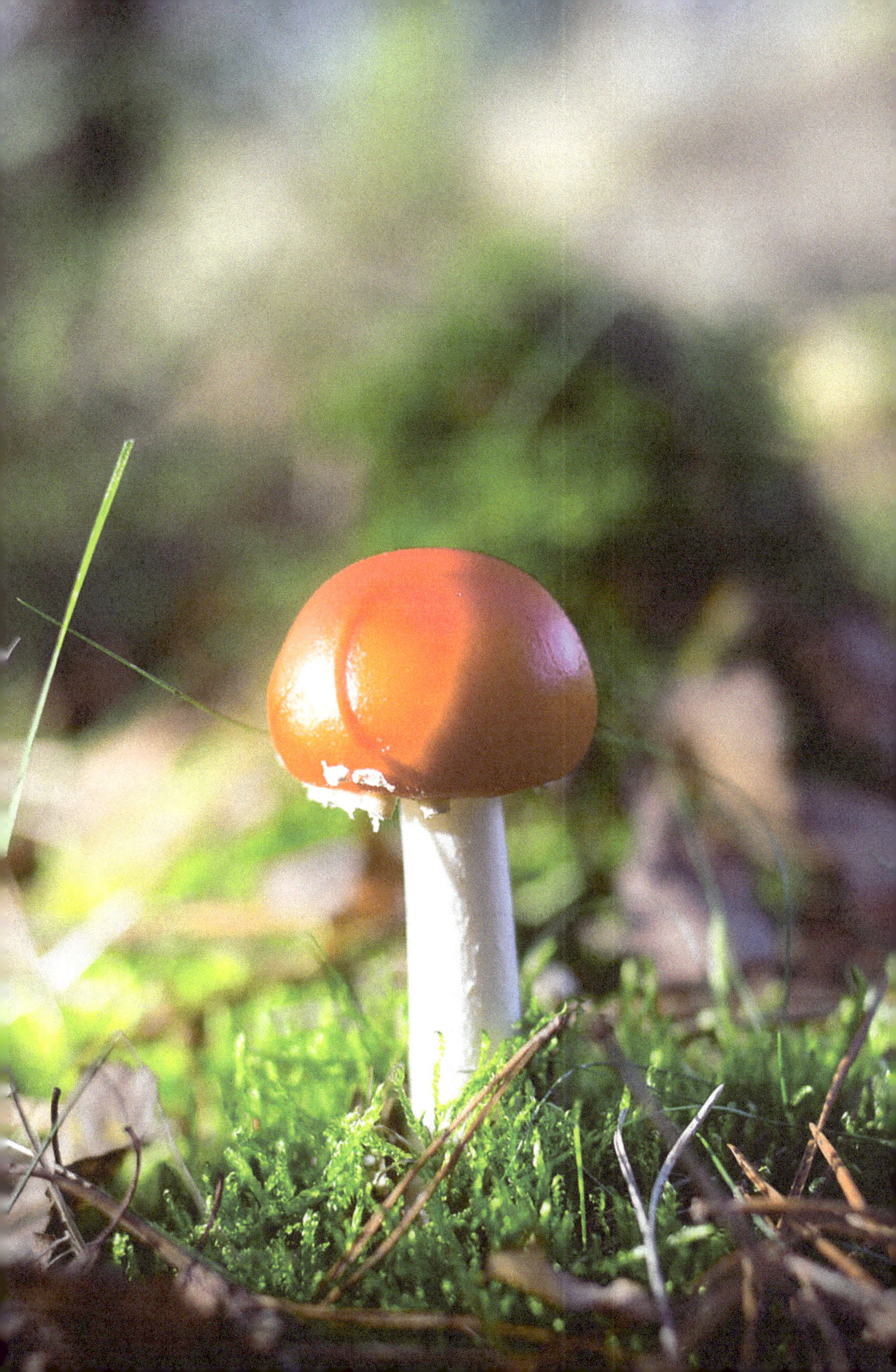

the same thing they do on land: They attract water vapor that accumulates into large droplets. When the density of spores is sufficiently high, they form clouds. Moisture-loving mushrooms make rain.

The clever design mechanism of spore discharge is, like most designs in nature, multifunctional. Fungal spores are not only important for reproduction, they are also rainmakers. Mushrooms release the spores when the climate conditions are right, and at the same time improve the viability of the next generation of mushrooms by positively affecting the climate. That is, by ensuring that there will be rain, they also ensure the next generation of fungi's future. By influencing the weather, they make sure their offspring have a better chance of survival.

And while scientific proof for this process is recent, many indigenous societies have known about this for centuries. Often, in rain dance rituals, the soil gets kicked into the air to lift the spores that had landed on the ground. But that is not all. A recent article in the Journal of Astrobiology and Space Science Reviews, builds a convincing case that fungi may have colonized Mars. They write that four investigators working independently have reported what appears to be fungi on the Martian surface. At the moment, more evidence is needed to confirm the observations, but it would not surprise me one bit. Fungi are one of the oldest life forms on Earth. They have had 470 million years of refining their spore design. That's about 470,000,000 field tests launching millions of microscopic spore shuttles each time, if we assume they follow an annual cycle. And not without success, because experiments have shown that fungal spores (and a variety of other organisms) remain viable after long-term exposure to the radiation-intense environment of space. That mushrooms have already traveled to Mars, just shows how sophisticated NI really is.[6]

A Story of Foxes

This story of spores may be surprising, but it is hardly unique. The more biology advances, the more we discover how organisms regenerate their environments in a way that improves the living conditions for all life on Earth. Satellite images of the tundra have turned heads when researchers noticed a strange phenomenon. The images showed remarkable and unusual green patches distributed across the landscape. Intrigued, the scientists set out to explore what turned these patches

---

[6] Off course, it could also be the other way around, that life first existed on Mars and that fungi traveled from Mars to Earth when the Martian environment turned hostile.

green, and they discovered that the patches centered around the dens of arctic foxes. It turns out that leftover food scraps and fox excrements close to their dens, fertilized the soil to such an extent that it created favorable conditions for more life to develop. The foxes' behavior led to cultivation of the land around their homes, like mini gardens, which led the researchers to conclude that arctic foxes are ecosystem engineers.

The small carnivores continuously upgrade their immediate environment by adding nutrients, making the soil around their dens richer. Richer soils lead to richer plants. Richer plant life attracts more insect life. Richer plant and insect life means more food for small mammals such as lemmings, voles, and other rodents—the artic foxes' favorite food. Over time, the foxes turn patches of the tundra into little green oases, thereby ensuring that there is more food for the next generations of arctic foxes. Just like the fungi, these canny canines regenerate the environment, leaving it richer than they found it.

A Story of Whales

One of the most wondrous examples of creating conditions conducive to life, however, comes from the stewards of the oceans—the great whales. It was investigative zoologist and journalist, George Monbiot, who first popularized the story through his compelling piece, "Why whale poo matters." In the 1970s, people believed that a great reduction in the whale population would lead to an increase in krill and fish, both of which are commercially important for our economy. The hunt was open. Industrial whaling became such a profitable business that it reduced the number of great whales at an alarming pace, bringing them to the verge of extinction in just a few decades. But the great decline in whales did not increase the number of fish or krill. On the contrary, as we are learning now that instead of increasing krill and fish populations, the great decline in whales may have led to a decline in fish stocks.

In the areas where whales were hunted most intensively, the volume of plant plankton went down. Plant plankton is the main food source for krill, which is the main food source for fish, and both fish and krill are the main food sources of many whales. So how do whales contribute to the production of plant plankton? Well, whale excrement is rich in iron and nitrogen, which are scarce in marine surface waters. Both elements are important fertilizers for plant plankton to grow. Now, although whales usually feed at great depths, they have to swim to the surface regularly to breathe and defecate. Their plunging up and down is called the "whale pump" in scientific literature as it causes vertical mixing of the water. This mixing supports the vertical transfer of nutrients from the deep sea to the upper photic zone, the only zone where photosynthesis is possible, and where plankton reproduce.

It is estimated that the whales' up and down movements contribute as much to mixing the water than the effect from wind, waves, and tides combined. Whales are thus important vectors of nutrient and material flux in the oceans. They are the stewards that keep the marine circular economy going. These aquatic giants thus not only affect the oceanic ecosystem, they influence the physical factors of the ocean as well.

Plant plankton absorbs carbon from the atmosphere, and when they ultimately die and sink into the abyss, they sequester that carbon onto the ocean floor where it is stored for millions of years. It is hard to estimate just how much "carbon drawdown" is accumulated by the oceans, but studies suggest billions of tons of carbon are pulled down every year. So, more whales means more plant plankton, which means more carbon sequestration.

But that is not the end of the story. Just like terrestrial plants, marine plankton gives off a chemical signal, called dimethyl sulfide (DMS), when it experiences stress from predation or UV radiation. DMS attract predators like albatrosses and other sea birds that eat the marine creatures who graze on the plant plankton. Not only do these birds help protect the plankton, they also leave droppings, rich in nutrients, that further enhance plankton's reproduction.

DMS is also an important chemical involved in global climate regulation. When the sun burns too hot, the chemical filters into the air, where it acts as a nucleus for condensation—a.k.a. a cloud. So, plankton makes clouds when the UV light stress is too high, and more white clouds means more reflection and a smaller surface of dark water to absorb the heat from the sun. This is known as the *albedo effect* (the amount of electromagnetic radiation that is reflected, rather than absorbed), and it is an important cooling mechanism of the planet. And the thread of interdependency continues—more whales means more plankton, which means more carbon drawdown, which means more sunlight reflected into space. And continues still.

WELCOME TO THE AGE OF BIO-LOGICS

New research suggests that the impact of industrial whaling not only altered marine ecosystems, but coastal ecosystems as well. With fewer Great Whales in the oceans, killer whales, who eat great whales, have since changed their diets. Killer whales, also known as orcas, have started to hunt for seals and otters instead, which has radically reduced the number of sea otters in the North Pacific. And sea otters play an important role in maintaining the health of underwater kelp forests. These kelp forests are one of the richest coastal ecosystems on Earth, and not only do these underwater jungles protect the coastlines from storms, they are also champions in drawing down carbon from the atmosphere, sequestering carbon as effectively as their terrestrial counterparts, the rainforests. Now, sea otters feed on sea urchins, the grazers of the kelp forests. But with fewer and fewer sea otters—having been eaten by the orcas who can't find enough Great Whales—sea urchin populations have exploded and are now decimating the underwater forests through overgrazing. So fewer great whales means fewer sea otters, which means dwindling kelp forests, which means less carbon storage and a weaker buffer against coastal storms.

Not only does this example illustrate how everything is interconnected and interdependent here on Earth, but it also illustrates how important keystone species, like whales and otters, are. These species maintain valuable ecosystems with their activities. That is why scientists call them ecosystem engineers. But that does not cover the magnitude of their contribution. Their activities create benefits that cascade well beyond their ecosystems, to the land and into the atmosphere. They are the guardians of a stable, life-friendly and viable biosphere because they play a vital role in climate regulation. And it is not only large organisms that generate substantial impact, microscopic creatures play vital roles too.

The International Monetary Fund (IMF) conducted a study that highlights how plant plankton not only contributes at least 50% of all oxygen to our atmosphere, they do so by sequestering about 37 billion tons of carbon dioxide each year. This is about the same as the carbon drawdown potential of four mature Amazon forests. The study also shows that if whales were allowed to return to their pre-whaling number of four to five million (it is estimated that there are about one million left today), it could significantly add to the amount of phytoplankton in the oceans and consequently to the carbon that is drawn down into the oceans each year. Researchers calculated that even a 1% increase in phytoplankton productivity—thanks to whale activity—would sequester hundreds of millions of tons of additional carbon a year.

With this knowledge, it's time to think beyond technological solutions to reverse climate change. Restoring the oceans so that whales and sea otter populations can return to their original numbers may be a solution that is not only cheaper, but more effective and less risky than many proposed man-made, high-tech alternatives like geo-engineering. According to the study, restoring whale populations could lead to a breakthrough in the fight against climate change. The researchers involved state that "healthy whale populations imply healthy marine life including fish, seabirds, and an overall vibrant system that recycles nutrients between oceans and land, improving life in both places. The 'earth-tech' strategy of supporting whales' return to their previous abundance in the oceans would significantly benefit not only life in the oceans but also life on land, including our own."

Not only that, fish stock and tourism would benefit from the return of whales and otters. The IMF study estimates that the current number of whales actually contribute more than $1 trillion to our economy in terms of carbon sequestration, ecotourism, and the fishing industry. Another study estimated that the carbon storage service of an underwater kelp forest is worth between $205-408 million per year, and this is probably a conservative estimate. We humans need to think in ecosystems instead of in isolated technologies, because so far, we have not been able to design a technological solution that does not cause other problems elsewhere. Besides, the associated economic benefits of ecosystem restoration may outclass even our best engineering approaches.

The accounts above also illustrate the critical role that keystone species play. Restoration efforts, therefore, will be easiest and most effective if they go hand in hand with strategies to improve life for keystone species that play an essential role in keeping these carbon sinks healthy and our environment thriving, because the real world does not operate in the reductionist machine logic that has dominated our thinking for so long. It is not only abiotic features (the non-living chemical and geological elements of the environment) that influence living organisms and the functioning of ecosystems. Organisms also affect the physical geography of the land, oceans, and even the atmosphere.

The living world affects the non-living world in a way that increases the health, wealth, vitality and viability of the entire biosphere. Fungi, foxes, whales, phytoplankton, and otters all play an important role in climate regulation, and we need them to play their part. Or, in the words of evolutionary biologist and futurist Elisabet Sahtouris: "The best life insurance for any species in an ecosystem is to contribute usefully to sustaining the lives of other species, a lesson we are only beginning to learn as humans."

We have so much more to learn from living systems, especially when it comes to change and innovation. The next example is one I regularly use in my workshops on the topic of bio-inspired innovation and living systems thinking. It never disappoints. No matter the audience—whether they are bank executives, HR managers, or innovation specialists, civil servants, engineers, agronomists, architects, design teams, CEOs, or students—the following science-based story is one that leaves participants both stunned and stirred. It is a story about wolves changing rivers.

A Story of Wolves

In 1995, wolves were reintroduced in the Yellowstone National Park in the US, after an absence of 70 years. They had been hunted to near extinction by humans by the early 1900s, which had a dramatic impact on the ecosystem. With no predator left to hunt them, the elk population had grazed much of the vegetation away—despite human efforts to control their population size.[7] But when the wolves were reintroduced, even though few in number, they had an astonishing effect on the environment. Naturally, the canines killed some of the elk, but that was not the pivotal point. It was that they changed the behavior of the elk. The elk started to avoid certain places, especially open areas in the valleys, changing not only where they grazed but also how long they stayed in one place, which allowed the landscape to recover. With much less grazing, trees were again allowed to grow. In fact, the height of some trees quintupled in less than six years turning bare valleys into forested landscapes once again.

But the change did not only occur above ground. Below the soil, the returning trees grew enormous root systems that stabilized the soil, reduced erosion, and lay the foundations for the underground internet spurring tree growth even more. Both above and below ground, the trees were creating habitat for other species to return. As the landscape became richer with more trees and berry-bearing

---

[7] An elk, also called wapiti, is one of the largest species within the deer family.

bushes, the birds returned, as did small mammals like mice and rabbits. This in turn increased the number of weasels, hawks, foxes, and badgers. Scavengers like bald eagles and ravens returned to feast on the carrion the wolves left behind. Beavers came back and built dams with the new trees, creating habitats for numerous other species like fish, amphibians, reptilians, ducks, muskrats and otters. Bears returned because there was much more to eat.

The return of the wolves impacted not only the ecosystem; it changed the geography of the landscape as well. The returning trees reduced soil erosion and stabilized the riverbanks. The beaver dams in turn, affected sediment deposition in the rivers, which led to more pools, riffles, and meanders, which created not only more habitat for fish but also restored the riparian vegetation and floodplains. The rivers became more fixed in their course and their banks became much richer, supporting more life. So, the land-dwelling canines did not only increase the health and wealth of the terrestrial ecosystem, but of the aquatic ecosystem as well. The wolves changed the rivers.

The wolf story is yet another example that shows that everything on planet Earth is interdependent. The smallest change, like a few wolves returning, can impact both biotic and abiotic features of the ecosystem in a stunningly short time period, and we can see that change in living systems occurs non-linearly. As in, the indirect effects are often more important than the direct effects. It is *the changed behavior of the elk* that is at the core of the change process in Yellowstone, not the killing of the elk.

What's more, it shows that small changes can cascade into big change in less than a decade. It took only ten years for the river's geography to change after the reintroduction of the wolves, and it is not so much the physical interventions that are important (like the tree regrowth or the beaver dams) but the processes they enable that are relevant for cascading change. Beaver dams for instance, catalyze a number of important processes like groundwater recharge, gravel deposition, floodplain reconnection, wetland habitat formation, and riparian vegetation expansion. Again, nature shows us that the key to improving the health, wealth, vitality and viability of an ecosystem is by enabling and cascading processes of value adding, and the capacity of continuously cascading value adding processes is what I call *regenerative value creation*.

In line with the theory of Livnat, the living system examples of fungi, wolves and whales show that the byproducts of the organismal interventions are absolutely fundamental in this process of regeneration. Yet, most humans are blind to the effects of the byproducts that are created by our inventions and interventions.

So how can we design for beneficial byproducts? How can we change our business logic from degenerative (or zero sum) to regenerative? There is only one mentor experienced enough to show us the way forward and that is Mother Nature. There is a logic to how life works.

Bio-logic
—life creates conditions pro life

As far as we know, we live on the only known planet in the universe that contains life. And life here on Earth has managed to stay alive for 3.8 billion years. That is pretty spectacular. Not even a giant meteor crash, or a gigantic volcano eruption darkening the Earth for several years, could wipe out life. How has life managed to stay around for such a long time? And why is it that from all life forms that have ever existed on the planet, only about 0.1% is estimated to be still around? What distinguishes the living from the fossils?

While so much yet remains to be discovered, there is one thing the survival champions have in common that is particularly relevant for society. These ancient organisms arrange their business in a way that benefits their environment. But like the examples of wolves and whales show, this does not happen in a linear way. It works rather, like the popular saying goes, "the whole is greater than the sum of its parts." In science we call this phenomenon *emergent properties*, which are entirely unexpected and can only arise from the collaborative functioning of a system but do not belong to any one part or individual of that system.

In other words, emergent properties are properties of a group of elements, whether atoms, cells, or organisms, that you would not find in any of the individual items. Examples of emergent properties include ant colonies, ecosystems, and cities. You, too, are an emergent property because you are more than the sum of your cells. An ecosystem is the emergent property of all the organisms playing out their essence in a process of co-creation and co-evolution, and by playing their specific role, natural selection has favored organisms that add value to their environment to enrich not only their locality but the entire biosphere. These organisms continuously upgrade Earth's life-support system because this is the best strategy to ensure the success of their offspring.

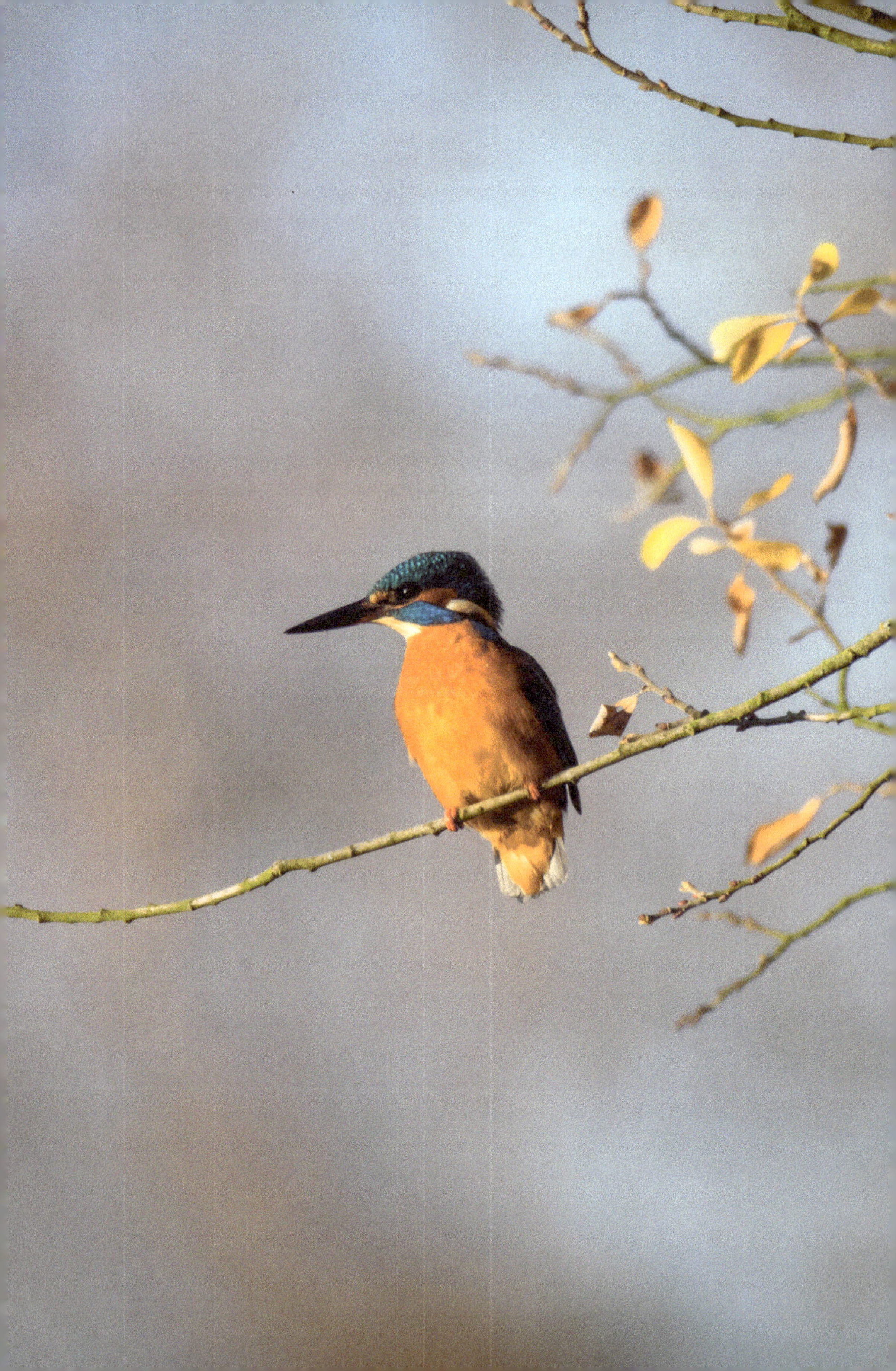

"Life creates conditions conducive to life." That is how the pioneering team of biomimics at the Biomimicry3.8 Institute summarizes this basic law of life into their biomimicry design lens, which is one of the best tools available to translate nature's time-tested and proven strategies into design principles for the business world. In the book *Regenerative Development & Design: A framework for Evolving Sustainability*, Pamela Mang & Ben Haggard unravel the mystery of life further by stating that sustainability is the byproduct of regeneration.

In biology, regeneration refers to a process of renewal that leads to a higher order of health, wealth, vitality and viability of a system. More health refers to increased healthiness and quality of life. More wealth refers to increased richness in terms. More vitality refers to increased vigor and aliveness, and more viability refers to increased "ableness" to stay alive. Regeneration can be looked at as a process of becoming more and doing more. It is both evolutionary (the system evolves towards higher levels of complexity) and developmental (the elements of the system express their inherent potential in the form of new roles and relationships). Viewing the world from this perspective sheds a new light on sustainable development. Because the more our understanding of nature grows, the more we are learning that zero sum—understood today as the goal of sustainability, namely, to eradicate negative or degenerative impacts—is actually not what leads to long term success. In the long run, only the ones that add value to the larger whole will remain. The immanence of biology permeates in the permanence of life.

Bio-diverse
—biodiversity inoculates against extinction

As any investment specialist will tell you, diversifying within and across asset classes is crucial if you do not want to have your entire fortune evaporate in one wallop. Scientific evidence now shows us that the natural world is no different. Communities with rich biodiversity, meaning high genetic and species diversity, are better able to avert extinction cascades than simple communities with low species richness because in poor communities, the disappearance of one species can trigger a chain of events, or cascade, where one loss leads to another and another and another. In species-rich and biodiverse ecosystems, however, chances are that something else will take over its role. The lesson to be learned from this is that biodiversity inoculates against extinction cascades, because it increases resilience and robustness.

The opposite of a biodiverse system is a monoculture, a uniform system built out of one species, like a wheat field. Its natural equivalent, is a prairie ecosystem. While both are grassland ecosystems, the former is composed out of one species only and designed by man, and the latter is rich in species and evolved naturally. Because biodiversity is nature's default state, man-made agricultural monocultures require massive inputs of labor, water, fossil fuels, petrochemical fertilizers, and pesticides to fight the natural order of things. A monoculture depends on stable conditions and is therefore incredibly fragile and susceptible to disturbances. All it takes is one flood, drought, disease or fire to turn the monoculture into a dead zone prone to erosion and degradation.

Prairies on the other hand, require no external input to be productive. Before their conversion into agricultural land, prairies produced enough food to feed tens of millions of bison with only rain and sunlight as inputs. Even more remarkable is their ability to cope with and recover from extreme weather events. Not even an intense wildfire can put a prairie ecosystem out of business. In fact, prairies thrive when they are exposed to intense disturbances. Being exposed to huge herds of grazing bison, extended droughts, and frequent wildfires generation after generation, has left the prairie ecosystem well equipped to deal with uncertainty and harsh conditions.

Not only are prairies incredibly resilient to deal with disturbance, they are also able to regenerate after major upheaval. Deep root systems allow plants to access water even in the driest of conditions, and to grow again even after they have been devoured or torched. The immense root systems of prairies are also nothing less than extremely effective carbon drawdown facilities, and the carbon fixed by grasslands tends to stay underground, even under fire. In areas that are prone to more frequent, intense, and widespread wild fires due to climate change, such as Australia and California, prairies may be a more reliable carbon sink than forests because, unlike burning trees, they do not release the stored carbon back into the atmosphere. Apart from producing food for a wide variety of species, from bees to bison, prairie ecosystems may offer us a robust and reliable technology to store carbon subsoil for long time spans. That is, *if* we restore and preserve these ecosystems and refrain from plowing in the future.

Prairie ecosystems can thrive on disturbance and disruption because evolution built a quality into the plants' DNA that anticipates change. This quality is referred to as *resilience* in biology, and it is nature's approach to dealing with uncertainty. It depends on the combination of three important features. *Diversity* because it is uncertain what part will be disturbed. *Redundancy*, because it is uncertain how many will be affected. *Decentralization*, because it is uncertain where the disturbance will hit. While most man-made systems are designed for stability and control, and therefore depend on predictability, prairie ecosystems have evolved to cope with uncertainty and unpredictability.

There is an important lesson for businesses and governments here: Monocultures are unfit to deal with disturbance and disruption, and are extremely fragile amidst change. Business monopolies and monocultures of thought and technology are just as brittle in the face of disruption as monocultures of weed in a farm field. Yet monoculture thinking and organizing is still the norm. Western science is still regarded as the only valid model for knowledge generation and decision making. Executive boards still consist of mostly of white men. And business metrics still account for dollars only. Lack of diversity leads to tunnel visions, homogeneity, and exacerbations, and prevents balancing feedback loops, which are necessary to prevent runaway change.

If we would take the time to learn from living systems, we would learn that nature innovates from a completely different paradigm than we do. Instead of *control & demand*, nature banks on *adapt & evolve*. Critics may claim that monoculture design is necessary because it allows higher production, but that kind of thinking still sprouts from a monoculture mindset, as it looks at productivity as one singular yield. Agricultural yield for example, is often expressed as tons of produce (think maize or wheat) per hectare.

The science of ecosystem services, however, adopts a more systemic perspective. One hectare of land can provide far more services than just tons of grain. It can produce oxygen and soil, purify air and water, cycle nutrients, detoxify pollutants, store carbon, and safeguard biodiversity. It can also support climate regulation, buffer floods, and cool heat waves. And let us also not forget its aesthetic, therapeutic, recreational, educational, and spiritual value. So, looking at a piece of land only in terms of "tons of produce" is like looking at another human being and only seeing the kilos.

We now know that rich, biodiverse ecosystems are far more productive than monocultures when we look at them from a system's perspective, and a recent study in the journal Science shows that species rich forests store twice as much carbon than single species plantations. Again, nature's biodiverse forest design outclasses our commercial model—the plantation. Biodiversity does therefore not only immunize against extinction, it boosts productivity, endurance, and resilience.

These insights have great economic and ecological significance, especially when it comes to the long-term health of the planet. Giving back half of the Earth to other life forms, like renowned biologist Edward Osborne Wilson proposes, not only ensures our future, it also safeguards the biggest R&D library of ways that work that we can draw from. Diversity and biodiversity matter. They are essential for dealing with uncertainty.

Towards business that is pro instead of anti-life

There is but one way forward, and that is to transform the human way of living to modes that are pro instead of anti-life. Seen in a broad historical perspective, current business practices are not enriching life; they are deteriorating life. Almost all economic activity today is part of a strategy that leads to tragedy.

But it does not have to be that way. By shifting our individual responses from reactive to anticipative, and from degenerative to regenerative, we can shift the macro patterns. No doubt, such a shift will be extremely challenging. Nonetheless, I am convinced that we can reimagine our value creation models so that they support, instead of impair, the web of life. So that our innovations add, rather than extract, value from nature. So that our business models increase, rather than reduce, the vitality and viability of both people and the environment.

In fact, it is already happening, and you will read in Chapter 5 about the business pioneers who are already working towards this future. Like the survival champions described in the previous chapters of this book, business can become good for the planet too, but we need to get serious about the transition, and there is not much time left.

The European Environment — state and outlook 2020 report (SOER 2020), the most comprehensive environmental assessment ever undertaken in Europe, shows that we have only *a ten year window of opportunity* left to radically reduce our consumption of natural resources, to lessen the impacts of climate change, and to scale up measures to protect nature in order to prevent irrevocable tipping points and runaway change. In other words, we are on the verge of shifting the planetary state to one that is unfriendly to human life.

And as the SOER 2020 report illustrates, current efforts to turn the tide do not get to the essence of what needs to be changed. They do not address the root of the problem. It is our logic of value creation that is in urgent need of an update. The illusion that humans are separate from nature—that humanity can live unplugged from the rest of life—has inspired the present logic of degeneration. It is the root cause of our global crises. It is a delusion that ecologies exist outside of us, because we are an ecology, and we are part of an ecology. It is when we realize that our business models are grounded in a degenerative value logic that we can start the effective transformation processes. The sooner we realize that we are an ecosystem, nested in and dependent on an ecosystem, the sooner we can start to devise meaningful, systemic, and life-enhancing approaches to innovation. The sooner we realize that we are the ones who need to evolve first before we can evolve our businesses, our technologies and systems, the sooner we can hack the degenerative logic that has been hardwired into our brains. If squid, octopi, and Boquila vines can do it, then why can't we?

Let's revisit a few important insights from the biology stories, and what they mean for the future of business. From fungi to forests, from arctic foxes to whales, *in nature long-term evolutionary success is the result of regenerative value creation*, or processes where organisms add value to their local environment in a way that enhances the entire biosphere. From a big history perspective, this means that "the code of life" is that it enables more life. Sustainability is not an endpoint but rather a by-product of regenerative value creation. By continuously adding value to the environment, organisms ensure that the following generations will be better off. This is the only investment strategy that is futureproof in the long term, and while predation and competition are part of the game, the stories about our cells, our canine companions, our forests, and our ocean life highlight that innovation and evolution depend primarily on collaboration. In fact, *collaboration and cooperation are more important for innovation than competition* because, as Martin Nowak brilliantly illustrates, without it there can be neither construction nor complexity.

The more our understanding of the natural world grows, the more we will come to realize that *life is what emerges from relationships*. The self is a society sustained by interdependencies. The richer the ecosystem, whether your own body or the environment you are embedded in, the more resilient it is. The networked way of life, or the centrality of networks for living and innovating, emphasizes not only the mutuality between our life and the life of all other creatures on this planet, but also the *crucial importance of byproducts for long-term success*. The challenge with most businesses is that they create products and provide services without giving attention to the byproducts that arise in their processes. The only way to genuinely move innovation forward is to spend as much attention on the byproducts as on the creations and transactions themselves. If we can change our micropatterns from degenerative to regenerative, we will improve the quality of life, richness, vitality and viability on both a local scale and a planetary scale. *The proof is in the patterns*. What happens on the microlevel is reflected on the macrolevel.

Leaving it better than you found it is the key, not only to survive, but to thrive, as the examples from the natural world illustrate. Contrary to popular conviction, *cognitive evolution might actually depend on enhancing friendliness, curiosity and tolerance*. Therefore, long-term business success might not depend so much on promoting your cleverest, but on fostering the most tolerant, curious, and friendliest employees—because cleverness alone is not enough to build collective intelligence and the intelligence of the collective.

While nature in general takes a very long time to upgrade its innovations, octopi and Boquila plants show us that shortcuts are indeed possible, and that these do not lie outside of ourselves. *It is possible to reprogram our brains and shift from a degenerative to a regenerative logic*. In fact, it is essential for our species survival. If fungi, plankton, and whales have learned how to influence processes in the atmosphere, surely, we can learn from them how to create a friendly climate, a climate that is beneficial to all of life.

By facilitating "earth-tech" approaches, like supporting whales' return to their previous abundance, we could experience a breakthrough in the fight against climate change, and by mimicking the life-friendly processes of the natural world, we can avoid the risks of unanticipated harm from suggested and untested high-tech fixes. *When we choose to focus on restoring the natural ecosystems in the ocean and on land, we are enabling nature's most powerful and sophisticated technologies to regulate the climate, and that type of R&D is millions of years ahead of ours*.

The stories I have shared in this chapter are only the tip of the iceberg. We are only beginning to understand how refined and hi-tech the living world truly is. From a historical perspective, we humans are a mere speck on the record of evolution. Still, we have been given two very powerful technologies for understanding and for creation: *our mind and will*. If we can harness our mind to full capacity, by improving our understanding of the way life works, and our will to full capacity, by learning to manage our egos, then we can tap into the power of NI.

This shift from degenerative to regenerative value creation is *one that starts inside.*

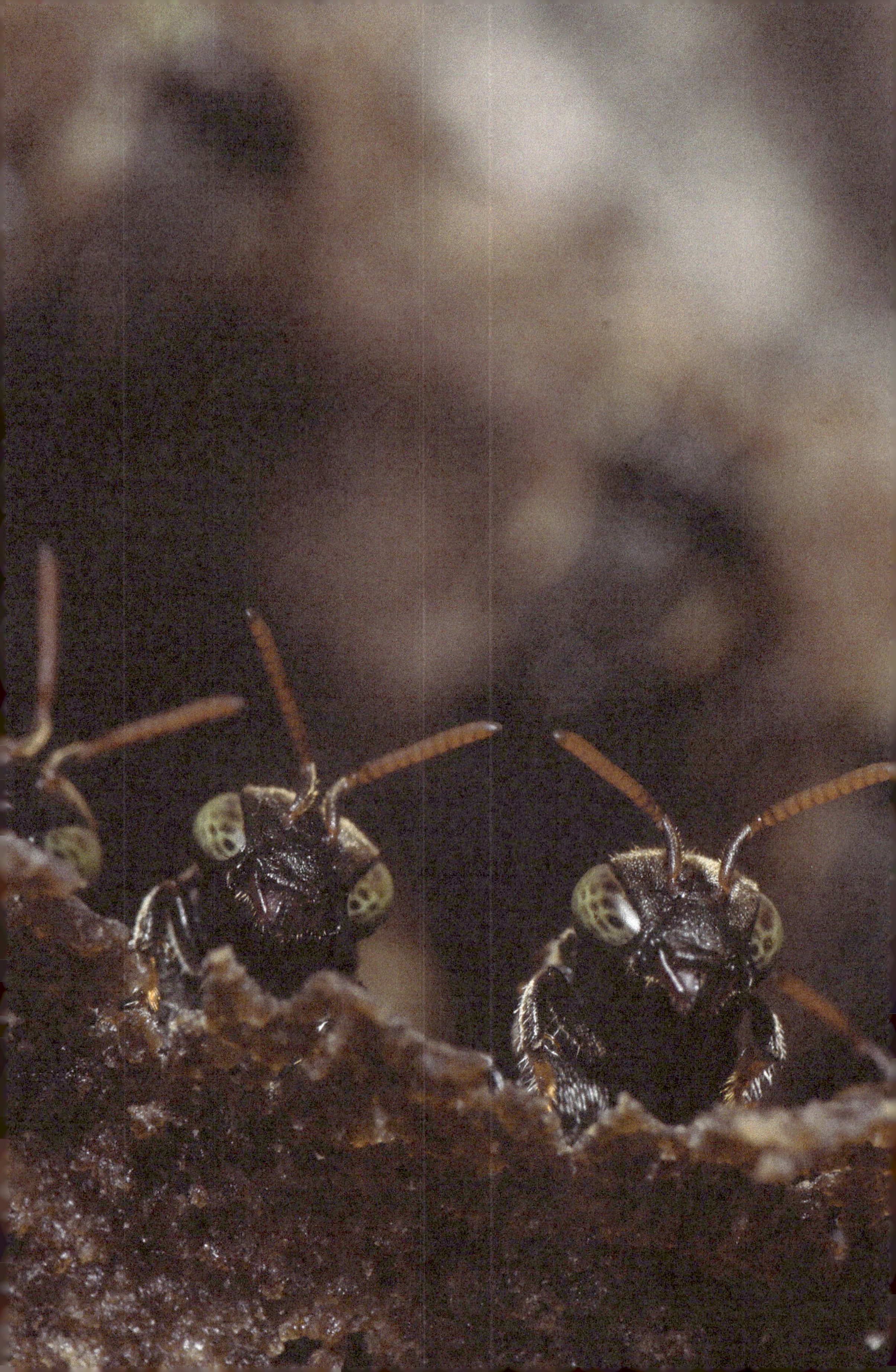

CHAPTER 4

BIOLOGY IS THE TECHNOLOGY OF THE FUTURE

Bio-inspired
—building the future on millions of years of field tests

Compared to the natural world, our world is poorly designed. Whenever we come up with a solution to a problem, we create different problems elsewhere, thereby perpetuating unsustainable ways of innovating. Yet, we are governed by the same laws that govern all life on our unique planet. And life has managed to sustain itself on Earth over eons, despite ice ages, volcano eruptions, and asteroid collisions. By now, it should be clear that we cannot solve our problems of unsustainability by using the same thinking that created them.[8] We need another kind of thinking, one that derives not from artificial but from natural intelligence.[9]

Since all life on Earth is subject to the same operating conditions, and natural selection has turned failures into fossils, those that have persisted hold the keys to the design that can stand the test of time and disruption. Janine Benyus and Dayna Baumeister, the great minds behind the discipline of Biomimicry call these survival strategies "life's principles" because they reflect what all life does on Earth. And while most companies have yet to discover this new way of innovating, nature has inspired organizations like VISA, Pax Scientific and the Land Institute, to pioneer some of the most cutting-edge and transformative inventions to date. These companies have learned how to harness the power of self-organization, of turbulence, and of regeneration.

What is more, learning from nature is now a daily practice in the innovation labs of multinationals such as Interface, HOK, Boeing, P&G, GE, Google, and Ford. In 2017, *Fortune* even called out biomimicry as one of the smartest ideas to benefit your business and career, stating that, "if you're not incorporating the most brilliant ideas from the natural world into what you sell, you're leaving money on the table."

While moving to Mars might seem exciting and adventurous, I would put my money on learning to become self-renewing right where we are. Imagine what we could accomplish if we could learn to adapt to changing conditions by developing rootedness, relationality, dialogue, and responsiveness—just like plants. Imagine the potential for flourishing if we learn to create conditions conducive to life—just like the animal stories that were shared before. Building the future

---

[8] Inspired by a quote that has been attributed to Albert Einstein.
[9] Off course, AI can build on the knowledge of NI.

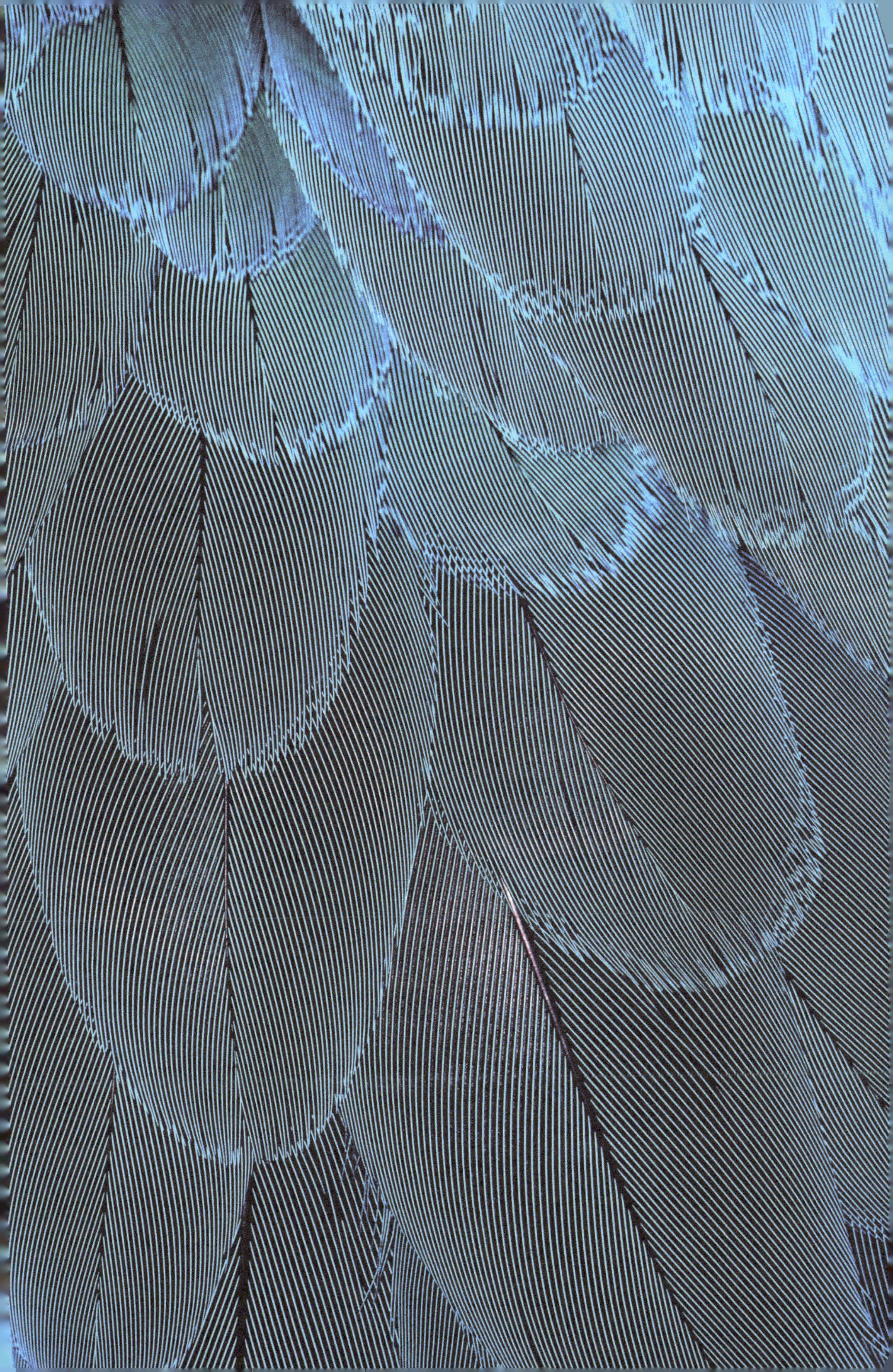

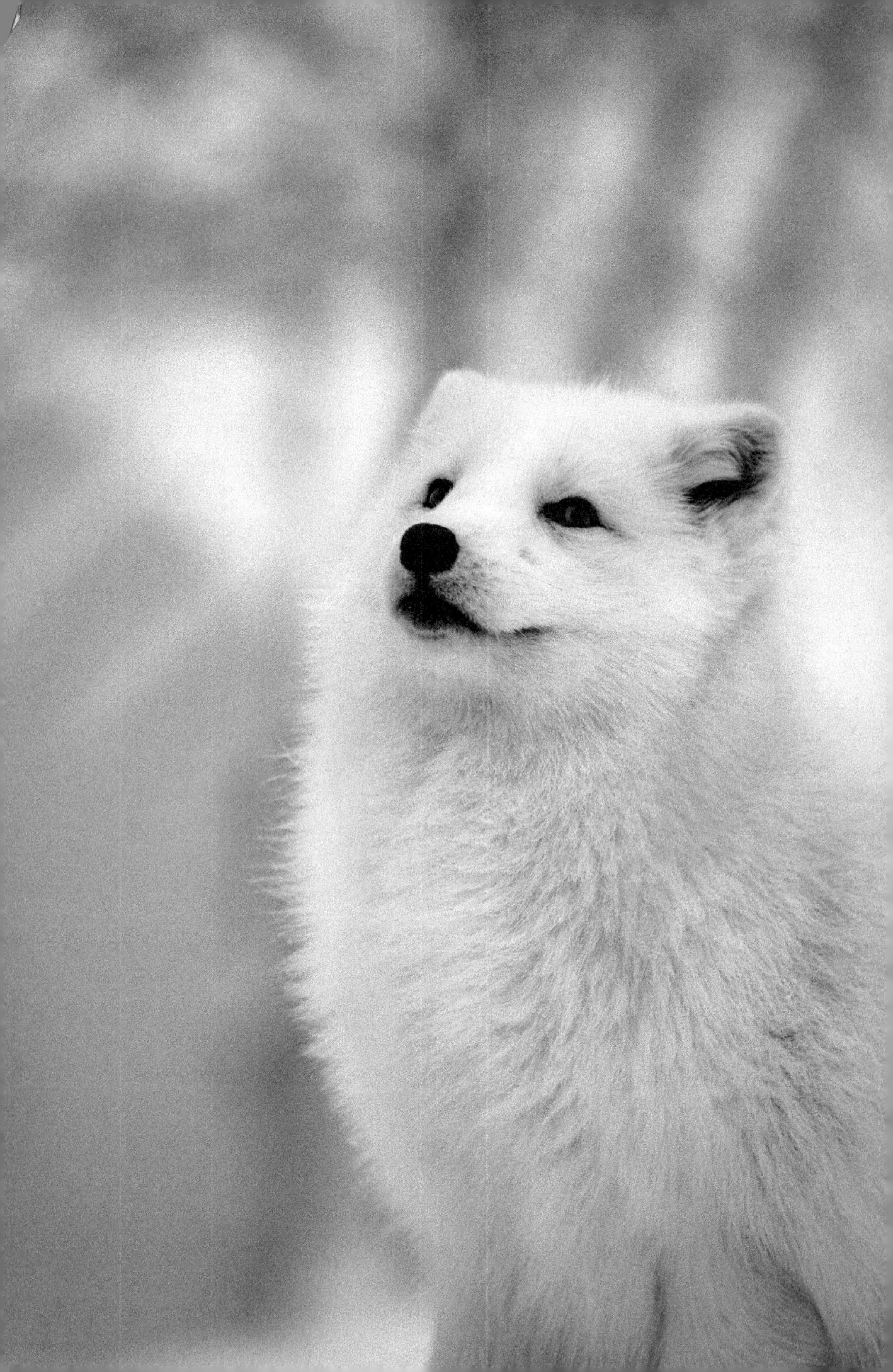

on millions of years of field tests seems to me to be the best chance we have for staying in this game called evolution.

Bio-logical
—it is only an investment if it leaves the world better off

The core principle of NI is *leave the world better than you found it*. Trial, error, imitation, and play is how nature innovates. Doing well by doing good is how she succeeds.[10] Bill McDonough, one of the founding fathers of the concept of a circular economy says that we are here to make goods, not bads. This is a completely different take on innovation, because, at best, organizations are managing *unsustainability* by doing less bad. As a general rule, the survival champions in nature do just the opposite. They regenerate. They create more health, wealth, viability, and vitality to ensure the success of not just the next generation but countless generations after that. Mushrooms make rain, whales cool the climate, wolves heal rivers, foxes plant gardens, and plankton make clouds. Nature's investment strategies for long term success are simple: only those that invest in the health of others to ensure their own and those that enrich their environment in a way that is beneficial for the biosphere survive in the long run. That is how NI works.

Calling the practices that degrade the planet's life-support-system "investments" is the most profound example of *virtual reality* I have ever encountered. Yet these VR-glasses appear to be glued to heads of business executives and politicians alike. We even teach this logic of degeneration at universities, meanwhile we refrain from teaching students how life works. The trickery of language. It is not an investment in our future if it is costing the Earth. So much of the world's natural habitat is lost for the sake of job creation and economic welfare. And so much dis-ease and sicknesses are spreading because people feel that their jobs are no longer meaningful. At this moment in time, our activities have brought us to the verge of world-changing tipping points that are far beyond the safe operating space of our planet.

It is time to shift our degenerative logic to a regenerative one, and to align with the way life works. What if we could create jobs that leave the world better

---

[10] In terms of staying around for 3.8 billion years.

than we found it? What if our products, our houses, our businesses, our politics added rather than extracted value to the environment? We can turn the tide by embracing NI and translating it into business models that do well by doing good. So how could your business become part of the solution rather than the problem?

Bio-chemical
—nature's chemistry is biocompatible and biodegradable

When it comes to chemistry, our logic is backwards. Chemist John Warner, President of the Warner Babcock Institute for Green Chemistry, narrows down the problem of traditional chemistry pointedly. From the 80,000 man-made chemicals in use today, fewer than 500 have been evaluated for toxicity. In the United States, only a handful of chemicals are regulated. Even more mind-boggling is the fact that not one university in the world requires its students to take a course in toxicology to become degreed chemists. The toxicity set free in the world is therefore one of unknown proportions and impacts. It is everywhere. From baby toys to perfumes to clothing and household equipment. You pay for products, and get the poisons for free. It is a merciless malice that affects everything in its wake. Toxicity is also a slow killer, gradually undermining health and quality of life, making it very difficult for our brains to recognize the problem. Cause and effect are simply too far apart for us to see the danger. Yet it does not have to be that way.

The living world is chock-full of chemicals. Adhesion, antifreeze, anti-oxidation, lubrication, flexibility, fire-retardation, self-cleaning, UV protection, water- and fire-resistance are just a few examples of the chemical ingeniousness concocted at ambient temperatures in nature's R&D lab. The seeds of fire-prone North American Jack Pine trees for instance, can withstand temperatures of up to 370 degrees Celsius. Hippos create their own sunscreen, which moisturizes and prevents infections. Arctic wood frogs freeze solid and defrost without damage. Spider silk is stronger than Kevlar, yet made at ambient temperature from dead flies and water. Nature's chemistry achieves astounding performance and is *non-toxic, biodegradable, and water-based*.

Mark Dorfman, biomimicry chemist and principal at Biomimicry3.8, highlights that nature's life-friendly chemistry recipe starts from three basic rules. First and foremost, all chemicals break down into benign and reusable components.

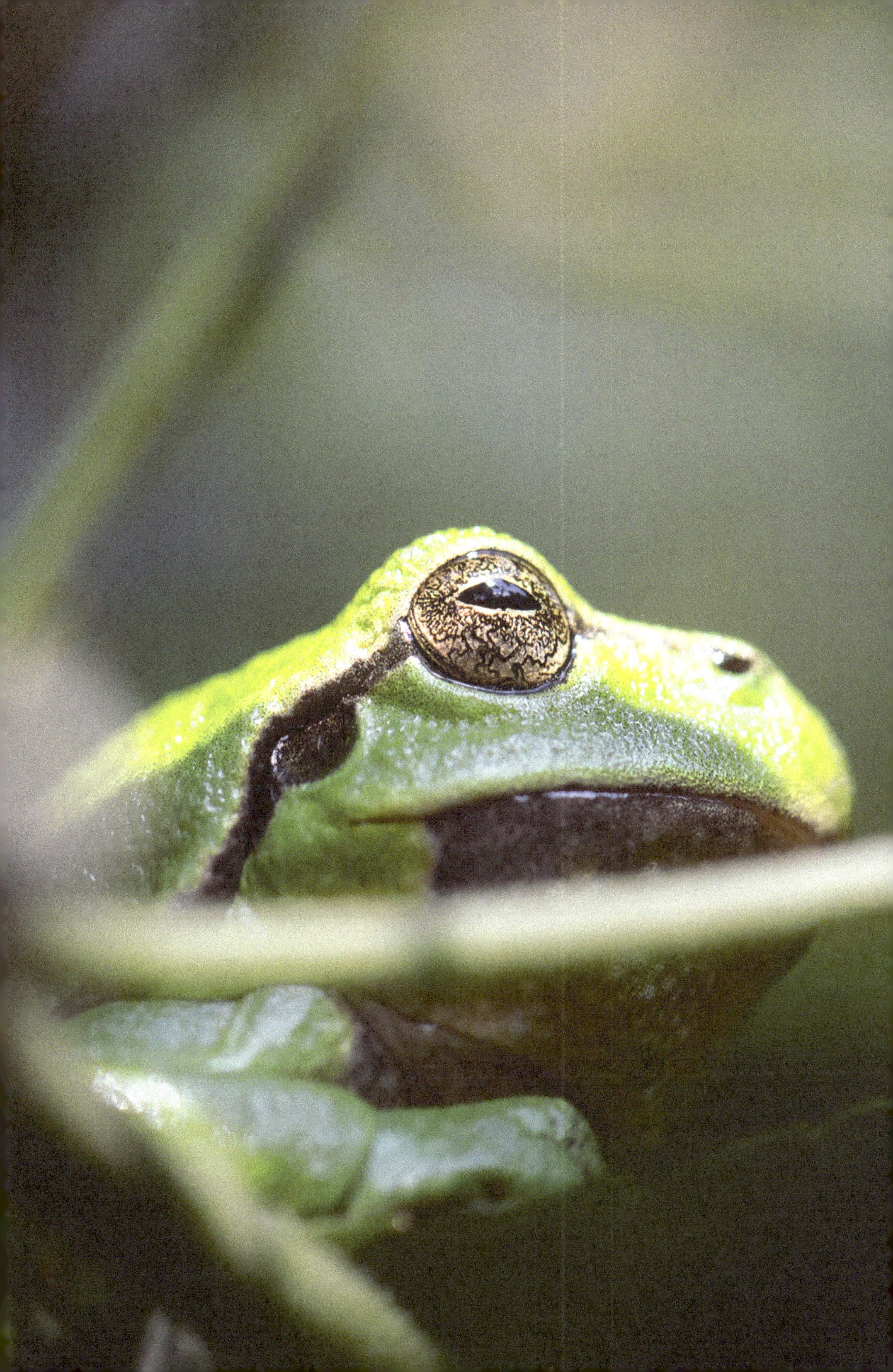

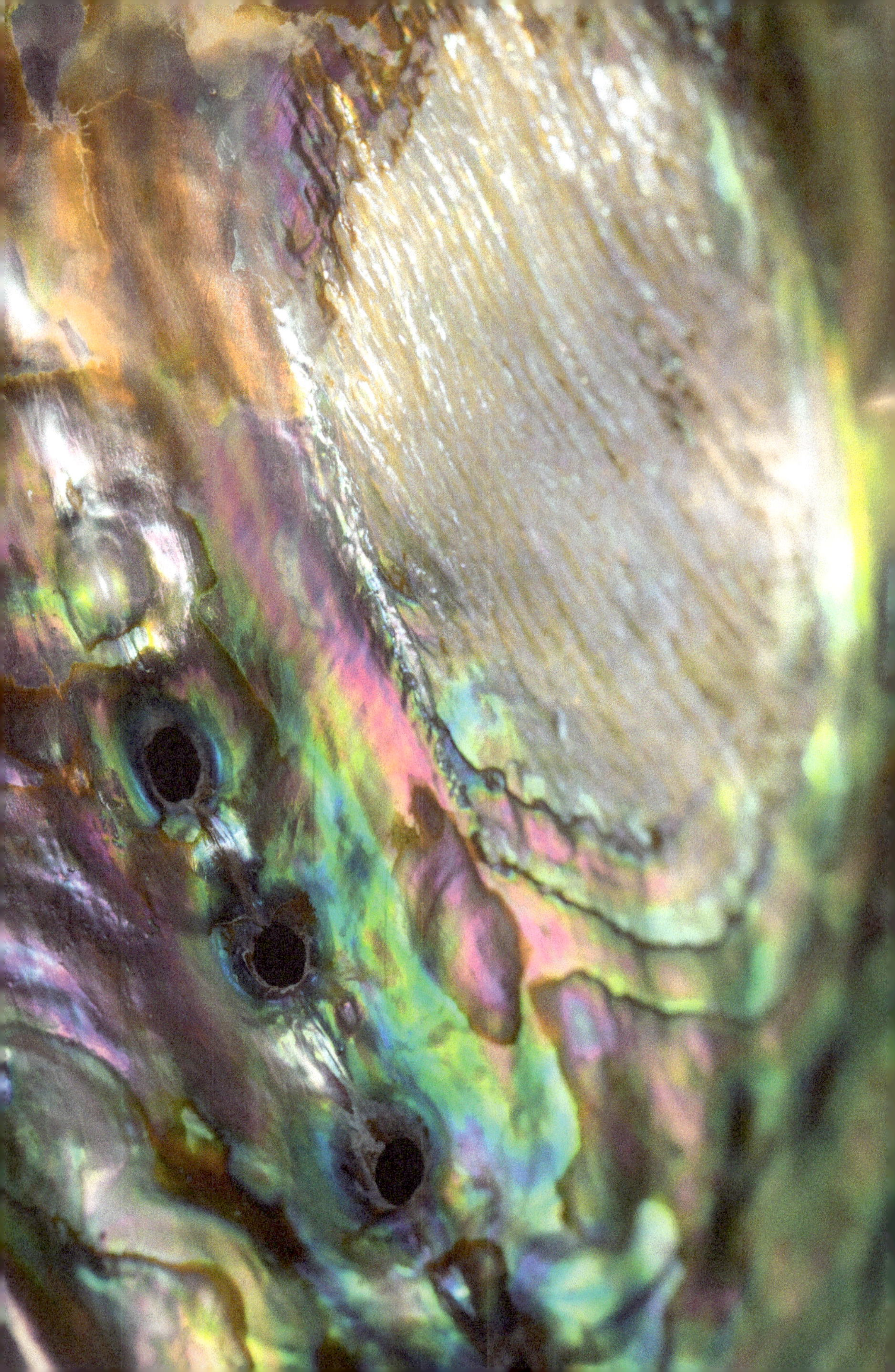

Second, nature uses water as a solvent for reactions. And third, she builds selectively with only a small subset of elements. While there are 118 elements in the periodic table, nature uses only 28 of them to create the billions of unique creatures that roam our planet.

Dorfman explains that nature's chemical strategies are, by necessity, life-friendly, because all organisms have to make, use, and manage their chemistry in the same place they raise their young. Generating life-unfriendly conditions is simply not an option that can withstand the test of time. And even though nature does create toxic chemicals occasionally—just think of a poisonous snake or spider—these poisons break down rather quickly into life-friendly components. They do not last, and they do not carry unintentional toxicities along with their primary function like man-made chemicals. Instead, toxicity in nature is the intended function for protection and predation. It can affect an organism but never an ecosystem.

Now that we are finally understanding the chemistry of life, businesses can shift gears and use nature's chemistry handbook to create life-friendly chemicals and processes. In fact, it is a fundamental requirement for a circular economy, because a circular economy without life-friendly chemistry perpetuates toxicity. If it is not life-friendly, it is not circular after all.

Bio-fabrication
—infrastructure is grown, not manufactured

Nature grows her infrastructure. From housing, to water cleaning facilities, from flood protection, to the Wood Wide Web, nature builds from the bottom up and in a circular fashion. Everything is food, and nothing is wasted. Absorb, assemble, multiply, disassemble. Absorb, assemble, multiply, disassemble. Nature's cycles spiral endlessly and add value at every turn. The process of natural selection leads to ever better designs and capabilities, to higher levels of resiliency and viability, to higher orders of wealth and complexity. Just like every winter is followed by spring, breakdown always comes before breakthrough. There are so many lessons in the way that nature creates. Features are built into materials, and materials work with the elements. Winds grow roots and make strong wood. Waves create superglue. Light and structure create color. Nature's portfolio is comprised of millions of unique designs, all devised for disassembly and conceived to color and sustain life.

What is even more astonishing, is that nature uses only two polymers to build all of life. Everything, from cell walls to muscles, from bones to trees, and from mice to elephants is made from only proteins and polysaccharides. These two basic polymers can be molded in the most versatile of ways. They can build soft tissues like skin or nerves, flexible materials like leaves or twigs, and strong materials like shells or horns. They can also build powerful parts like wings, or hearts, or complex parts like brains, or eyes. In contrast, our human industry depends on 350 polymers to make our things, none of which can come close to the versatility and functionality found in nature's designs, which can also self-assemble and are recyclable in perpetuity.

Little scarab beetles glitter and gleam like metallic in the sunshine, no different than a piece of jewelry, but there are no metals in their coats. The beetle bling is the result of the interplay of light and structure. Imagine if we could learn how to create silver and gold and metallic materials from only organic components, just like the little scarabs. In fact, the iridescent morpho butterflies are inspiring nanotechnology to mimic these photonic structures and properties to create color from structure. While precious metals need to be mined and are limited, biomass (living matter) can grow almost everywhere and is virtually unlimited.

Once you understand the ingenious ways in which nature builds, you will come to see that she uses very different design guidelines from ours. *Less material, more design*, that is one of her fundamental rules. Another one is that designs are always *multifunctional.* Feathers insulate, communicate, and improve lift. Noses breathe, read, and smell. Shells provide housing, protection, and make rocks. Trees make oxygen, shade, and soil. They purify air, clean water and prevent erosion. In nature, nothing fits just one purpose. Optimization beats maximization. Nature thus *optimizes functions while maximizing value.*

Yet, our human mass production approaches disregard the optimization principle, and we are experiencing disastrous effects as a consequence. Maximizing yields, which is the central adagio of current economic practice usually leads to diminishing value. In big agriculture for instance, food quality, soil, water and air quality all decrease when focus is on maximization (not to mention the harmful effects on biodiversity, human health and ecosystems). Mass production may lead to cheaper prices, but what you do not pay in money, you do pay in health, vitality, and quality of life.

Biomass is more than a mass of resources. It is a mass of functionalities and capabilities, all of which are tailored to improve life. *Minimum materials for maximum effect*, that is how nature works.

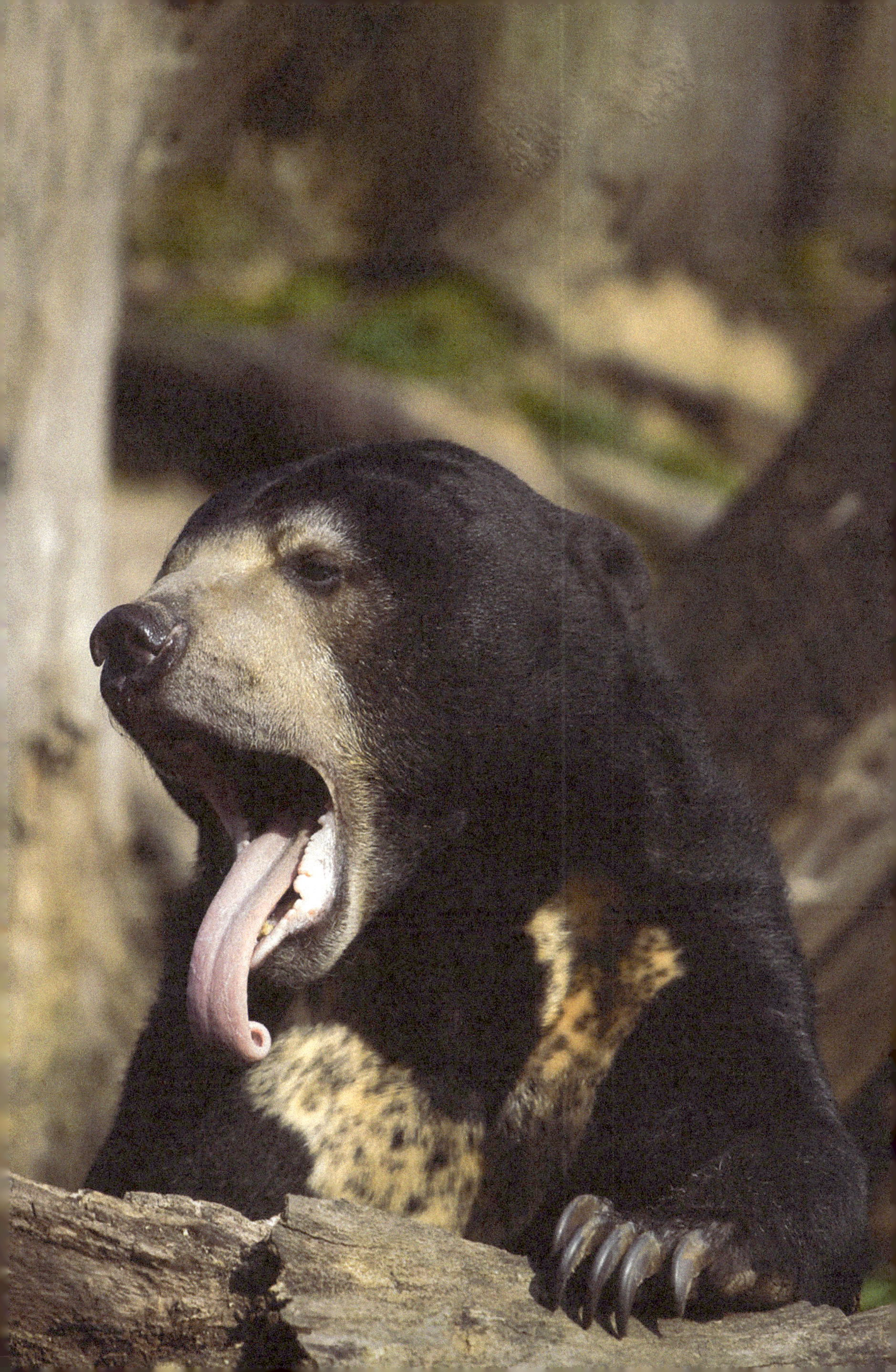

Bio-data
—nature's information systems advance collective intelligence

In our world, big data is the new gold. We are mining and storing data like we did with the precious metals. As data systems are becoming larger and ever more complex, learning from self-organized swarms and superorganisms (whose algorithms count in the big scheme of things) becomes increasingly relevant, especially since large amounts of data don't necessarily lead to smarter decisions nor appropriate responses. Nature's information systems on the other hand, are both effective and efficient and advance the intelligence of the collective while supporting the continuation of life.

Viruses went viral for the first-time billions of years ago, but they did not wipe out life. Termites outweigh humans ten to one, yet they do not deforest the planet like we do. There are anywhere between 100 and 10,000 trillion ants in the world today, and their footprint does not jeopardize the future. Ants live in cities, sometimes housing millions of individuals and, as far as we know, there are no issues of homelessness, unemployment, burn-out, congestion, or smog. And while we like to think of superorganisms as vassals working under the spell of a queen dictator, we now know that *distributed leadership, collective intelligence*, and *collective decision-making* is what makes ants so successful.

It is also not surprising then that bee democracy precedes ours. And not only does bumble bee governance arrange communal life effectively, it increases the health, wealth, and viability of the world's ecosystems. The same applies to other ancient super cooperatives like social insects, coral reefs and the complex Wood Wide Web. These have much to teach on how to disseminate information and resources in a lasting way.

From the internet of bugs to the internet of things, how can we build, access, and assess big data in a way that promotes the quality and future of life on our globe? What are the formula and algorithms that support life? How can we use big data for good and build the collective intelligence that is required to learn to flourish together with all other inhabitants on Earth? In nature, information is everywhere, and organisms know how to use it well. Schools of fish equal schools of efficiency. Termitaries excel in proficiency. Microbial logistics stand out in efficacy. And they all leave the world better off. Nature calculates, plans, negotiates, orientates and iterates via a sophisticated system based on data that matter. Big data require big questions, and biology shows us that AI without NI is not futureproof.

Bio-hacking
—a fast track to evolutionary change

Change usually starts from within. If there is one prime pattern in nature, it is that. Wolves turned into dogs, because they became more tolerant and friendly. Fungi and trees evolved into forests, because they became reciprocal. Whales became the managers of the marine circular economy, because they became better stewards. And we humans got so successful because we became more imaginative and collaborative. These examples show that the communication between our DNA and our behavior is a two-way stream: DNA influences our behavior and our behavior also influences our DNA.

While Livnat empirically shows that new skills can be anchored into our genetic codes so that they become innate, octopi and Boquila lianas show us that we do not need generations for that to happen. They have *learned to hack and reprogram their own genes to become better versions of themselves.* In our world, what really needs to be hacked is the way we think. As the previous part on patterns in Chapter 2 illustrates, the value logic in our heads is mirrored in the world. So, the question is: How can we install an evolutionary mentality in our mindsets, and a developmental culture in our organizations so that we can proactively hack and reprogram the thoughts, customs, and practices that are not fit for the future, and are no longer appropriate in today's world?

People in leadership positions are likely better placed than most to help cascade positive change and new ways of thinking across society. But, like Whitney Johnson, an influential management expert says: "We give a lot of airtime to building disruptive products and services, to buying and/or investing in disruptive companies, and we should. Both are vital engines of economic growth. But, the most overlooked engine of growth is the individual. If you are really looking to move the world forward, begin by innovating on the inside, and disrupt yourself."

We individual humans can evolve into better versions of ourselves. After all, octopi and Boquilas learned to rewire their genes millions of years ago.

The practice of rewiring the human brain has actually been an ancient one, rooted in traditions such as mindfulness, meditation, yoga, and recently, positive psychology. While most of these practices have long been regarded as esoteric, today's scientific technologies show that they do alter the brain. Both mindfulness and meditation have proven to bring about a multitude of benefits that increase

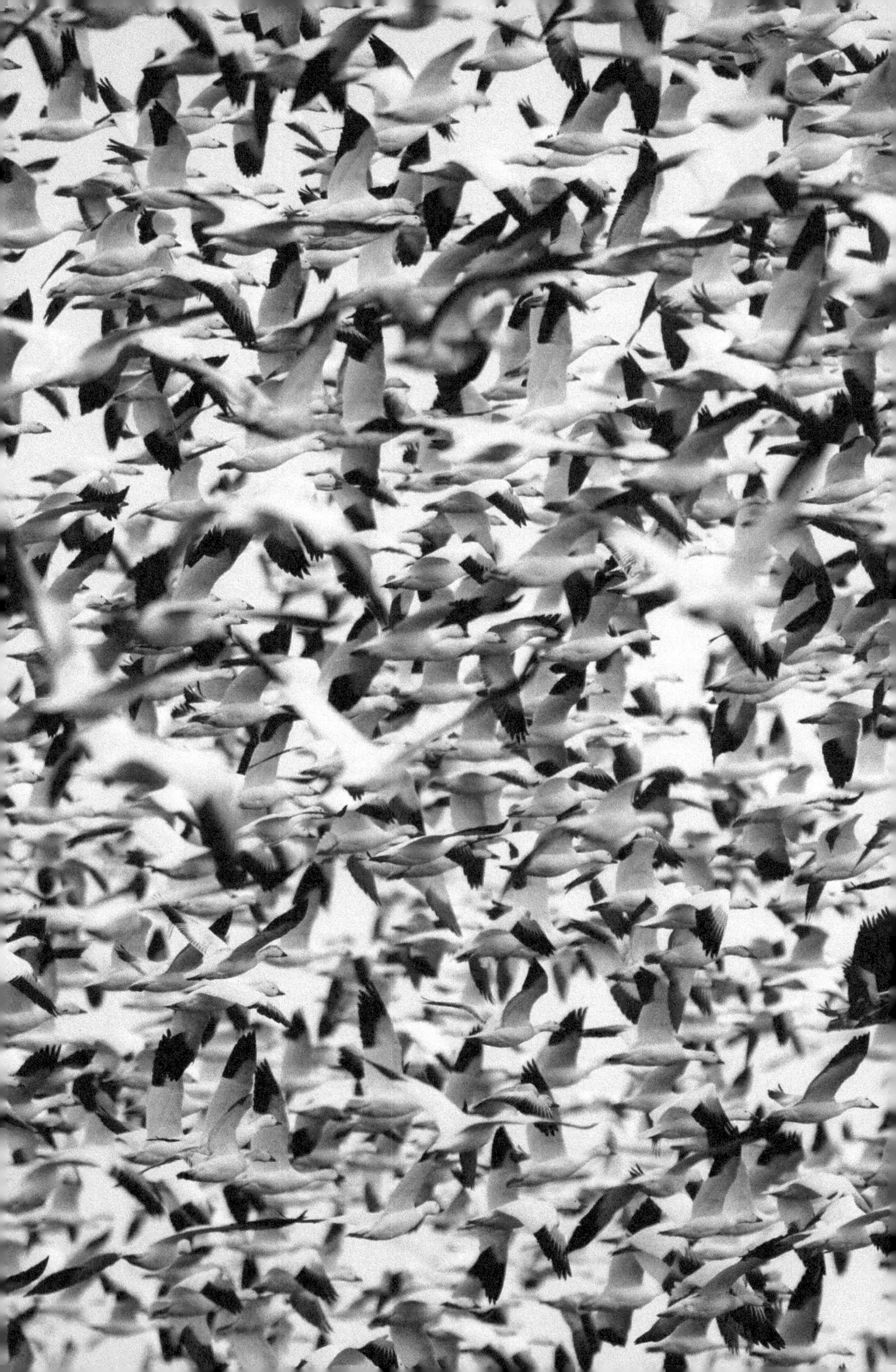

well-being and self-realization of practitioners, which explains the recent surge in corporate meditation programs, because meditation also improves employee performance. But more often than not, such methods are only used to "manage the dysfunction" rather than transform what is no longer appropriate. For this reason, many enlightened employees are leaving their companies as their jobs fall short in meaningfulness, purpose, and positive impact.

From a psychological point of view, hacking our own brain might be a good strategy because we are more prone to view things pessimistically. Humans have a natural inclination to care more about preventing losses than increasing gain. We give more weight to negative information and experiences than to positive ones, and we tend to select information that fits our pre-existing beliefs. Not only are we programmed to give more attention to and remember more information about negative events, we also tend to view people who say negative things as smarter than those who are positive, giving greater weight to criticism. It is no wonder that change management processes have such low success rates.

Sports psychologist Rens Ter Weijde of Purpose+, points out that there are two important barriers that prevent us from flourishing as individuals and organizations. The first barrier is that the brain has developed mental shortcuts to preserve energy, reinforcing old world views and habits of thought. Ben Haggard and colleagues at of Regenesis pinpoint this difference in *thinking* versus *thoughting*. While thinking creates new thoughts, thoughting only downloads old ones. Thinking is more energy-intensive, so the brain automatically goes to thoughting unless you train it to do otherwise. Jumping to conclusions requires much less energy than questioning one's own values, beliefs and worldviews. The second barrier is that our limited mental bandwidth is not able to deal with today's information overload. As a result, the traditional top-down, corporate hierarchies will become increasingly ineffective and will be replaced by flat horizontal company cultures, where leadership and ownership are shared and distributed. Because only the latter can harness the power of collective intelligence and agility.

Bio-philia
—nature not only makes us healthier; she makes us happier and smarter too

It may sound contentious, but nature is better for your health than the health care sector. And this assessment doesn't come out of thin air. Evidence of the impact of nature on our health, happiness, and wits is mounting. Nearly 1,000 studies "point in one direction: Nature is not only nice to have, but it's a have-to-have for physical health and cognitive function," according to the Yale School of Forestry & Environmental Studies.

For instance, a multitude of scientific investigations show that wandering through forests reduces blood pressure and heart rate. What is more, forest immersions reduce the levels of cortisol (our stress hormone) and increase the levels of serotonin, the "happy" chemical that operates in our nervous system. Eva Selhub and Alan Logan, researchers at Harvard and authors of the book *Your Brain on Nature*, state that, "spending time in a forest can reduce symptoms of psychological stress, depression and hostility while improving sleep, vigor and vitality."

The restorative impact of nature is so effective that merely looking at nature through a window, boosts mental energy. In fact, employees who have a view of nature from their desk, perform better than those without. Their job satisfaction is higher while absenteeism is lower. Likewise, the ability to focus and concentrate is higher when people spend time in nature compared to urban environments. Research showed that creativity and problem-solving capacity of students rose by 50% after spending four days in the wilderness, meanwhile, those that spent four days in the city did not show this increase. Tests given in schools also showed that children in the presence of plants scored much better than those without.

Not only are cognitive abilities enhanced in nature, our immune system is also improved. So much so, that the number of killer T-cells (the cells in your body that eliminate cancer cells) is significantly higher after a hike into the woods. And when going out into the wild is not possible, merely looking at nature footage already increases feelings of contentedness, joy, wonder, awe, amusement and curiosity, while reducing feelings of tiredness, anxiety and stress. What is more, scientists have recently discovered that low childhood exposure to nature is associated with worse mental health in adulthood. The study, involving 3,585 participants from four European cities, demonstrated that growing up without regular exposure to nature leads to higher levels of nervousness and feelings of depression in adult life.

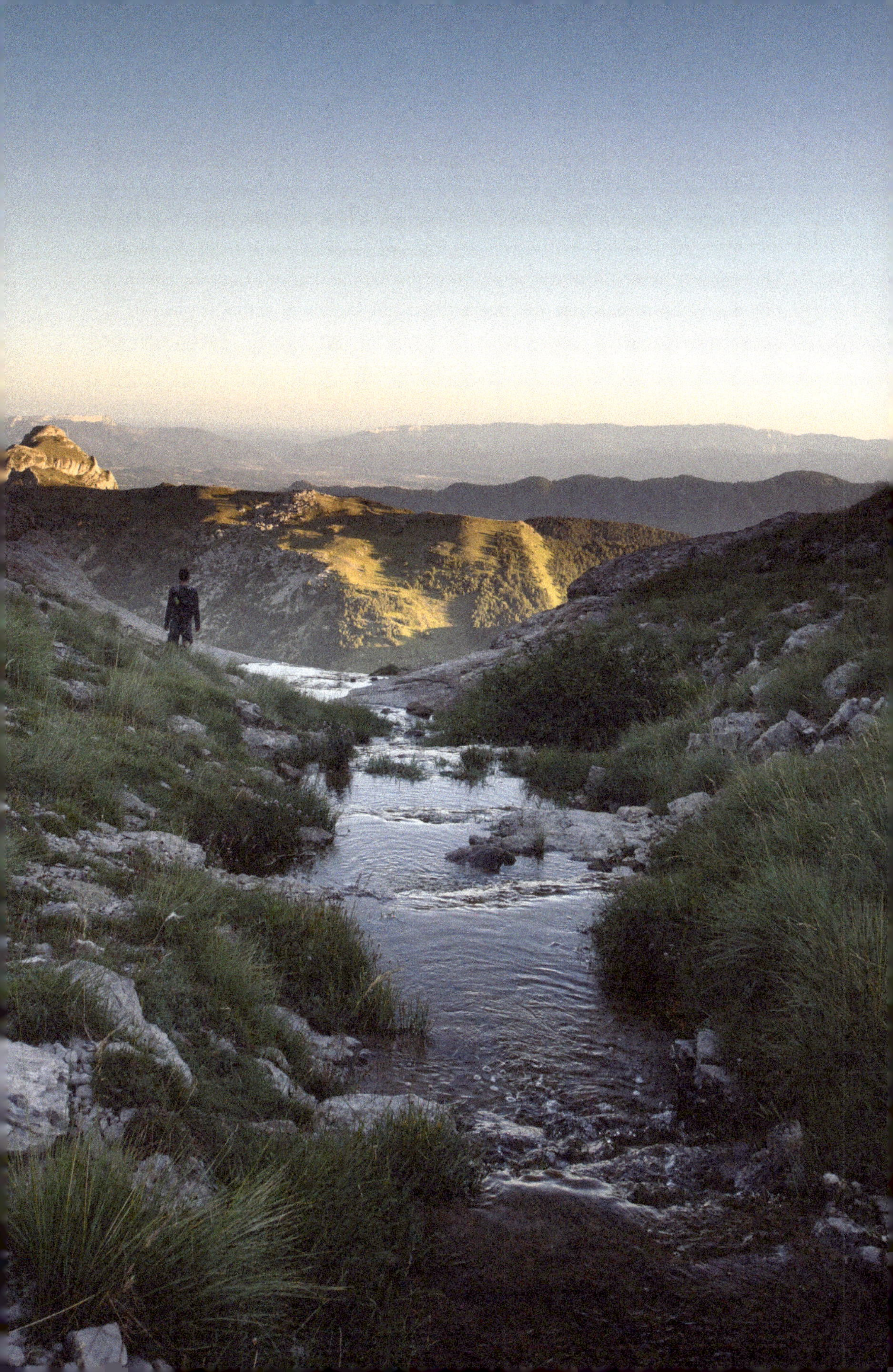

Nature thus not only makes us healthier; she makes us happier and smarter too. Applying these insights to how we construct our human dwellings, is central to biophilic design, a discipline that investigates how we can design buildings and spaces that energize, restore, heal, and improve our being—just like nature. The need to rethink the way we design the human habitat became painfully obvious when researchers discovered that our buildings actually make us ill. They even formulated a name for it: "sick building syndrome." Not only do the pollutants and toxins of modern building practices lead to discomfort and health problems, so too does our disconnection from nature.

Sometimes it takes going to space to figure out what we humans need to stay well. Enter the space research program that is investigating how we can get to Mars, where the most difficult challenge to solve in terms of long space journeys is not so much technical as it is psychological. The mental deterioration associated with deep space travel is an important obstacle to solve before we can send astronauts to the red planet, a mission that has been tickling our imagination since the landing on the moon. As it turns out, one of the solutions that offers the best prospect of solving the issue is to supply the mission with a large amount of plants.

Experiments with plants in space, like aboard the International Space Station, have demonstrated noticeable, positive effects on astronaut's moods. So much so, that the search for bioregenerative life support systems in space has significantly intensified over the past years.

This did not surprise Stefano Mancuso from the University of Florence, whose laboratory has been investigating the effects of space travel on plants. He writes in his compelling book *The Revolutionary Genius of Plants* that, "Plants are the engine of life. We humans are totally dependent on them and whatever destination we choose as the next step of our expansion into space, we cannot go there without plants."

It all boils down to the simple fact that regular nature exposure is beneficial, nature deficiency is harmful, and man-made structures devoid of nature are detrimental to health, happiness and cognitive capacities. Developing urban spaces at the expense of nature is designing out health and smarts. But it does not have to be this way. What if we could redesign office spaces, industrial sites and cities to be more life-friendly and nature inclusive? Wouldn't you prefer to live in a building covered with plants instead of a cement box, and smell flowers instead of cars? Wouldn't you prefer to wander streets that buzz with life instead of concrete dead zones? I would. More so, I think we can. If we have the courage to think beyond conventional urban planning and construction approaches to develop regenerative building and planning practices, we can achieve a better quality of life. If we learn to design roads like rivers, buildings like trees, and cities like forests, we not only boost health, we boost bliss and wits too.

Renaturing human nature and rewilding urban habitats should be the focus of urban planning and development, because the nature of the future and the future of nature are interdependent.

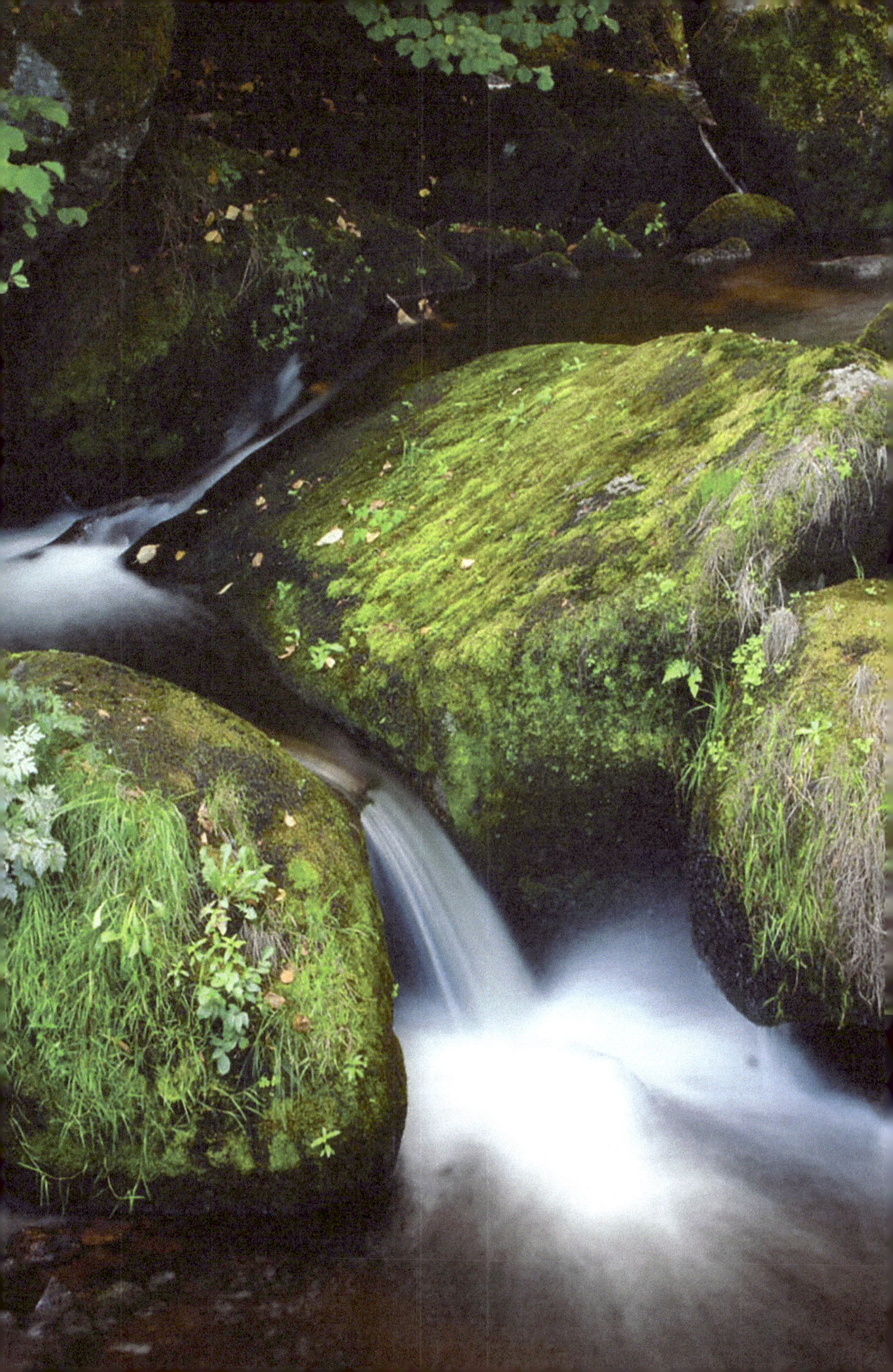

CHAPTER 5

IMPROVING BUSINESS AND THE WORLD THROUGH NI

NATURAL INTELLIGENCE

Health Care

While usually featured as the bad guys in thrillers like *Jaws*, sharks are actually very refined and robust organisms. They have been around for almost half a billion years and are excellent hunters, thanks to their extraordinary, streamlined body. This streamlining expresses itself on the macro scale with a hydrodynamic body shape that creates vortices to propel them forward in a very energy efficient way, and on the micro scale where a shark's skin structure reduces drag, or resistance, and increases thrust in a very clever way. Their skin is made up of tiny, overlapping scales (known as dermal denticles) that are arranged in a distinct diamond pattern with tiny riblets. This roughness of the sharkskin prevents water from sticking to the shark, which would slow it down. No surprise then, that some sharks can swim as fast as 50 kilometers per hour. But there is yet another interesting feature of shark skin. Its surface properties prevent microorganisms from attaching to the shark.

As highlighted in the introduction, we now know that the conventional way of "controlling" bacteria (a.k.a. killing them via antibiotics and disinfectants) has contributed to the creation of superbugs like MRSA, the hospital bug that is resistant to antibiotics. As these practiced biocidal methods are making bacteria more resistant and resilient, it becomes clear that we need new strategies to manage bacterial growth and to create healthy environments. And it appears sharks might show us an alternative way.

A company called Sharklet Technologies Inc, based in Colorado, is developing thin films that mimic the properties of the sharkskin to inhibit bacterial growth by means of microstructure in place of chemicals. By imitating the diamond pattern into coatings, Sharklet® products inhibit bacteria from attaching, colonizing, and forming biofilms—without the use of toxic additives, chemicals, antibiotics, or antimicrobials. This company has invented a technology that has the potential to radically reduce the spread of infection in hospitals, schools, and nursing homes, especially when Sharklet is applied to surfaces like bathroom doors and to medical equipment like wound dressing, catheters and tubes. What is more, imitating the shark skin technology significantly contributes to sustainability as fewer chemicals and toxic disinfectants are needed to maintain a healthy environment.

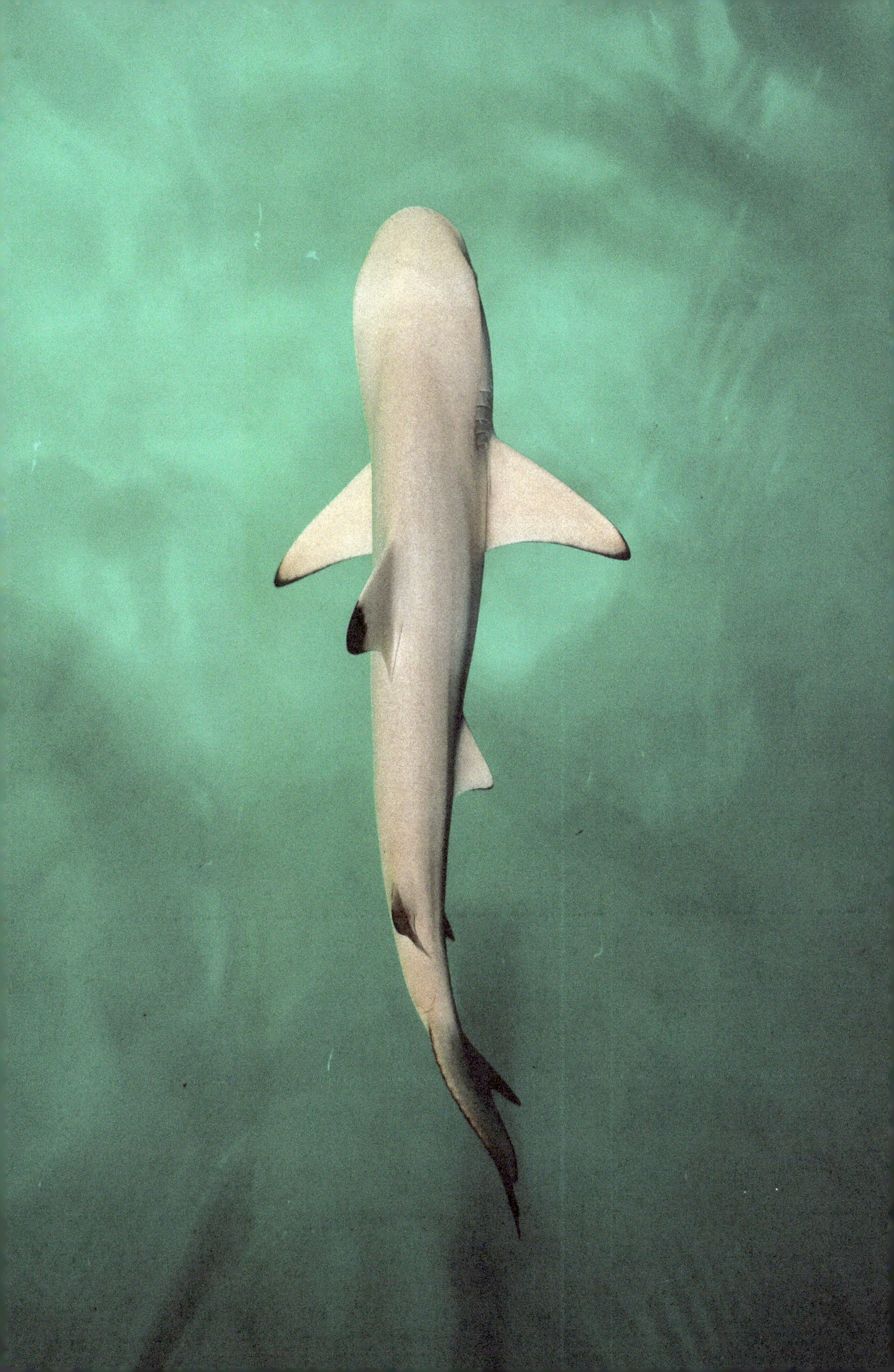

But it is not only big, impressive animals like sharks that might teach us a thing or two to improve our health care system. Little creatures like mosquitos and slugs, often considered an annoyance, also possess superpowers and state of the art equipment which might contribute to better and more comfortable medical procedures. Take needles for instance. Even though they are cleverly designed and get the job done, having a needle inserted in your body is never pleasant, is it? That is because the smooth cylinders of needles present a large surface area that interacts with your nerves, more often than not resulting in discomfort and pain.

Mosquitos, however, have evolved a natural bio-micro-electro-mechanical system that functions like a needle, but penetrates the human skin painlessly. Most of the time, we do not feel them piercing our skin, because mosquito syringes have been designed to minimize contact area. Less contact with nerves, means less pain. The mosquito syringe system is very sophisticated. It contains multiple parts and only the tiniest of parts are used to pierce the skin of their victims, touching the nerves of the skin at significantly fewer points than our one-piece needles. High-speed video observations of blood sucking mosquitos show that they only insert two micro-saw parts with nano-sharp teeth to perforate the skin and not the whole feeding device which is called fascicle. Not only is this elegant bio-micro-electro-mechanical system nearly pain free for its victims, the force needed for injection is extremely small, costing the mosquito very little energy. Inspired by this low-invasive model, Japanese engineers have designed a microneedle after the mosquito feeding device to reduce pain during injections and blood transfusions.

Now, let's move from needles to surgery, to explore how nature can show us how to improve survival and recovery. In 2017, a headline of *Popular Mechanics* read, "Slug Snot Could Be a Valuable Medical Tool." Indeed, researchers at Harvard have found a way to create a revolutionary surgical adhesive for wound healing inspired by the slimy slug. When people are cut open for surgery, internal tissue needs to be closed again efficiently. While stitches or staples work, they still damage healthy tissues. In fact, many medical adhesives are toxic to cells, inflexible when they are dry, and have difficulty binding to biological tissue.

But slug-inspired, wound-mending adhesives work as a non-toxic, bio-compatible superglue, and research shows that their high mechanical performance in wet environments, and compatibility with blood, cells, and tissues allow these materials to meet key requirements for next-generation tissue adhesives. In other words, this new medical technology for healing and surgical repair inspired by slug mucus might one day help you or a loved one heal better, quicker, and more comfortably.

And while these last two examples are still in the proof-of-concept phase, more and more bio-inspired technologies are entering the market, offering more elegant and efficient solutions in comparison to their manmade alternatives. Like Tissium for instance (formerly known as Gecko Biomedical), a privately-owned life sciences company, based in Paris, that is dedicated to the rapid development and commercialization of biomorphic programmable polymers to address various unmet clinical needs. They develop sealants that are biocompatible, biodegradable and on-demand programmable to help achieve immediate hemostasis during open vascular surgery.

Or Veryan Medical, a company established in the UK, that develops bio-inspired solutions for vascular disease in areas with strong unmet medical needs by using its advanced understanding of the physics of blood flow. By mimicking the natural shape and geometry of the human vascular system, Veryan Medical has developed a helical shaped stent technology, called BioMimics^{3D} the swirling flow® stent. Their stents are more flexible, more kink-resistant, and more fracture-resistant than conventional straight ones. The helical shape also supports the swirling of the blood flow through the stent, which has been shown to prevent future blockages, a process also known as restenosis.

Of course, the best health care investments are the preventative ones, the ones that prevent disease in the first place. And there's no better teacher to learn how to do that than fungi. While we often turn to plants for their medicinal and immune supportive properties, humans are actually closer related to fungi than to plants. This relationship might be why fungi have such enhanced medicinal benefits for humans.

Fungi are several hundred million years older than plants, which further explains their extraordinary capacity to stay healthy. The fungi part that lives subsoil, the *mycelium*, is a network just one cell wall thick, yet is in direct contact with a myriad of possible hostile organisms like viruses and bacteria. To survive, these organisms have developed amazing properties, the likes of which we have not yet encountered. A recent scientific overview of medicinal mushrooms and fungi reported approximately 130 medicinal functions—including antitumor, antioxidant, antidiabetic, antiviral, antibacterial, anti-parasitic, antifungal, anti-hypercholesterolemic, immunomodulating, radical scavenging, cardiovascular, hepatoprotective, and detoxification effects.

The article highlights that numerous bioactive polysaccharides, or polysaccharide–protein complexes derived from medicinal mushrooms, appear to enhance innate and cell-mediated immune responses and exhibit antitumor activities in both animals and humans. And it's not just in the lab, several of these medicinal mushroom compounds have been subjected to Phase I, II, and III clinical trials, where they have shown their efficacy on patients. Long before these trials, fungi have been extensively and successfully used in Asia to treat various cancers and other diseases.

Mushroom therapy does not entail serious side effects like chemo or radiation treatment (though toxicity requires careful consideration), which calls into question why the Western world has been blind towards the fungi's medical properties. According to a recent publication in the *Biomedical Journal*, the reasons why they are ignored in the West, even though there exists excellent evidence to suggest a scientific basis for the effects of medicinal mushrooms, may be related to economics and IP rights.

Paul Stamets, my favorite mycologist and a brilliant scientist and entrepreneur, has put forward the idea that mycelium is the neurological network of the biosphere. He proposes that fungi are therefore the bridge between the immune system of our body and that of the environment. Given the plethora of recent scientific findings on the beneficial impact of forests—the place where fungi thrive the best—on our health supports this idea. If the mycelium network has evolved extraordinary immune system properties, then spending time in the woods is likely to enhance our immune system as well. In fact, a question that has been circling my thoughts for years is: Why does Lyme disease have such detrimental effects on humans, but not on the forest dwelling animals that have been infected and act as carriers?

If the human immune system is connected to the purported immune system of the forest, which developed more than 300 million years ago, then we'd better think twice before continuing our deforestation efforts. Because we lose not only the trees, but also many of the fungi that can help us combat illnesses, prevent cancer and infections, clean up pollution, and help restore degraded soils.

Because mushrooms are the forest guardians, they fuel numerous life cycles and are essential for processes of regeneration because they facilitate the transition between life and death. As decomposers, they turn dead matter into fertile soils, setting free the nutrients for other life forms to develop. Like Stamets says, "Without fungi all ecosystems would fail. Knowing how to work with them, will be critical for human survival." He concludes that "MycoDiversity is BioSecurity."

Putting his knowledge of fungi to practice, Stamets founded Fungi Perfecti, a family-owned company dedicated to promoting the cultivation of high-quality medicinal and gourmet mushrooms. Fungi Perfecti is also a good example of a company on a regenerative mission. Not only do they set out to preserve and protect as many ancestral strains of mushrooms as possible from pristine woodlands, Stamets also invests in cutting edge research to help save the bees.

Together with researchers from Washington State University and the United States Department of Agriculture, Stamets discovered that extracts from the living mycelial tissue of common wood conk mushrooms, known to have antiviral properties, significantly reduced viruses in honeybee colonies. After observing bees foraging on mushroom mycelium, the research team set out to explore whether the bees were deriving medicinal or nutritional value from those fungi. They tested extracts from the mycelium of multiple polypore fungal species known to have antiviral properties and the results are astounding. In field tests, bee colonies that were fed fungi extracts, exhibited a 79-fold reduction in the deformed wing virus and a 45,000-fold reduction in the Lake Sinai virus compared to control colonies. Clearly these findings indicate that honey bees self-medicate using mushroom-derived substances. Bees thus not only need access to poison-free flowers, they need access to immune-boosting mushroom mycelia too.

Energy

When it comes to man-made innovation, we like to use language like "state of the art" and "hi-tech," and when we refer to other life forms, especially those that are very different from us like bacteria and algae, we often use words like "primitive." Funny, because fluorescent microalgae, one of the oldest lifeforms on the planet, can convert sun light into energy with 95% efficiency, using only benign and locally available resources. In comparison, the majority of installed PV (photovoltaic) cells today operate in the 10-20% efficiency range. So, who is primitive here?

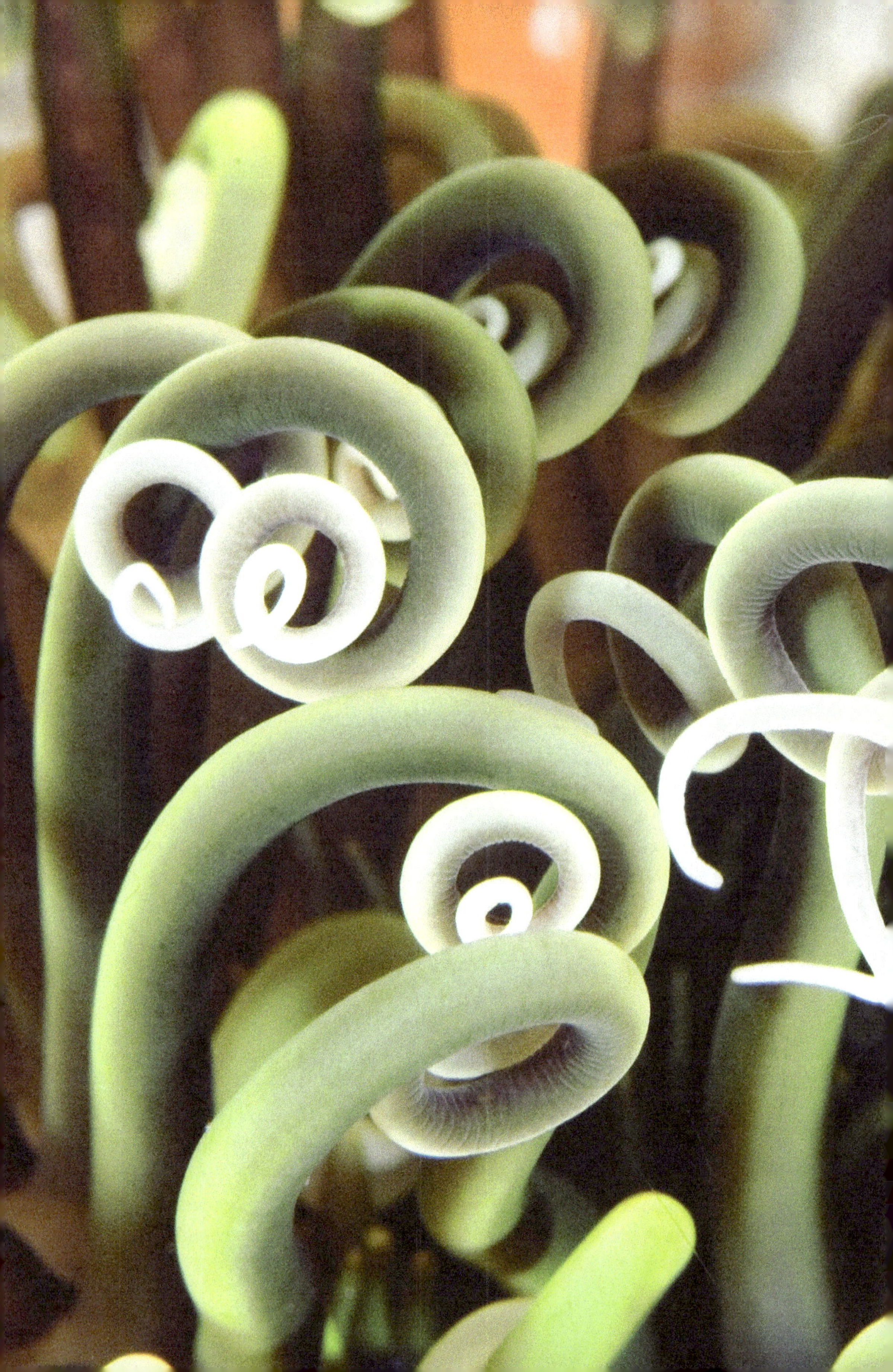

After dozens of years of R&D, scientists are finally looking at algae technology as inspiration for advancing PV efficiency. They have discovered that a mass of light-harvesting antennae, called phycobilisomes, cover the microorganism's surface and are responsible for converting light into energy, and that each antenna is made up of stacks of complex building blocks. One of the scientists involved in the research, Professor Albert Heck, Scientific Director of the Netherlands Proteomics Centre at Utrecht University, highlights that the solar converting system of these algae is more sophisticated than the most sophisticated Swiss watch.

Heck acknowledges that the algae's hi-tech nature is a product of billions of years of fine-tuning—and that engineers could learn a lot from it. Once scientists understand how these tiny aquatic creatures achieve such super-efficient energy harvesting from the sun, they might radically advance the performance of our PV systems. Which would accelerate the transition to renewable energy and a low carbon future.

While some scientists have struggled for decades and decades to improve energy efficiency, others have struggled to control turbulence—the non-linear dance pattern of fluid movement —because engineers want fluids and currents to move in an orderly and linear fashion. Nature, on the other hand, does not move in linear lines. She swirls, spirals, and spins. NI, therefore, is about harnessing turbulence instead of fighting it.

Jay Harman, inventor, entrepreneur and CEO of Pax Scientific, a fluid dynamics research and design firm in California, understood this years ago. Capturing the force of nature, that is what fluid dynamics should be about, not controlling or resisting it. Harman points out that while engineers have covered the earth with straight pipes, canals, chimneys, and buildings, nature never, ever, uses a straight line for any purpose. Inspired by the whirlpool shape that can be found everywhere in nature, Harman reverse engineered the spiral shape into a patented mixing device called impeller.

In 2013, the impeller was already installed and used by more than 200 cities to mix and destratify layers of stagnant water in over 600 large-scale drinking water storage tanks. It proved to be much more efficient than conventional systems, saving municipalities up to 90% in energy costs to keep the water fresh and up to 80% in disinfectant use for the creation of municipal tap water. Imitating nature did not only pay off in terms of environmental benefits, according to Harman, PAX Water has won several industry awards and doubled its sales every year since.

PAX is not the only company working the magic of turbulence. In Belgium, a young company called Turbulent, founded in 2015 and gathering an impressive list of awards, is developing efficient hydropower plants for rivers and canals with a low height difference (between 1.5 - 5 m), also inspired by the whirlpool principle. Turbulent developed a hydropower impeller design that turns the incoming water flow into a low-pressure vortex, allowing aquatic life to pass unharmed while generating electricity. Their power plants are small, affordable, fish-friendly, easy to install, and easy to transport to remote locations.

In particular, their bio-inspired design can practically be implemented anywhere where there is a small height difference in canals and rivers, and they can produce electricity every hour of the day and every day of the week. So, they produce a nearly constant supply of electricity in contrast to the intermittent supply of wind turbines and solar power. According to the pilots that are already up and running, these decentralized power plants can generate electricity for dozens to hundreds of households, and investments are paid back in five years or less. Hydropower inspired by nature pays off. The founders of Turbulent are now setting up a production line in Belgium.

In the meantime, another Belgian, a physicist called Jean-Pol Vigneron was captivated by the light emitting insects we call fireflies. Together with his research team, he discovered how these small insects were able to shine light through their exoskeleton. It appears that the scale-like structures that cover the firefly's exoskeleton have a jagged form with a tilted slope, which sticks out at different angles thus emitting more light. The team emulated the light-emitting microstructure into a jagged over-layer for LED lights. The firefly design increased light extraction by more than 50%. Researchers at Penn State University in Pennsylvania have now fine-tuned the technology and filed a patent. They hope to collaborate with manufacturers in the field to commercialize the firefly technology. Given that electricity for lighting worldwide accounts for about 5% of the greenhouse gas emissions, the firefly technology might help to significantly reduce these emissions.

There is another small critter, one that very few people have heard of, that can radically help our society shift to a low carbon future. I am talking about the tardigrade or water bear. This microscopic, water-bound invertebrate has amazing superpowers that allow it to survive freezing cold, sweltering heat, dehydration, and other extreme conditions for large periods of time. That is why biologists call them "extremophiles." Like the name says, water bears need water to do their thing. When conditions get tough, like during extreme droughts, tardigrades sit these out by suspending their metabolic activity. This reversible metabolic state is also known as cryptobiosis, and it helps the tardigrade survive dozens of years without water. As soon as water returns, the dormant water bear springs back to life. To prevent damage during droughts, tardigrades protect their biological material with special proteins and sugars.

Imitating tardigrade tech for stress tolerance can serve a number of fields, from improving food storage to the stabilization of sensitive pharmaceuticals in a dry state. The San Diego based company, Biomatrica, offers technologies to stabilize biological materials at room temperature without the loss of sample integrity and inspired by the long-term survival strategies of organisms like the tardigrade. Nova Laboratories Ltd in the UK secures vaccines in a glassy substance of sugars, storing them in a non-liquid form, thereby eliminating the need for refrigeration. This candy coat keeps the vaccines effective for months— even in hot temperatures. While these bio-inspired technologies are particularly handy in tropical countries, they also open the pathway to significantly reduce refrigeration costs in labs worldwide, the cost of which is currently estimated at about $30 billion a year. Given that refrigerant management is the most significant global solution for cutting greenhouse gas emissions, tiny creatures like the tardigrades show us how to save energy, money, and the planet from runaway climate change.

Agriculture

The degenerative impact of innovation-as-usual approaches is painfully illustrated in agriculture. If we continue current industrial mass production practices, we have only 60 harvests left on Earth according to soil specialists. Not to mention that agriculture is ranked as the number one driver of the destruction of nature. No less than one million species are threatened with extinction, according to leading scientists in a landmark new report from the Intergovernmental Science-Policy Platform on Biodiversity and Ecosystem Services (IPBES) that was released in 2019. It states that while more than a third of the global land surface is devoted to agriculture, land degradation has already reduced the productivity of 23% of that area. As nearly 75% of the world's freshwater resources are used for agriculture, the synthetic chemicals associated with crop protection and promotion have infiltrated the freshwater resources at a magnitude never seen before, affecting all life in its wake.

A citizen science project in Belgium in 2019 for instance, discovered that dead songbird fledglings, found in nest boxes, had 36 different chemicals associated with crop protection in their bodies. Even more worrying is the fact that 94% of the studied bodies contained DDT, an insecticide that has been forbidden since 1974. This not only shows that human-induced eco-toxicity can last long after our changed policies, it also shows that they can affect the whole food chain. In fact, the IPBES study estimates that up to $577 billion in annual global crops are at risk from pollinator loss. The answer to some, is intensification and precision agriculture. Unfortunately, these measures sprout from the same degenerative logic that caused the problems in the first place because they keep toxifying the land, require huge inputs of fossil-based energy, fertilizers, and pesticides and thus accelerate both the climate and the biodiversity crisis. Luckily, there is another way.

It turns out that ancient indigenous communities were practicing a form of agriculture known as *polyculture agroforestry* in the Amazonian rainforest 4,500 years ago, which, researchers have concluded, is responsible for the overwhelming abundance of edible plants that can be found there now. This indigenous farming practice was very different from the clear-cutting of forests that spread through the Americas after the arrival of the Europeans. Rather than deforesting and depleting the soil, these indigenous farmers maintained a closed canopy and continuously enriched the soil, so they could reuse it over and over again. So much so in fact, that this type of soil, called Amazonian Dark Earth, is much more fertile than unmanaged Amazonian soil. Even though these indigenous communities have been absent for thousands of years, the Amazonian rainforest is still the most affluent in the places that they once inhabited. Not only does this show that agriculture and nature conservation can go hand in hand, it also shows that humans can play a positive role in the ecosystem and that regenerative

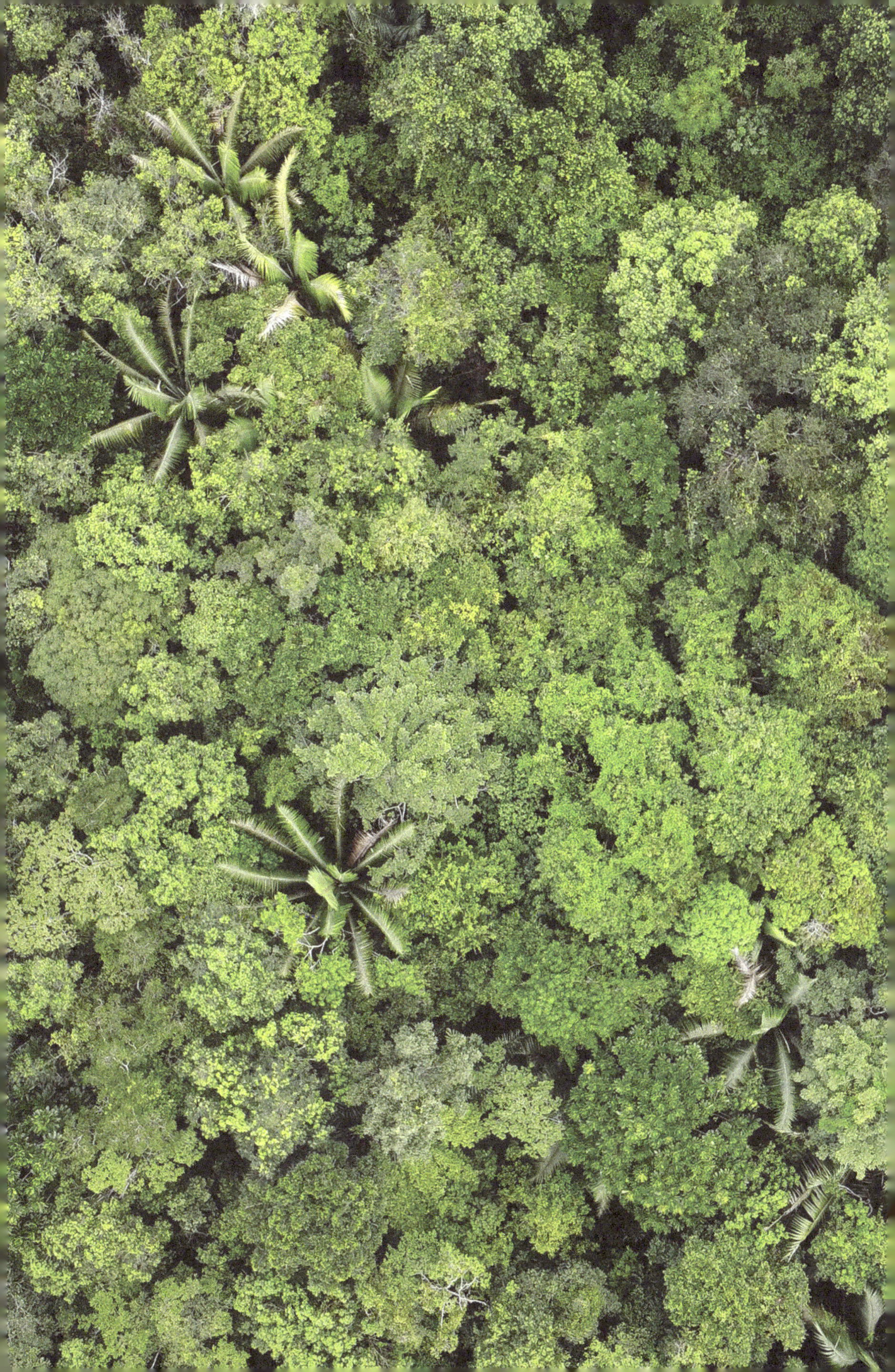

agricultural systems can endure for thousands of years. In fact, it is the best example that *permanent agriculture* (permaculture) works.

According to the researchers involved in the study, the indigenous agricultural systems have an enduring legacy on the hyperdominance of edible plants, which makes them conclude that this agroforestry model of food production can serve as a model of sustainability for modern farmers. And while critics claim that such models cannot feed the world, agroforestry can increase yield and improve food security at the same time. That is because all polyculture practices increase crop resilience to several climate change effects, such as drought, flooding, or rising temperatures. They enhance water infiltration and storage, reduce evaporation, and temperature extremes, support biodiversity, and increase livelihood resilience.

There are already millions of permaculture practitioners in the world that are redesigning landscapes according to these polyculture and agroforestry principles, most of whom are small holders or home growers. You might wonder why we aren't practicing this type of agriculture on a large scale. That is mostly because it requires a very different business model than conventional agriculture. Permaculture farms can easily produce up to 80 (if not more) different edibles in relatively small quantities, compared to big agriculture, and there are many harvests throughout the year. The current agrarian economic model, however, has been designed for large quantities of one or a few crops that are harvested once a year.

The fact that permaculture land also produces a wide range of ecosystem services, (carbon storage, safeguarding and promoting biodiversity and increasing food security) while industrial agriculture leaves the land uncovered and sterile for a large part of the year (making it very fragile in the face of climate change) is not presently taken into account in our current economic model.

It seems that permaculture pioneers are not only innovating the way we produce our food, but they are also pioneering new business models in an economic environment shaped for mass production, the latter being the reason that this more regenerative way of producing food has not yet entered the mainstream. Nevertheless, examples of largescale permaculture farming do exist. One of the most renowned examples is probably New Forest Farm, a 43 ha perennial agricultural system run by Mark Shepard in Wisconsin, which is considered one of the most ambitious, large scale, sustainable agriculture projects in the United States.

His book *Restoration Agriculture* offers an insightful story of how to shift from farming at the expense of nature, to farming in collaboration with nature, and shows that many solutions to the challenges of modern agriculture are remarkably low-tech. Working with perennials instead of annuals and transforming monocultures in biodiverse polycultures, results in healthier animals, superior quality meat, dairy, and produce, a resilient income, and a whole lot of ecosystem services like carbon capture, water storage and pollination. And in contrast to conventional agriculture, the soils on his farmland get richer over time, leaving the environment better off than before.

Another example is Polyface Farm in Virginia, where Joel Salatin, one of the most well-known and published co-owners of the farm, calls himself a lunatic farmer, because he often does the opposite of what is considered to be conventional farming practice. Instead of the current efficiency-based model of meat production—fattening up high numbers of livestock in industrial stables, isolated from their natural environment—Polyface farm's goal is to approximate the natural model of herbivory. Wild herbivores exhibit a few key characteristics that keep them healthy and robust. First, they horde together for protection against predators. Second, they don't eat where they poop. They move daily to fresh forage. And third, their diet consists of diverse plant forage only. They eat a wide variety of herbs, grasses, shrubs, trees (and bark in winter). They never eat grains (like maize or soy), animal products, or fermented feed stocks like industrially grown livestock. Because these animals can roam freely, they can regulate their health themselves instead of being pumped full of antibiotics.

Salatin calls his meat production system "salad bar beef," because his cattle eat forage only and are herded into a new pasture roughly every day. This more natural model of livestock management regenerates the land, thickens the forage, and reduces weeds and pathogens. It also promotes cow health and therefore increases the nutritional qualities of the meat. Polyface Farm services more than 5,000 families, 50 restaurants, ten retail outlets, and a farmers' market with its salad bar beef, pigaerator pork, pastured poultry, and forestry products, showcasing that this nature-inspired way of meat production is economically viable at the same time as it is ecologically regenerative.

Even small-scale permaculture initiatives offer a good alternative to the degenerative industrial model, not only for ecologically sound and healthy produce, but also for the farmers involved. While BigAg renders a very poor income for farmers, the 400 edible species rich food forest Ketelbroek, in the Netherlands, produces a farmer's income that is ten times higher than a conventional monoculture farmer receives. Other food forest farmers report less spectacular numbers but still much more than what they would get for monoculture crops. What is more, such farmers are never exposed to carcinogenic chemicals, because they are not used. It's a win for all. The farmland gets richer in soil, produce, and biodiversity over time, and the farmer's family is better off and can live and work in a healthy environment.

There is endless logic to mimicking nature's models in agriculture. Research shows that *Silvopasture*, an ancient farming practice that integrates trees and pasture into a single system for raising livestock, is the highest ranked carbon mitigation solution in agriculture. According to Project Drawdown, it is the ninth most potent way to pull carbon dioxide out of the atmosphere. The researchers involved, state that Silvopasture far outpaces any grassland technique for counteracting the methane emissions of livestock and sequestering carbon subsoil. That is because pastures with trees sequester five to ten times as much carbon as those of the same size that are treeless, storing it in both biomass and soil. Moreover, adding trees to grasslands helps decrease the effects of droughts, because trees root deeper than grasses and pull up water from below. They provide shade and wind breaks, protecting livestock and soil, which amplifies the productivity of the farm by increasing meat and dairy production. So Silvopasture is a climate win-win, because it averts *and* sequesters emissions, it helps in managing climate risks *and* it can increase income over the long term.

In southern Spain, Silvopasture models are called *Dehesas*, and a study on such farms in Extremadura showed that mixed systems, rotating cattle, sheep, and Iberian pigs on pastures with evergreen trees, have been found to be the most sustainable in general terms. Diversification of agricultural produce not only increases productivity; it also builds resilience to market risks. Finca Casablanca, in Extremadura, is an extensive Dehesa farm, combining olive trees with beef cattle and native pigs, which has been developing a novel grazing model, to prevent overgrazing and facilitate tree regeneration. They collaborate with the local University of Extremadura to study and improve the system and are considered an exemplar of sustainable agricultural practice in the region.

Silvopastoral systems that include trees into grasslands also help to adapt to erratic weather conditions and increased drought. Project Drawdown calculated that if Silvopasture expands an additional 200 million hectares by 2050, over 31 gigatons of carbon dioxide can be sequestered. Farmers could also realize financial gains of $699 billion globally from revenue diversification on an investment of just over $41 billion to implement.

The forest model is not the only natural model that we can draw inspiration from to develop productive landscapes. The prairie model might inform regenerative agriculture too, because it is a productive, self-regulated, nutrient cycling, and resilient model that maintains healthy soils, stores carbon and promotes biodiversity. The Land Institute in Kansas is developing an agricultural intensification system that equals the ecological stability of the prairie, and has a grain yield comparable to that of a monoculture. Instead of relying on annuals, they mimic natural systems and work with perennial plants, those that live longer than just one year and consequently, grow deeper roots. Their mission statement brings several of nature's lessons together beautifully: "When people, land, and community are as one, all three members prosper; when they relate not as members but as competing interests, all three are exploited. By consulting Nature as the source and measure of that membership, The Land Institute seeks to develop an agriculture that will save soil from being lost or poisoned, while promoting a community life at once prosperous and enduring."

The Land Institute focuses on ecological intensification by using naturally occurring plant communities as models for polyculture production. By mimicking nature, they are convinced that previously unattainable levels of ecological intensification are possible with perennial polycultures instead of annual monocultures. To put this in practice, the researchers at the Land Institute are breeding new perennial grain and seed crops adapted to ecologically intensified polycultures. They aim to develop an agricultural system that can produce ample food, while also reducing the negative impacts from industrial agriculture and a changing climate. Their focus is twofold: perennializing existing annual grain crops and domesticating wild perennial species which are productive and resilient crop candidates.

One of their first commercial new perennial grains is Kernza® wheat, and Patagonia Provisions was the first company to turn this new perennial grain into an organic beer, appropriately named Long Root Pale Ale. A number of restaurants in the US also serve this new perennial grain.

In Finland, the Baltic Sea Action Group initiated the Carbon Action project, which develops and researches ways of accelerating soil carbon sequestration by enhancing the microbial life below ground. They build on the logic that the

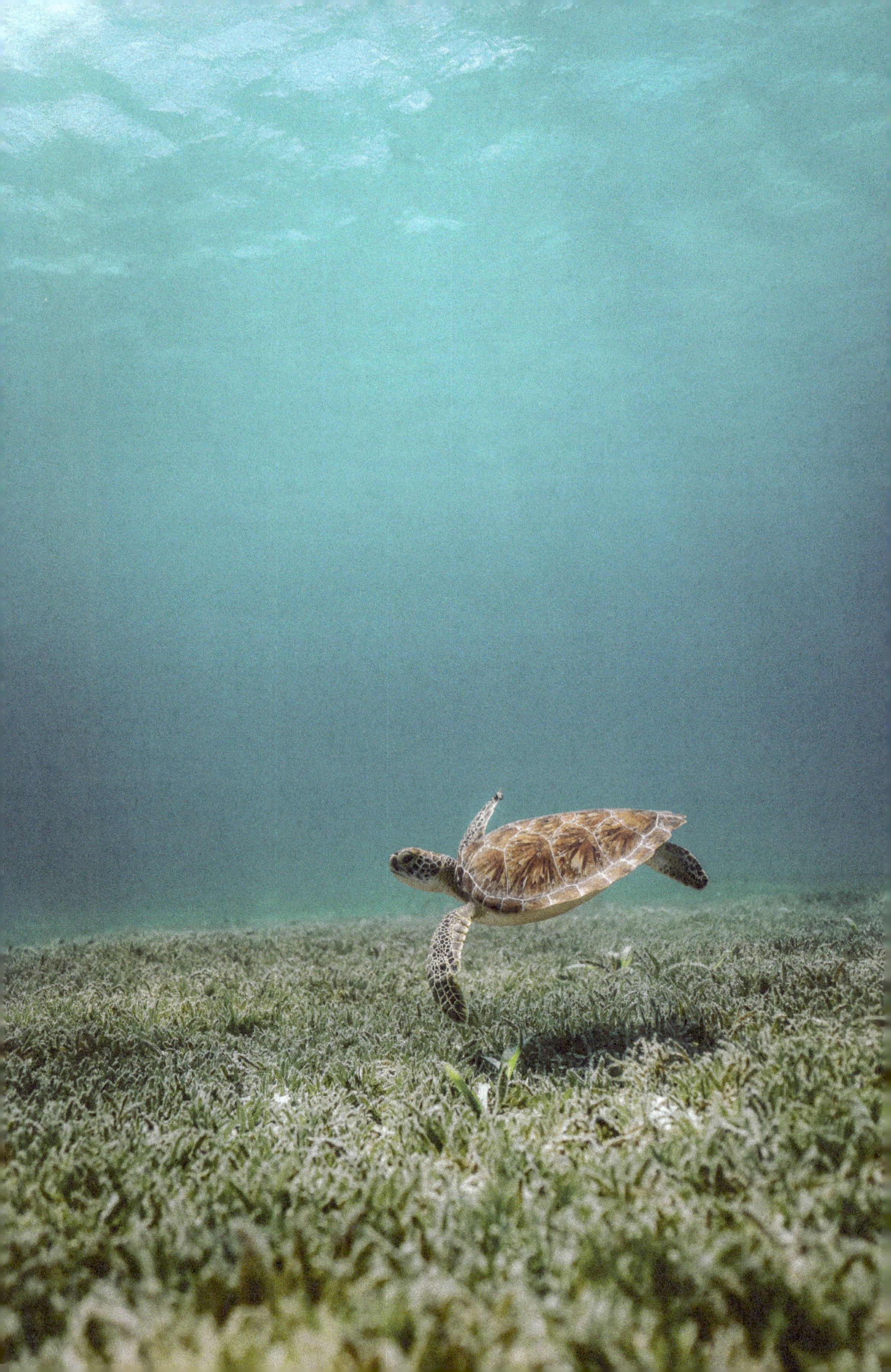

soil can store more carbon than all the plants and the atmosphere combined, and that the microbes play an important role in stabilizing the carbon in soil. One hundred farmers are now experimenting with how they can advance carbon drawdown by adopting regenerative farming practices, and they work with a multidisciplinary team of scientists to measure the effects. One of the aspects that is being investigated is how biodiversity above and below ground is connected, and how that affects carbon sequestration and stabilization.

Buildings and Cities

Nature builds with resources that are readily and locally available, at ambient temperature, and without harmful emissions to the soil, water, and air. Take seashells and corals for instance. These are little shelters of calcium carbonate that have been made by living organisms like mollusks, crustaceans, and polyps. These marine organisms grow their exoskeletons by extracting carbon, magnesium, and calcium from the sea water. After their death, their exoskeletons sink and assimilate on the ocean floor. Over time, their tiny houses turn into giant layers of stone. Marble, limestone and chalk are therefore rocks made by life. These rocks are very important for urban development, as we mine them to create cement—the major building material of today's world.

Our manufacturing process, however, involves heavy equipment, explosives, fossil fuels, and requires heating the limestone to more than 1,400 degrees Celsius. For every ton of cement produced, we thus release a ton of carbon dioxide into the atmosphere, which is problematic since we produce about 15 billion tons of cement every year. Nature in contrast, uses carbon as a building block to create mineral structures that absorb rather than emit carbon in production. It is a drawdown technology that has been successful for about 450 million years, creating a life-friendly climate for the world in the process. In other words, by sequestering and storing carbon on the ocean floor, marine life has managed a feedback loop that contributed to a stable climate,[11] creating favorable conditions for more life to evolve.

---

[11] The Earth's atmosphere operates somewhat similar to a greenhouse. Gases in the atmosphere such as carbon dioxide trap the heat in the atmosphere, creating a greenhouse effect.

We do exactly the opposite, our industrial system sends more heat-trapping gasses into the atmosphere, making the building sector one of the largest contributors to global warming. In fact, conventional cement production is the third largest emitter of carbon dioxide emissions to the atmosphere annually.

But there is another way. Nature shows us that the problem is the solution. By emulating nature's production process, the cement industry could turn emission into sequestration and evolve to become one of the most effective, human-created drawdown technologies. Fortunately, some companies are already doing just that. Blue Planet, a Californian company, is developing and commercializing scalable solutions for carbon drawdown that are both economically and technically sustainable.

Blue planet uses similar mineralization processes as marine ecosystems to create carbon negative building materials for residential and commercial construction. They claim their technology is more efficient and cost effective than traditional approaches of carbon capture, because it does not require an energy and capital-intensive purification step. Blue Planet's bio-inspired aggregate has been applied and tested at San Francisco International Airport. Calera is another established business in California that makes cement by turning carbon into materials.

Already pioneered in the 70s, Seament, nowadays called Biorock technology is also a method based on mineral accretion and has been used to restore coral reefs, fishery habitats, and increase shoreline protection. Hundreds of Biorock projects have been established across the Atlantic, Pacific, and Indian Oceans, and in Southeast Asia to support corals, oysters, seagrasses, saltmarsh, and many other marine species and to protect coastlines from rising sea levels.

The patented technology inspired visionaries from London-based Exploration Architecture to develop the concept of the Biorock Pavilion, which is the first building to be grown in the sea. As architect Michael Pawlyn rightfully postulates, it makes sense to make more things out of atmospheric carbon. Not only is it a vast stock of raw material, turning carbon into buildings and other products might become one of the key tools to reduce carbon dioxide levels in the atmosphere.

Sea creatures are not the only ones to build with local resources. Termites, labeled the greatest insect builders by *Guinness World Records*, build mega cities of impressive magnitudes. Their mounds, hardy infrastructures that can withstand rain, wind, floods and scorching sun, can rise more than six meters high in the sky, can span 30 meters in circumference and are made using only locally sourced mud and other fine-grained material. In Botswana, termites build islands. Islands constructed by termite bioengineering are raised above the level of seasonal flooding in the floodplain of the Okavango alluvial.

Not only do these tiny creatures change the physical properties of the landscape, they enrich the soil, allowing shrubs and trees to colonize the mounds storing carbon in the process. In fact, research pinpoints termite mounds as hotspots of plant growth and animal activity, which decreases the farther one gets from the mound, and recent evidence illustrates that termite bioengineering prevents desertification and makes the land more resilient to climate change. Because termites store nutrients, moisture, and seeds, drylands with termite mounds can sustain vegetation with less rain than those without, and can recover faster after harsh conditions. In other words, termites not only enhance the environment surrounding their cities, creating cities that create more life, they also make the landscape more resilient to climate change and weather extremes. No wonder they have been able to survive for millions of years.

But their engineering talent does not stop there. Termite mounds in Africa are exposed to roasting temperatures during the day and close to freezing temperatures at night. Yet the fungus grown inside for food, needs a stable climate of about 30 degrees. The termites achieve this via a smart design of ventilation tunnels that they open and close during the day. Australian compass termites create optimal thermoregulation by aligning the long axis of the mound north-south, hence the name. This way, they can capture the warmth of the morning sun after the cold night while exposing minimal mound surface area to the sun at midday.

Architect Mick Pearce who designed the Eastgate office and shopping Centre in Harare, Zimbabwe, together with engineering firm Arup, emulated the termite ventilation system. The building is passively cooled and extremely successful in maintaining an inside temperature in the range from 21-25 degrees Celsius, while outside temperatures fluctuate between five and 33 degrees. The passive cooling system inspired by termites does not only result in dramatic cost savings of avoided energy expenditure, it is said to use 90% less energy than a similar sized building next door, the $35 million Centre also saved 10% on up-front costs by not purchasing an air-conditioning system.

Since the building of the Eastgate Center, scientists have uncovered that the thermoregulation system of termite mounds is even more sophisticated, as it is found that the ingenious termite architecture allows the mound to inhale and exhale via a convective flow, powered by the sun. So, the mound functions like an external lung, which is a very effective way of regulating both ventilation and humidity. Despite decades of R&D, engineers and architects still have not been able to design cooling systems for buildings without the negative side effects of noise pollution, mold and bacteria contamination, or energy consumption. Learning from the termites how to optimize thermoregulation for buildings, might help engineers to design better, more efficient, and passive ventilation systems.

Bio-inspired building design is, of course, not new. One of the most famous ancient buildings inspired by nature is probably the Crystal Palace, which was built inside Hyde Park in 1851 to house the first Great Exhibition in the UK. It was designed not by an architect but by a horticulturist, the celebrated Joseph Paxton, the head gardener from the sixth Duke of Devonshire. Paxton's design was inspired by the leaves of the giant Amazon water-lily. The huge floating leaves are incredibly strong and can each carry a load up to 45 kilograms without breaking or deforming, even though they are only paper thin. That is because the radial nerve structure of the leaves with its ribs and struts has evolved for optimal strength and support as the leaf needs to stay afloat to collect energy from the sun. Paxton understood the design logic behind this structural integrity, which is what he mimicked to create the large arched vaults of the Crystal Palace. Imitating the load-bearing capacity of the water-lily's nerve had a lot of advantages. The pillars and load-bearing walls were no longer needed, rendering the space more open for exhibitors, thereby saving materials, money and space.

A more recent experiment with bio-inspired design comes from the University of Stuttgart, where researchers combined biomimicry and robotic construction to create two pavilions at the Bundesgartenschau horticultural show in Germany that are of superior material efficiency and strength.

The first, a largescale wooden pavilion, has a shape inspired by sea urchin architecture. Urchins have a distinctive skeleton that is made up of self-similar and interlocking plates. Imitating this structure into the pavilion accounted for 376 unique plate segments that fit together in a very efficient and load-adapted structure, which is also astoundingly lightweight. Even though the entire pavilion spans 30 meters across, it is column-free and weighs just 38 kilograms per square meter. So, the pavilion is incredibly material efficient and completely reusable, just like the sea urchins that inspired it.

The second building is a fiber-composite pavilion that is even more impressive. Its structure is inspired by beetle wings. In contrast to conventional building practices which usually use massive structures to carry loads, most load-bearing structures in nature are composites of fibers like cellulose, collagen, or chitin. To build the beetle wing pavilion, the researchers set out to emulate the natural composites using glass- and carbon-reinforced fibers as load-bearing structures for a plastic membrane. The pavilion spans 23 meters across and weighs only 7.5 kilograms per square meter, while still passing the required strength tests for construction. The beetle wing design is significantly less resource-intensive, and its weight is many times lower than that of comparable steel or wooden structures. Because of its lightweight nature, there was no need for heavy means of transport or lifting equipment, which further saved on energy, emissions, and costs. Building like nature leads to superior benefits in terms of design, strength, resource efficiency, environmental qualities—and it saves money.

I have mentioned before that refrigeration management, of all solutions, is the most impactful climate solution, because the HFCs used in air conditioners have 1,000 to 9,000 times greater capacity to warm the atmosphere than carbon dioxide. Developing alternatives for refrigeration management is therefore exactly where the building sector can make a huge impact that profits both people and the planet. Termites are not the only organism to show us how we can cool our buildings without using energy. One of the champions in climate regulation lives in the desert, which is no surprise given that they have to manage scorching sun during the day, freezing cold during the night, and have an extremely limited supply of water. I am referring to the cacti. These plants are immobile—they cannot retreat to the shade to keep cool, nor can they huddle together to stay warm—and thus have had to come up with very smart building strategies to deal with such climate extremes.

Biologists have discovered that the iconic ribbed structure of the cacti helps them stay cool during the blazing heat. Obviously, the ribs shade a large part of the plant's surface, but it is the differences in temperature between the sun exposed and shaded planes of the vertical ribs that produce the rising and falling air currents, which cool the cactus through enhanced heat radiation. The dense covering of spines, common to many cacti, further increase the shading and also provide protection from animals, and collect water (a scarce resource in arid environments) from fog. Lastly, the vertical ribbed design of cacti results in a very small top surface that is exposed to the midday sun. So, the whole shape and design of a cactus is optimized to enhance cooling and water collection and retention. It is through smart design that these organisms are able to deal with climate extremes and survive in harsh environments like deserts.

In Phoenix, the University of Arizona Health Sciences Education Building is clad in an exterior skin, inspired by the rib folds of the native saguaro cactus. The designers of the building, CO Architects, looked at the local environment for inspiration to improve cooling and energy efficiency. The self-shading nature of the native cacti inspired them to mimic this ability into an external cladding system, which aids heat radiation, just like the exterior of the native cacti.

Another feature of building like nature, is circularity. While conventional building practices produce an enormous amount of waste that cannot be reused after the building's useful life is over, nature reuses every single element to create something new. In Driebergen-Zeist in the Netherlands, Triodos, a bank committed to invest in sustainable projects only, is building its new headquarters according to the principle of circularity. Together with Rau Architects and EDGE Technologies, they are building an office building that will be completely reusable after its useful lifespan is over. They have become a partner in the pioneering project Madaster, which creates passports for the materials used to guarantee effective circularity. The building is thus designed for disassembly, and consists mainly of wood and glass, which can all be easily reused in the future thanks to the material passports that have been created.

It is one thing to design *like* nature, but it is another to design *with* nature, the latter being equally important in facing the challenges of the 21st century, especially when it comes to urban living. Contemporary cities induce high-stress levels, mental health issues, high crime levels, and ill health, and problems with "urban heat island" effects, and air and water pollution are on the rise. Giving space to include nature in spatial planning and urban design, like in the disciplines of *biophilic architecture* and *nature-based solutions*, effectively addresses many of these challenges.

A research overview by Jana Söderlund and Peter Newman shows that the *socio-psychological benefits* of biophilic design include improved mental health, reduced stress, attention restoration, increased wellbeing, decreased violence and crime, faster healing rates in hospitals, and greater altruistic behavior. The *environmental benefits* include improvements to water, air, biodiversity, and reduced energy consumption and urban heat island effects while the *economic benefits* from biophilic design include better workplace productivity, improved health, increased retail potential, increased property values and employee attraction, and increased livability in dense areas.

The Children's Psychiatric Center (KPC), conceived by Osar Architects in Genk, Belgium was designed with the wellbeing of patients and staff as a priority. When exploring how to create a healing environment that makes children feel safe and which relieves stress, they realized that working with nature was the most effective solution. To achieve that, they embedded the building in its natural landscape, and wove the inside and outside together in a smart way with green roofs and no less than six sunken gardens, creating sheltered, green garden niches specific to children of different ages. KPC also decided to integrate a mini farm in its gardens, because interaction with plants and animals have a positive impact on the patients.

And nature's benefits go well beyond improved health and wellbeing. Numerous studies also highlight that one of the most effective solutions to curb the devastating effects of climate change in cities, especially in the case of urban heat island effects, is to renature cities. That is why the European Commission set up a policy plan to promote nature-based solutions.

There really is no case for designing nature out of our living and working habitats.

Green Chemistry and Manufacturing

In her book *Biomimicry: Innovation Inspired by Nature*, Janine Benyus comprehensibly sums up the gist of present-day manufacturing as "heat, beat, and treat." It has been the dominant logic of the industrial age, and it has been hardwired into the brains of most industrialists. Not only does this method of making stuff require vast amounts of energy, it also releases enormous amounts of toxic pollutants into the environment, the atmosphere, and into our bodies.

Nature's methods of production are very different. She builds with what is locally available and uses only a subset of elements from the periodic table to grow an extraordinary variety of effective and multifunctional materials at ambient

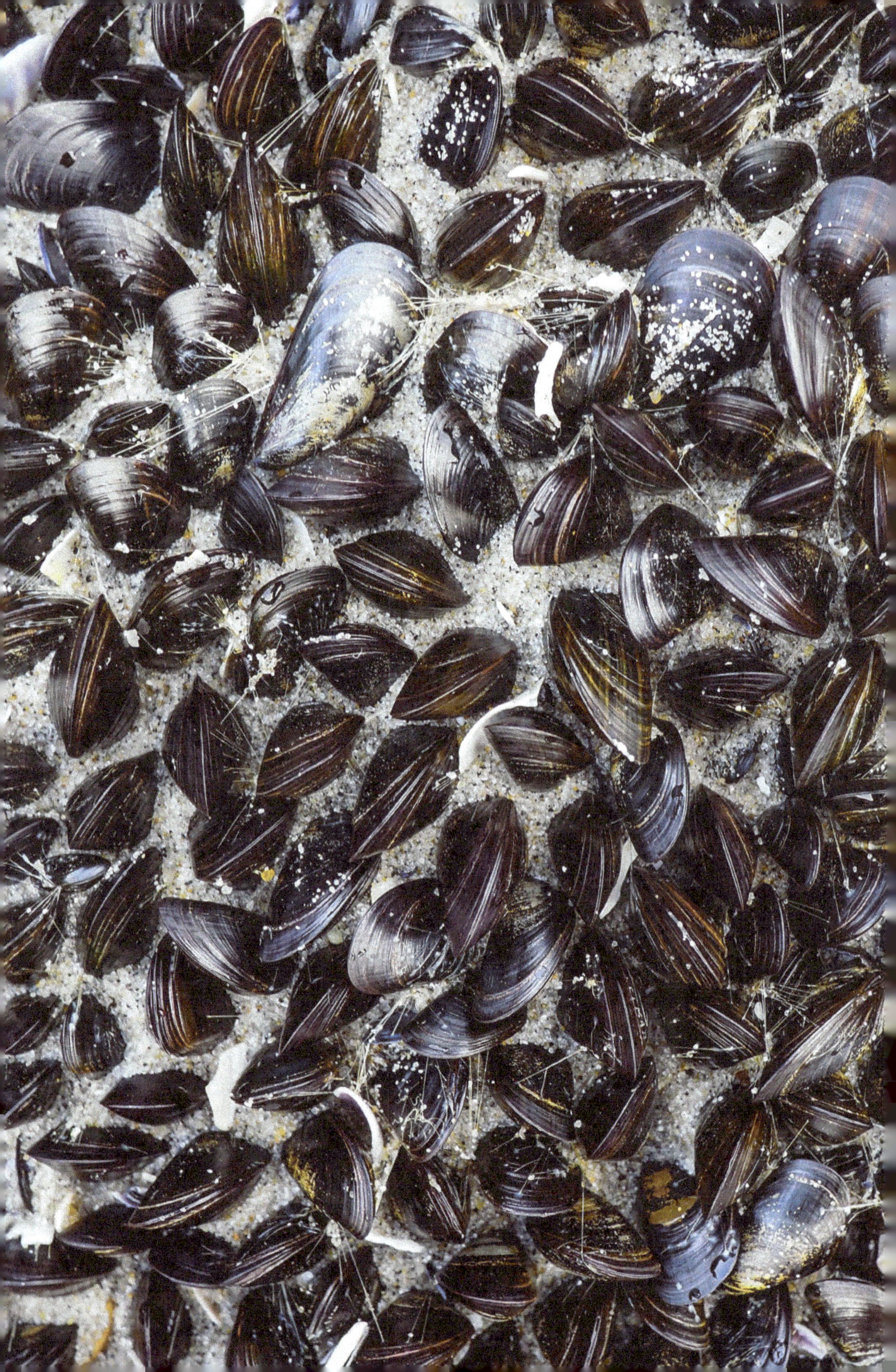

temperature. Even more noteworthy is what nature does not do: She does not generate eco-toxicity. Everything she makes is bio-compatible and bio-degradable, and all elements can be reused infinitely. No waste to burn off or get rid of and no byproducts, like nuclear waste, to be stored in highly secure, costly, safe places. In nature, everything is in one way or another part of the circle of life.

So, the question is not can chemistry turn green, but rather why do we keep holding on to a model that is clearly energy intensive, harmful, and in many ways primitive when compared to nature's chemistry laboratory? Here, the education system can play a crucial role. By training chemists without any knowledge on how life works, we perpetuate the unsustainable heat, beat, and treat system. To change our chemistry and manufacturing approach, we thus have to completely redesign our chemistry curricula.

The Warner Babcock Institute for Green Chemistry is pioneering how chemistry can be done differently. By developing environmentally benign chemicals and technologies to eliminate the use and generation of hazardous substances, the institute is transforming the world of industrial chemistry. To accomplish that mission, they look to nature, because in nature, all chemistry is green.

According to John Warner, the president of the Institute, nature always shows the best model. He explains that although he learned as a chemist that molecules can be stretched to do something that does not suit their fundamental structure, they will always have the tendency to go back to where they were before. Nature does not work that way. She does not force molecules to interact but facilitates them to express their own unique essence. And so, the way they work at WBI is to "ask" a molecule what their role should be by studying its fundamental structure.

If a molecule has strong adhesive properties, then it already knows how to be a "paint" molecule, meaning that the manufacturing and product development process will be far easier and more straightforward than when you force a molecule to do something it does not want to do. Warner pinpoints this new way of thinking powerfully by stating that, "We have to let go of ego and let the inherent properties of materials teach us what to do."

Not only is biomimicry combined with green chemistry one of the most promising avenues for innovation and creativity, WBI illustrates that next to being environmentally friendly, green chemistry can also create significant cost savings. When hazardous chemical substances are designed out of materials and processes, all the hazard-related costs are also removed from the manufacturing process, such as those associated with handling, transportation, disposal, and compliance.

Furthermore, I speculate that when we completely shift to non-hazardous green chemistry, health care costs will drop dramatically in the future. Currently our homes are full of carcinogens, such as formaldehyde and VOCs (volatile organic compounds). And scientists studying the levels of these volatile and particulate chemicals in households state that air quality inside the average home compares to that of a polluted major city.

A company called Columbia Forest Products, the largest manufacturer of hardwood plywood and hardwood veneer products in North America, aspires to change this and has a longstanding tradition of innovating for sustainability. Their mission statement is the following: "Our ideas will be groundbreaking, and our stewardship will be forever mindful of the ground we live on." Aligned with their mission, they have come up with an alternative to formaldehyde for use in plywood products. Their formaldehyde-free glue is called Purebond® Technology and has been inspired by mussels.

Mussels live in intertidal zones, where they are exposed to enormous stresses from crashing waves to scorching sun. Yet these mollusks have developed a technology to stick to the wet surfaces of rocks despite continuous battering waves or desiccating heat from the sun. This amazing ability is the result of sticky proteins that the mussels secrete, known as byssal threads, which provide both incredible strength and extraordinary flexibility. Dr. Kaichang Li, a professor at Oregon State University's College of Forestry, discovered a plant-based alternative that can achieve the same performance as the mussel glue. This environmentally friendly alternative to formaldehyde delivers outstanding adhesive properties and exceptional water resistance, showcasing that bio-inspired design can lead to superior product performance as well as enhanced environmental quality.

The need for bio-compatible and bio-degradable polymers is painfully obvious when looking at the plastic industry. Since 1950, humans have made 8.3 billion tons of plastic. The petrochemical industry produces about 300 million tons of plastic per year but recycles only 3%, therefore, leaving the other 97% to break down in our oceans and landfills, where they harm the food chain and our environment. In 2014, bioplastics accounted for only 0.2% of the global polymer market. One of the difficulties that bio-plastics face is that they are difficult to shape into complex 3D forms. Most bio-plastics are also not biodegradable, which is why they are still marginal.

The Wyss Institute for Biologically Inspired Engineering at Harvard has developed a new bioplastic that does not suffer from these shortcomings. Their fully degradable bioplastic called "Shrilk" is made using chitosan (found in shrimp shells) and fibroin proteins (found in silk) in a way that mimics the microarchitecture of insect exoskeletons. Shrilk can be used to manufacture objects without the environmental hazard posed by conventional synthetic plastics, and it can rapidly biodegrade into useful nutrients for plants. It is a low-cost, versatile material that exhibits exceptional strength and toughness and it is ready for licensing.

Another bio-inspired chemical for next generation materials is AirCarbon™ developed by Newlight Technologies Inc in California. They have figured out a process to turn greenhouse gas into a high-value material for consumer products as alternatives to synthetic fibers and plastics, and in a scalable way. The company's regenerative mission goes further than mere sustainability. For one, AirCarbon reduces greenhouse gases in the air when the product is made with renewably-sourced power and greenhouse gas, which creates a net positive carbon impact. And two, Newlight aims to create and encourage new standards in transparency, so clients can track, trace, and verify just how much carbon was diverted from the air in the process of making AirCarbon. To do so they have set up a highly advanced tracking system that provides third-party verified and audited carbon impact traceability for every product they produce.

Their technology to make material from air and greenhouse gas was inspired by a unique microorganism from the Pacific Ocean, one that did just that. And after AirCarbon's lifetime is over, it will degrade into benign components that can be building blocks for something new. Or like Newlight puts it: "There is no silver bullet to solving our environmental challenges, but we want to start by leaving things better than how we found them. AirCarbon is a natural energy material, so if it ends up in the environment, microorganisms in the soil and ocean eat it as a nutrient, like a tree leaf, because they make it themselves for growth."

The ocean is full of amazing materials that have been made by life-friendly chemistry. Abalone shells are not only beautiful to look at because of their color-shifting iridescence, they are also exceptionally strong and fracture resistant. Even though the abalone shell consists of 95% of the same material as chalk, they achieve 3,000 times the toughness thanks to a clever, intricate microscopic structure. In fact, these small, ocean-dwelling mollusks create materials that are twice as tough as our high-tech ceramics, and they do this at ocean temperature, with only locally available resources. Even more remarkable is the fact that abalone shells are incredibly resistant to cracks. Instead of breaking like man-made ceramics do under great stress, they deform and self-heal from within. They achieve their incredible strength and ability to self-heal through a sophisticated microscopic architecture that combines stiff, inorganic minerals (like calcium carbonate) with the stretchy and flexible organic materials of proteins and polysaccharides. The organic layer acts as a living mortar that can quickly stretch into cracks, gluing them back together after fracture. These layers of living organic matter amid brittle layers of minerals thus manage cracks from within, making the composite extremely hardy and strong. So, in nature, weak interfaces make materials tough. Scientists around the world are studying natural strength and composition of biological materials like shells, bones, and sponges for insights to create stronger and more adaptive (self-healing) materials.

Engineers from the McGill University in Canada for example, applied abalone microarchitecture to create a bio-inspired glass that is 200 times tougher and more deformable than standard glass. Unlike man-made manufacturing and construction, where strength is derived from mass, nature derives strength from structure and shape. Because like Julian Vincent, professor and President of the International Society for Bionic Engineering says, "In nature, material is expensive, and shape is cheap." What is more, while our industrial processes use about 350 synthetic polymers, which are hard to recycle and mostly life-unfriendly, to create our consumption goods, nature uses only a handful of polymers to create about 8.7 million different species that roam the Earth today, and all are biocompatible and completely bio-degradable. Some of the most common polymers in nature include cellulose (found in algae, plants, and trees), chitin (found in fungi, crustaceans, and insects) and keratin (found in all vertebrates, including humans). By adding smart nano and micro-structures to those few common polymers, nature creates an extraordinary variety of functions and performances of materials, which add up to a huge diversity of designs—from diatoms to a great whale, from bacteria to a sequoia.

Life builds to shape—which in many instances, far exceed the performance of their modern engineering analogs—like in additive manufacturing, but with benign materials, life-friendly chemistry and reverse logistics (aka no waste).

Human Resources and Organizational Development

One of the most fascinating behaviors in the world of social insects, is that of swarm intelligence. Tiny creatures like ants, bees, and termites can solve complex problems and produce engineering solutions that outsmart ours—without such a big brain and without central command. For instance, fire ants configure waterproof floating rafts by linking their bodies together and trapping air between them to survive floods. Such rafts can house 100,000 ants, and can survive for several weeks before they hit dry land and start a new colony, as many witnessed after the floods induced by Hurricane Harvey. Termites build structures the equivalent of skyscrapers with a stable interior climate cooled by solar powered ventilation. And bees select new hives via collective decision-making processes.

A central feature in these social insects is that there is no central control or top down management. There are no managers that organize and control work. There is no queen bee, ant, or termite that gives orders. Instead, individuals self-organize by following a set of simple rules, by banking on transparent authentic communication, and by using quorum voting systems to make decisions. Their flexible work organization and effective, consensus-building group decisions make them incredibly adaptive, robust, and resourceful to changing circumstances. In fact, social insects have been so successful that they have colonized every inhabitable location on our planet, in numerous quantities no less.

For good reason, swarm behavior is a popular research topic. One of the leading institutes in this regard is the Swarm Lab at UC Berkeley, led by Professor Jan Rabaey, which applies swarm logic to improve wireless sensor networks. Other popular applications of swarm technology include using ant algorithms to improve traffic on the internet, freight logistics, or manufacturing processes. The possibilities of swarm technology are limitless and applying them to HR and organizational development might be the most effective way to boost agility, creativity, motivation, and responsiveness in organizations.

A new take on HR is needed because technological innovation is fast-paced and changing exponentially, while social innovation is slow-paced and changing logarithmically. In other words, technological innovation is changing faster than organizations can absorb, which has been postulated as one of the greatest management challenges of our time. It is becoming increasingly clear that in these VUCA (Volatile, Uncertain, Complex and Ambiguous) times, old-fashioned ways of managing a company are no longer effective. Chains of command in traditional, hierarchical organizations are too long for agile responsiveness, lengthy chains of command that are also associated with increased communication failures. In pyramid models, the most powerful decision-makers operate the furthest from the frontiers, lacking the local details that are needed to make good decisions. At the same time, one of the most overlooked and untapped resources in organizations is the talent of the employees.

Waggl Inc, a company with offices in California, Peru, and Brazil, develops crowdsourced communication software to advance shared decision-making processes and effective communication inside organizations. Like the name suggests, it was the "waggle dance" of bees, which is used in decision-making, that inspired them to develop a real-time, transparent engagement platform that sources and prioritizes the knowledge of employees for organizations that want to tap into the collective intelligence of their workforce. And that unlocking of the collective intelligence of employees can pay off big time is illustrated in the example of HCL Technologies, an Indian multinational IT service and consultancy company.

In 2007, Vineet Nayar took over the leadership of the company and introduced a radical cultural transformation. To overcome employee disengagement, he set in motion a series of changes to unlock the collective intelligence of the HCL work force. These changes were all centered around the promotion of internal communication and innovation to spark creativity. He promoted the use of the company's intranet. He set up a brainstorm site where employees could point out problems and promote solutions. He organized weekly polls to check in with staff and set up direct communication lines between employees and management. He set up an innovation group that used stand-up comedy to spark creativity and he launched a virtual innovation bank so that employees could see the impact their ideas were making. He also introduced radical transparency, inviting employee sourced review for projects, plans and managers. He himself answered hundreds of questions a week. By tapping in into the collective intelligence of the HCL work force and favoring transparent communication, both the quality of the work and the motivation of the employees improved. Nayar stayed on until 2013 and increased revenues from $743 million to $4.7 billion, including a 25% increase after the global recession in 2009. Unlocking the swarm intelligence of a company therefore not only advances agility, it promotes success too.

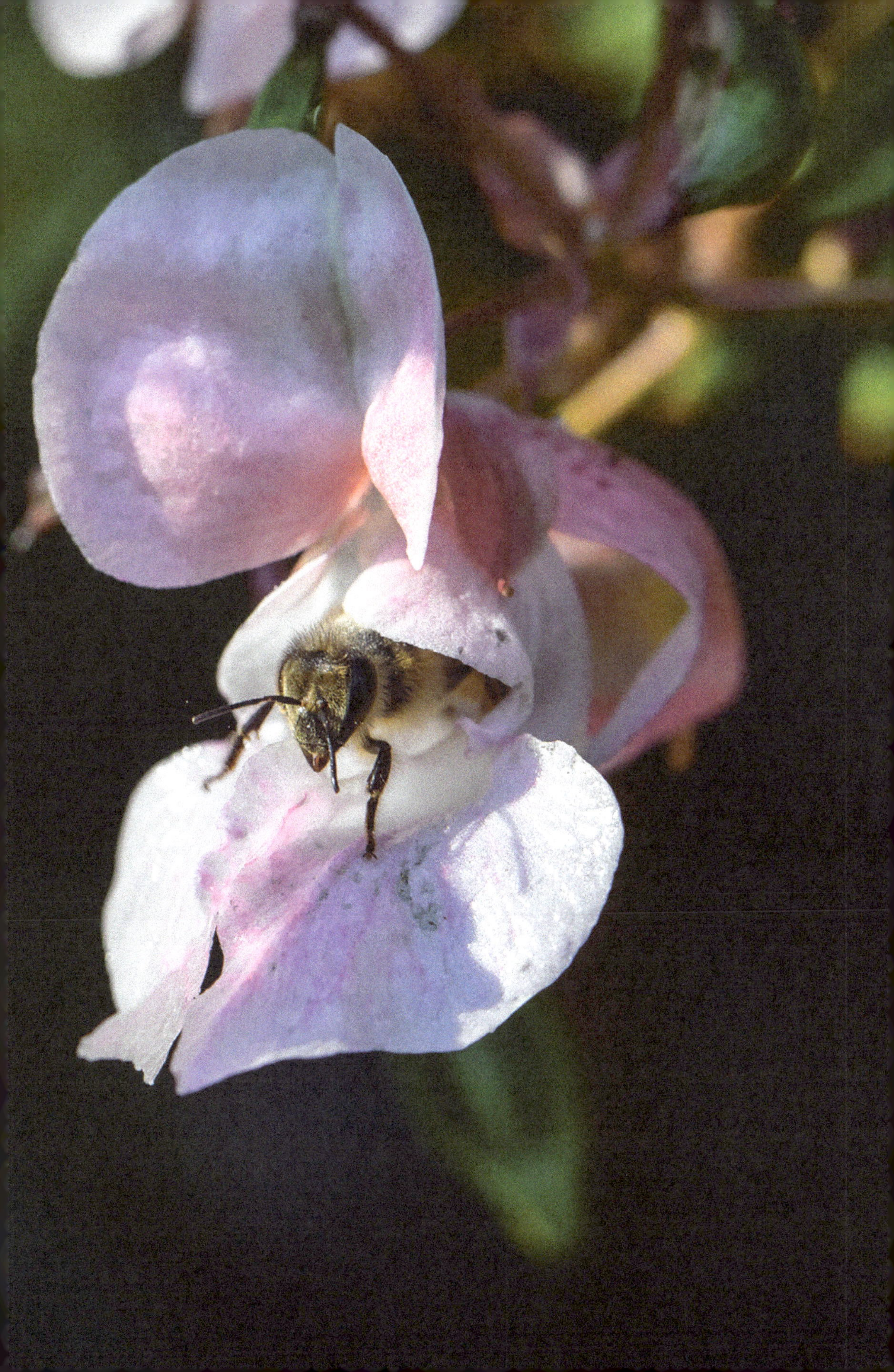

NATURAL INTELLIGENCE

History shows that weighty overhead costs push companies to look for alternatives, such as moving the work to low cost countries. However, this further amplifies the degenerative impact of business, as these countries often have lower standards for social and environmental sustainability. But there is another way. It is the way of swarm intelligence, which is centered around principles of self-organization and self-management.

The French company FAVI, which produces gearbox forks for the automotive industry, has been self-organized since the eighties. There is no management, no executive committee, no HR, and no planning department. There are only employees and a CEO. The workers organize themselves into mini-factories that serve a specific client and they are responsible for the whole trajectory, from order to delivery. While all its competitors moved to China to enjoy cheaper labor costs, FAVI remained in Europe and holds a 50% market share for its product.

Frederic Laloux, who researched self-organization in companies, claims that the quality of FAVI's products is legendary while it's on time delivery is close to mythical. Over the last 25 years, not one order has been shipped late. And even though they face strong Chinese competition, the workers at FAVI generally make 16 or 17 months of salary a year. This is because there is no costly management, and the company upholds a model of profit sharing with its employees. No surprise then that there is virtually no employee turnover.

Another organization that works this way is Buurtzorg, a pioneering home-care organization in the Netherlands. Their slogan is "Humanity over Bureaucracy," meaning that nurse-led adequate care for the patient is central, and administrative red tape is kept to the bare minimum. Buurtzorg employs about 10,000 nurses and all teams are completely self-managed. The model is built around a holistic and tailormade care approach where the first priority of any nurse is to get to know the patient and his or her environment. This is not done through questionnaires or any other formal approach but by patient and nurse having a coffee together. The vision behind the Buurtzorg model is that patients are better off if they are part of a caring community (Buurtzorg means neighborhood care in English).

Giving full autonomy to the nurses to plan and deliver the care for patients pays off in more than one way. Studies showed that patient satisfaction rates are higher than those of any other health care organization in the Netherlands and that staff commitment and contentedness scores very high, as well as productivity.

In the Buurtzorg model, patients needed care for less time, regained autonomy quicker, had fewer emergency hospital admissions, and shorter lengths-of-stay after admission. In addition, Buurtzorg had lower overhead costs than other home-care providers (8% of total costs, compared with 25%) and less than half the average incidence of sick leave and employee turnover according to several in depth studies.

So, how can self-organization work so effectively? The key to success is to find a set of effective, simple rules that can guide employees in their decision-making processes. The following are a few of the foundational principles that arrange Buurtzorg's business:

1. Mindful activities do not need automatization.
2. Mindless activities (like administrative tasks) do not need to be made important.
3. Every decision is checked with the entire team.
4. Solutions are adopted as long as everyone in the team agrees, when a better idea comes along, it is revised.

At Waggl, employees organize their work according to five values:

1. Put family first and team second above individual gain.
2. Be humble and respect others.
3. Act with honesty.
4. Thrive with change.
5. Be excellent and never give up.

Whether you choose values, principles or simple rules (simple rules is the lingo of biology), as long as people genuinely support and follow them, they function as effective guidelines for organizing co-operations. Instead of excessive bureaucratic protocols managed by a team of top down managers or an HR department, these simple rules give direction to employees to self-manage their time and activities. In many cases, even time off (employee holidays) is organized this way.

Self-managed teams thus respond to information, instead of orders. It works because we like working with competent, conscientious, motivated, and responsible team mates. Even though employees are accountable to each other all day long, bearing much more responsibility than in top down hierarchies, it is a much more rewarding system that allows employees to flourish. And cutting down on the red tape frees up resources to pay better wages to the employees.

It is a more effective investment system, because fewer resources are wasted on administrative hassles, and more is invested in lasting impact. The shared responsibility and leadership of self-managing teams also advances capacities like communication, collaboration, and teamwork.

Charged as the head of a group of bankers aiming to redesign the financial credit model in the sixties, Dee Hock, the founder and former CEO of the VISA credit card association, was intrigued by the thin line between chaos and order that most complex living systems operate under. Inspired by this widespread model in nature, he and his colleagues came up with principles to guide the creation of a new credit system that included the following:

1. Equitable ownership by all participants.
2. Self-organization.
3. Distributed power, function and governance.
4. Infinitely malleable, yet extremely durable.

The idea of a "chaordic organization" that blends characteristics of chaos and order was born, and even though principles like self-organization, distributed governance, and shared ownership were at the time quite unorthodox in the sector, the new credit model worked and grew to be very successful. From 1969 to 2004, it grew from 15 to 50% market share, and the VISA products were co-created by 21,000 owner/member financial institutions. By 2019, VISA operated in more than 200 countries, with 3.4 billion cards accepted at 61 million merchant locations, resulting in 138.3 billion network transactions, and a total volume exchanged of $11,6 trillion.

On a deeper level, the concept of chaordic organization is even more remarkable as it creates space for both collaboration and competition. Or, in the words of Hock: "Paradox and conflict are inherent characteristics of chaordic organization." That is why VISA stayed clear of monopolizing the credit market, as monopolies and monocultures do not appear in nature. Pristine forests are always composed of a diversity of trees and shrubs. Prairie ecosystems always include a diversity of herbs and grasses. Healthy coral reefs house an abundance of species. The principle here is "favor diversity, not monopoly," and it took great lengths for Hock to safeguard this principle as it goes against monopoly thinking, which is still prevalent in the business world.

Critics may claim that there are ample examples of businesses where self-organization does not work. And indeed, success heavily depends on finding the right simple rules and creating the right enabling conditions for the organization to be self-organized. Critical in this, but often forgotten, is that communication requires short and authentic feedback loops, and that an effective strategy is needed to deal with defectors—those that do not cooperate. In fact, this latter point highlights the importance of human development (HD) to develop abilities like care, attentiveness, responsibility, diligence, fairness, compassion, and effective communication skills to upgrade collaboration skills.

More importantly, leadership needs to be shared. In successful self-managed organizations, it is not the boss that hires and fires, but the team. It is the only way to maintain and support reciprocal relationships. It is a much more honest system, because if someone is only taking and not adding value, then the team is able to replace this person with someone else. This might seem harsh, but this system actually supports a better match between people's talents and their job content, and it favors emancipation and maturation, which benefits the organization as a whole. Working in self-managed teams also requires mastering abilities like self-awareness, self-knowledge, and self-management.

A remark I often receive during my workshops with executives is that self-organization might work in teams of highly educated staff, but that it is too challenging for workforces without such background. A small social enterprise in Belgium called Okazi, challenges that viewpoint. Okazi employs people that cannot find work in the regular economy. The enterprise has a strong sustainability ambition and aims to promote product re-use and upcycling. At the moment, the organization is in transition from a top down, hierarchical managed business, to a self-organized organization. And doing so with success. Even though management believed they had reached maximum sales at their popular re-use shop in Hasselt, a careful redesign of the shop interior, guided by the employees themselves, increased sales by 30%.

By empowering the talents of their employees, the organization as a whole prospered. In time, Okazi aims to become a fully self-managed organization. A carefully planned and supported transition process is guiding the employees towards that end, and they recently started a process to rethink the role of their Board of Trustees, because a self-managed organization needs other types of support to thrive in a rapidly changing world.

The Okazi example shows that self-organization can work with all members from society if the transition process is conceived as a developmental approach. In fact, that is where work is most needed. The mechanistic world view model has been so deeply ingrained in our mental models that we need a whole new approach to organizational development. It is time to shift from HR—which still reinforces the mechanistical thinking model, as if humans are nothing more than "resources" to the organizational machine—to HD or Human Development.

Regenesis Institute in the US explicitly works on developing potential with the communities and businesses they work with. Development is different from education. It is not about new knowledge and functional skills to do a better job. It is about who we need to become, in order to play out a regenerative role in the business and environmental ecosystem that we are part of. One of the projects that Regenesis was involved in is called Playa Viva, and it's located on the coast of Guerrero, Mexico.

David Leventhal, the owner, originally planned on creating a responsible resort, one that would be respectful of the environment and beneficial to the people in the neighboring village. When he arrived, the village was economically depressed, the land was degraded, people were discouraged, and the young people were leaving for the big cities looking for work. At first, his idea was to help the community by employing locals in his project. The downside of such a project approach is that it often locks-in functional thinking: Everything is seen in terms of how it can serve the project.

When Regenesis got involved, they helped their client see that the local community was a place with ancient roots, traditions, and that Playa Viva could actually reignite the relationships of people and place. This transformed his conception of the project that he wanted to enroll. Instead of seeing himself as a benevolent owner, he saw himself as a regenerative member of the community and he committed himself to supporting its development as an integral part of his project. With local artisans and builders, he developed unique tree house structures for the resort that utilized local materials, were raised above storm surges, and created minimum footprints on the land. He helped train the local farmers in organic and biodynamic methods in order to restore land that had been degraded by palm oil production, and he established relationships with local fisherman to ensure sustainable management of the fisheries. This increased the quality and value of their production, while ensuring a steady supply of local produce for Playa Viva's kitchens.

One of the most remarkable, positive impacts of this more regenerative way of working, was how they turned the problem of turtle poachers into a solution. The village was an important nesting site for endangered turtles, and poachers had long harvested the eggs and meat. Rather than fighting them, Leventhal hired the poachers as rangers to protect the turtles and provided them with uniforms and off-road vehicles. With their newly acquired prestige in the community, they were able to sponsor education programs around turtle stewardship, which crystalized as a new identity for the local community, and which allowed visitors to engage in a truly authentic eco-tourism experience.

As the community of Guerro has come back to life, young people have begun to return, because they can finally find meaningful work in the place they grew up in. Meanwhile, the owner's life has been transformed by this relationship with the community, where his project is one of many, all working together to return life to the place to which they belong.

This whole new way of thinking and working was achieved by a very simple framework, called nested systems, that is inspired by living systems. It begins with three baseline questions:

1. Who do I have to become to unlock the full value-adding potential of the project?
2. What does the project have to become to unlock its full value-adding potential to the local community?
3. What does the community have to become to unlock its full value-adding potential to the wider system it is part of?

So instead of thinking functionally, it is about thinking developmentally. It is about developing new capabilities and roles, which is a very potent way to transform from something that *is*, to what it could *be*.

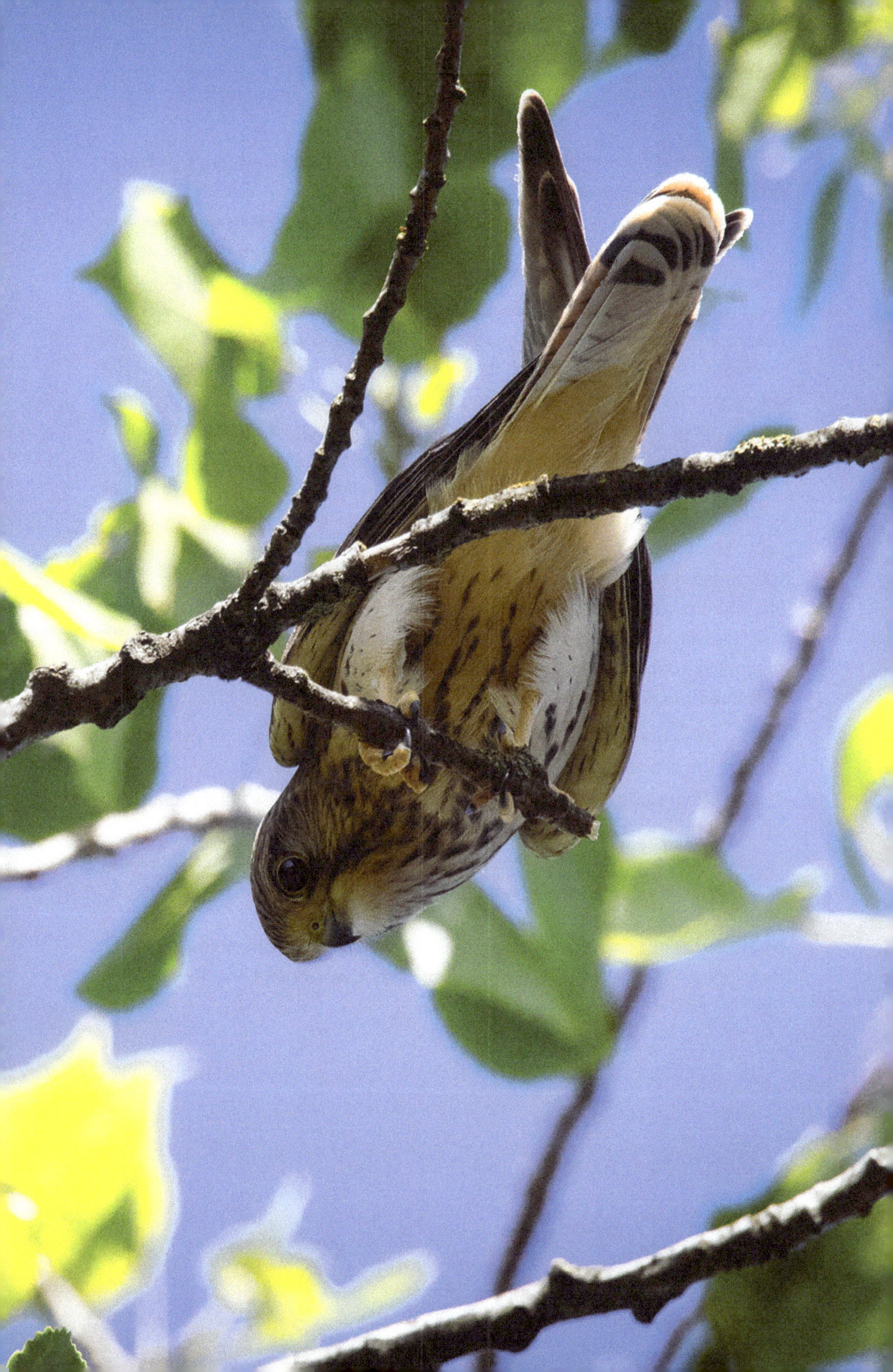

CHAPTER 6

CHANGING THE LOGIC OF VALUE CREATION

The nature of innovation and innovation in nature

To transition from degenerative to regenerative value creation requires us to change the nature of innovation. An interesting way of looking at the transition that is required is through the lens of the Levels of Work, developed by of Charles Krone (Table 1). This framework was first published by Ben Haggard and Pamela Mang in their book *Regenerative Development and Design*. It starts from the premise that any living entity—be it an organism or a system—must work to operate, maintain, and improve its operations, and ultimately regenerate itself in order to be successful in a world that is volatile, uncertain, complex, ambiguous, interdependent, and nested (so VUCAIN instead of VUCA to emphasize our current blind spot).

Operate

A tree for example needs to inhale carbon dioxide to photosynthesize. By *improving its metabolic processes*, the tree becomes more efficient in turning carbon dioxide into sugar, which allows it to grow better. Not only does the tree share some of its sugars with its wider community, it also produces oxygen as a byproduct. So, the outcome of improved metabolic processes is efficient generation of life. Another example is an herbivore, like a buffalo, that needs to eat plants in order to be able to operate. By improving its metabolic processes, the buffalo can harvest more energy from the plants that it consumes. That is why they evolved a complex digestive system containing four stomachs.

But the buffalo not only eats plants, it stimulates plant growth as well. Experimental evidence shows that buffalo saliva stimulates growth in plants and contributes to the overall health, fitness, and nutritional value of the plant. It also prolongs the growing season of plants, and recent evidence shows that buffalo have a stronger influence on the timing of plant growth than weather and other environmental variables. So, the outcome of innovation on the level of metabolism is, again, efficient generation of energy in the buffalo and of growth in the grasses, on which the buffalo depends.

Maintain

To maintain its operations in the near future, the herbivore needs to *be resilient to changing conditions*. So, it has evolved in a way that it can eat a wide variety

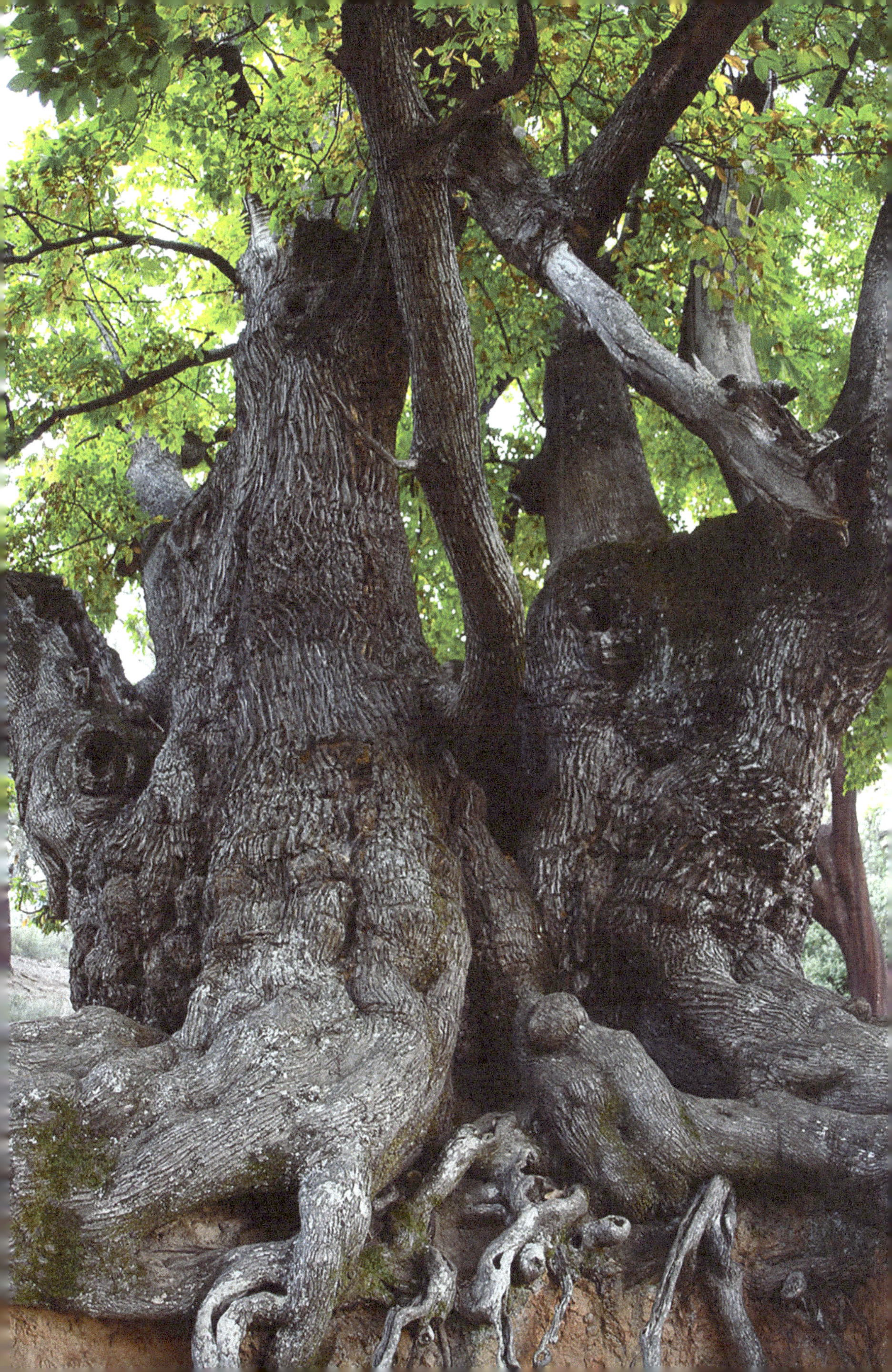

of food sources. If a drought leads to less grass, the herbivore eats herbs and shrubs instead. If a thick snow cover buries the ground cover, buffalos can survive on twigs and bark from trees. To further improve resilience, herbivores like buffalo, bison, and deer, migrate and move around over great distances. If they are able to express their natural behavior, meaning they are not confined in nature reserves or influenced by people, they will eat a little and then move on. The simple rule they follow is "never take all," which prevents them from overgrazing and depleting the food source for future generations.

Many indigenous cultures adhere to this simple rule. They have adopted principles like "never take more than one third of the life you are harvesting" so there is always something left for others and there is always enough left to not jeopardize the future of the resource. This is also about resilience. Buffalo and other herbivores can go on for days without food because evolution equipped the animal for changing conditions by built-in energy reserves. The same applies for trees. When a tree experiences a drought, it learns to store water for future occasions. The trees that are not resilient to change, die off, leaving only those that are equipped to effectively deal with change.

And some of the survival strategies are really remarkable. Trees in fire prone environments, like in Australia, can regrow even after being reduced to dust. All it takes is just a tiny bit of root to survive subsoil, from which an entire new tree can regrow. And regrowth happens fairly quickly. Only months after a blasting fire, the forest looks green again with shoots coming out of surviving trunks and roots. So, on the maintain level of Krone's framework, innovation in nature acts on the level of building resilience to change and disruptions.

Improve

We now know however, that long term evolutionary success is the result of plants and animals *creating positive impact which benefits the wider environment*. While some herbivores, like bison, have specific qualities of value-adding, like extending the growth season of plants and thereby increasing the nourishment for other grazers, all herbivores leave behind dung that fertilizes the soil. Deciduous trees do something similar by shedding their leaves in autumn, which not only insulates and thus protects the soil, it also improves organic matter which enhances soil fertility. This way, the herbivore improves the living conditions for the plants and the tree improves the soil microbial life. Both processes enhance a vital regulating feedback loop, one that keeps the climate friendly for life.

This feedback loop regulates carbon drawdown from the atmosphere into the ground, and it works like this: Adding dung and organic matter makes the topsoil richer. More nutrients mean more plant growth, more photosynthesis, and more carbon that is transported into the soils. Richer soils also mean a richer subsoil microbial life, which in turn promote the stabilization of carbon in the soil, which makes it an effective and stable carbon sink. On the improve level of Krone's framework, innovation is then about creating positive impact which benefits the wider ecosystem.

Regenerate

And lastly, the herbivore plays a regenerative role in the ecosystem. Even if it prefers to eat grass, it also likes to nibble on small twigs and branches of trees, which induces a cascade of positive impacts. As a reaction to getting pruned, the trees generate a lot more produce like acorns, seeds, nuts, berries, and other types of fruit. This brings more wealth into the ecosystem that serves as food for other animals like insects, birds and mammals. When food is abundant, these animals produce more offspring, which means that there is more food for carnivores. The carcasses that carnivores leave subsequently leave food for scavengers. Pruning also stimulates a process of rejuvenation in the plant, which increases its health. So, the herbivore adds value to its immediate environment in a way that increases the health, wealth, vitality and viability of the wider ecosystem.

Even trees have a way of regenerating life. When they can grow into a healthy biodiverse forest ecosystem, they develop services that not only affect the wider landscape around them, but the entire biosphere. By purifying and regulating the air and water cycles, forests contribute to climate regulation, an important process that affects the overall health and viability of the biosphere.

These last two examples highlight the role of innovation on the regeneration level of Krone's framework, as it enables the *evolution of the wider system*. Positive impacts get cascaded, and as a result, the wider system becomes healthier, richer, more viable and vital.

How regeneration works exactly however, is still largely unknown as we currently only partially understand the nature of interdependencies and feedback loops. Yet it gives already a first idea on how innovation works in the long run. So, while all four levels of work are important, long term evolutionary success, as we have seen earlier, only happens when living entities invest in positive impact and regenerative value-creation. *It is about unlocking the potential to become more and do more.*

The **Nature of Innovation Framework**, organized according to Charles Krone's levels of work (here called nature of efforts). The left-hand side, Natural Intelligence, summarizes how nature innovates. This summary is derived from the science of biology and builds on the theory of regenerative development and design. The right-hand side, Industrial Intelligence, summarizes current industrial innovation logic. This summary builds on insights from transition science. Not only is the nature of innovation in the socio-economic system different from the nature of innovation of life, the outcomes created through current innovation practice are also significantly different. And whilst Industrial Intelligence is addressing the levels of 'maintain' – albeit inefficiently, and 'improve' – although only scarcely – there is no equivalent for the level of 'regenerate' yet. This illustrates the innovation challenge of the 21st century for business: how to create business that benefits and enables benevolent evolution of the wider ecosystem so that quality of life, richness, vitality and viability of all life on the planet is enhanced?

NATURAL INTELLIGENCE		LOGIC	INDUSTRIAL INTELLIGENCE	
"For life" Biocentric, Living systems-based, Systemic, Relational, Anticipative		Framework of Krone	**"For profit"** Anthropocentric, Mechanistic, Reductionistic, Linear cause & effect, Reactive	
OUTCOME	NATURE OF INNOVATION	NATURE OF EFFORTS	NATURE OF INNOVATION	OUTCOME
Higher order of health, wealth, vitality & viability of the wider ecosystem	Enable evolution of the wider system	Regenerate	/	/
Benefit to the wider ecosystem	Create positive impact	Improve	Create positive impact	Benefit to the wider socioeconomic system
Resilient to changing conditions	Build resilience	Maintain	Sustainify operations	Slow down degeneration
Efficient generation	Improve metabolic processes	Operate	Improve production processes	Efficient degeneration

CHANGING THE LOGIC OF VALUE CREATION

Regenerative value creation is where current business innovation falls short. The focus of most innovation strategies does not go beyond the levels of *operate* and *maintain*, which are about existence—about surviving to live the next day. Innovation-as-usual keeps organizations in the outdated take-make-waste model of improving production or in the sustainifying operations (reduce negative impact) model inspired by the ambition to reduce harm. Both result in degeneration of the life support system on which we all depend. Compared to how life works and innovates, present day sustainability strategies and programs at best slow down degeneration. Most of the time though, sustainifying efforts preserve the dysfunction as they are about "doing things better" instead of "doing better things."

Luckily, in recent years, creating positive impact has found its way to pioneering companies and organizations as movements like purpose-driven business and impact investment show. Yet, these are mostly focused on creating positive socio-economic benefit, which is not quite the same as creating positive impact for the wider ecosystem. The champion survivors in nature not only generate positive impacts, they create conditions for regeneration. Tapping into NI, therefore, helps to elevate our thinking, especially when it comes to sustainability and the sustainable development goals. Because in nature, sustainability is a byproduct, not a goal in and of itself. It is the byproduct of regenerative value-creation.

Therefore, the innovation challenge of the 21st century for business is in how to shift the nature of innovation from the lower levels of existence (operate and maintain) to the higher levels of potential (improve and regenerate). How to develop businesses that benefit the wider ecosystem? How to develop business models that enable regeneration—the benevolent evolution of the wider ecosystem so that quality of life, richness, vitality and viability of all life on the planet is enhanced?

While there is no roadmap, I do know that innovation-as-usual is not going to get us there. We will need to shift from functional thinking (how to fix a problem) to developmental thinking (how to develop potential). While existence refers to what already *is*, potential refers to what *could be*. Much of the current sustainability (and for that matter, environmental conservation work) is situated in the layer of existence. Work is focused on slowing down degeneration, or the restoration and conservation of that what is currently present. Both approaches, however, fail to address the depletion that has already occurred.

For instance, man has had a profound impact on ecosystems from the moment humans domesticated fire and started to hunt collectively. The fact that most megafauna are extinct and that pristine, old-growth forests are extremely rare, is a testimony to human impact. Working on issues related to sustainability from the mental models associated with the levels of existence only is thus problematic. It fails to appreciate the potential that can be developed, which leaves the implication that the only way forward for society, is to do more with less.

Most sustainability work also starts from a perspective of problem solving. Mang & Haggard point out that the problem with problem solving is that it might get rid of what we do not want, but it does not do anything for what we do want. It is like riding a horse sitting backwards. You will see what you are riding away from, but not where you are going, and this basically sums up the *pattern of reactivity* (innovation leads to unintended side effects, which then need to be "fixed"), which is associated with innovation-as-usual. That is why regenerative work centers around developing potential instead of problem-solving. When living entities unlock their potential for value-adding, they create conditions that enable them to do more than survive—they become more and therefore generate more. Once an organism begins to add value to the larger systems in which it is embedded, it starts to create the conditions that allow it to thrive.

Regenerative thinking is therefore very different from sustainability thinking, because it starts not from a mindset of problem-solving but from a mindset of potential, not from a mindset of responsible consumerism (what can I extract sustainably), but from a mindset of stewardship (what value-adding processes can I enable). A regenerative practitioner therefore looks beyond self-actualization in order to live out a value-adding role in the wider system. Like whales, wolves, beavers, otters, bees, and other keystone species, this way of operating is to become a steward of the evolution of the whole. Regenerative development is not about forcing a system to become something but about calling forth the potential for evolution. In that sense, it avoids the pitfalls of manipulation and exploitation, mindsets that reinforce degeneration. That is why NI needs to encompass more than bio-inspired problem-solving approaches, such as nature-based solutions or biomimicry; NI needs to expand the thinking from *what can I do*, to *what can I enable*, and more importantly, *who do I have to become* to achieve positive and regenerative impact.

Regenerative development is thus about advancing to a different level of performance, and also a different level of being. It is not new technology but a new mental model and a new role for human beings that can assure a future for us on this planet. If this is the first time you encounter this innovation framework and the underlying theory of regenerative development, then it might sound very abstract and vague. So, in the next part, I will delineate a few examples of how the different levels of innovation can play out in practice.

From status quo thinking to regenerative thinking —*What can you do?*

There is a popular proverb that says that if you have ever slept with a mosquito in your room then you know that no one is too small to matter. Given that all our gardens combined could potentially add up to the largest nature reserve on Earth, it follows that part of the solution to the devastating nature-loss worldwide lies in our own little gardens. In fact, it is a central adage from permaculture, that you can change the world in your backyard.

The action researcher in me wanted to test whether this premise would hold true when put into practice. Keen to work on a practical solution, I set up an experiment in our backyard. The central question of my quest was, can we turn this poor and degraded piece of land into an edible, thriving ecosystem that supports all of life? And so, our garden became a project in a real-world context where I could apply all the knowledge on bio-inspired innovation, systems thinking and regeneration I had gained over the years.

Because books can convey theory but not experience, I enrolled in a permaculture design course by Taco Blom, from the Dutch-Belgian Permaculture association at his CSA Samenland (togetherland) in Belgium.[12] This turned out to be an incredibly valuable investment. Not only because Taco is a walking encyclopedia of plant knowledge, but because his understanding of the systemic nature of ecosystems is unparalleled, and his hands-on experience outclassed that of all my biology professors combined. The first thing he taught his students was to observe the land by investigating its context, stressors, and potential.

When we moved into the house in 2011, the garden was an impoverished monoculture of grass where only a couple of bushes survived. The absence of any weeds indicated long-term use of herbicides. The absence of biological life—when we dug a hole of one square meter to assess the soil, we encountered

---

[12] CSA is short for Community Supported Agriculture.

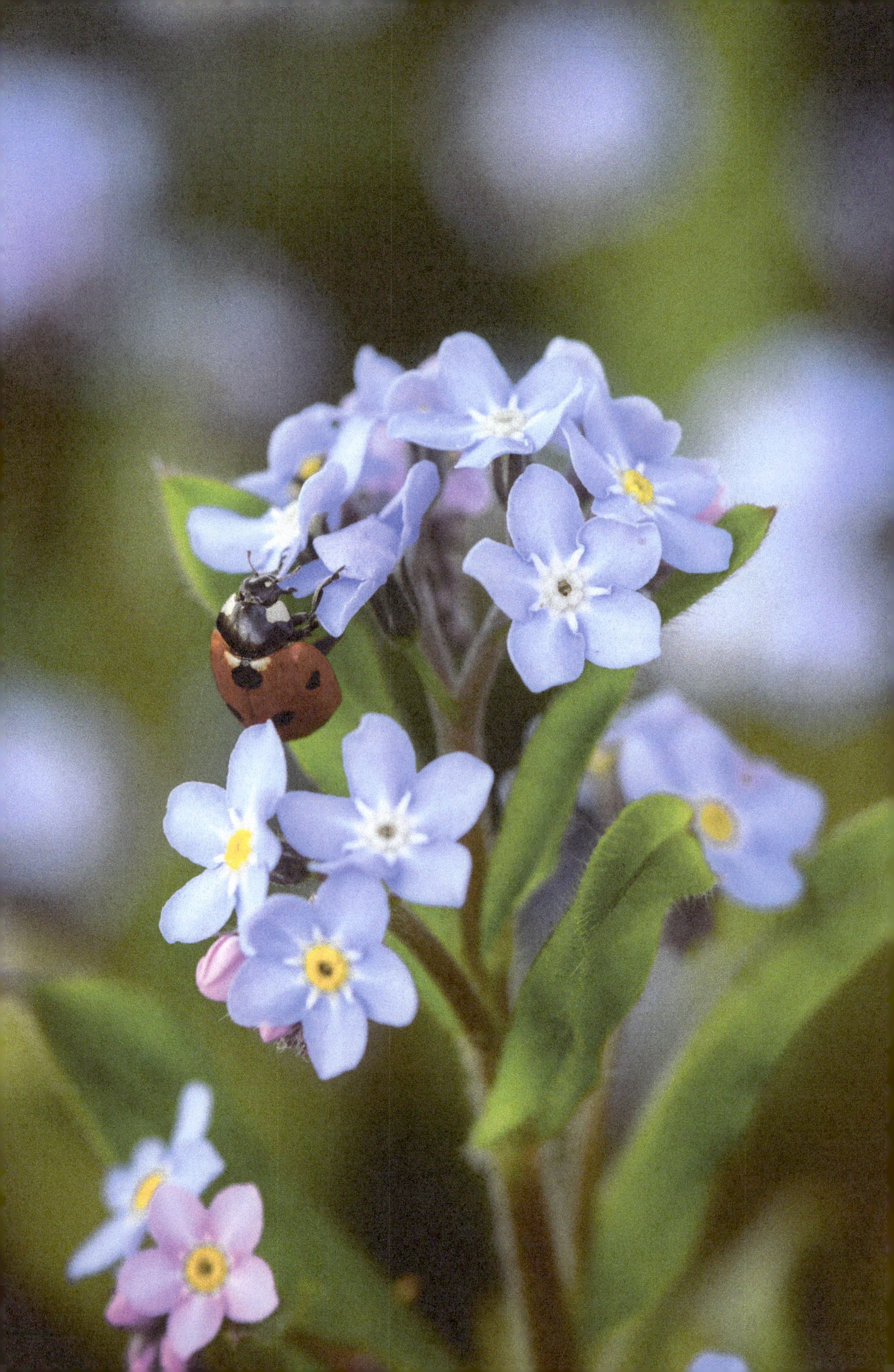

no earthworms—indicated a severe state of degradation. The sandy soil denoted that water stress is an important factor to consider, and the presence of American black cherry (regarded as an invasive pest species in Europe) at the edge of our plot, indicated a severely disturbed system. These weed trees are pioneers and are often the first ones to colonize waste lands, because they can grow under harsh conditions. Their role in the ecosystem is to make conditions less harsh, so other species can come in through a process of natural succession. Specifically, these pioneers provide organic matter to enrich the soil and they mobilize nutrients so that these can become accessible for other plants.

Therefore, the first thing we needed to do in our redesign adventure was to imitate the role of pioneer plants to improve the soil by adding organic matter. We did so using a variety of methods including mulching, introducing green manure plants, and adding compost. Soon enough, more life returned to the garden, bringing with them more capabilities for restoration and regeneration. Because the topsoil became more fertile, earth worms returned, which attracted moles. Both species are very important for aerating the soil. The next year, the ants returned. At first only the very small kind but recently also bigger ants. Ants are important for a number of reasons. They contribute to soil fertility, disperse seeds, protect plants, biologically control pests, and provide habitat for other important insects.

What is more, many ant species collaborate with bacteria and fungi, especially those that play an important role in the Wood Wide Web, and creating the conditions to get this below ground internet up and running was one of our first priorities, as it was central for optimizing communication, health care, and resource management in the ecosystem. Richer soil leads to a richer plant community, which in turn attracts more insects. More insects attract more birds, more amphibians, and mammals. These organisms further enrich the garden, not only with their manure but with the seeds and skills they bring with them.

Six years into the redesign process, there are close to a dozen nut trees that we have not planted in the garden. It was the squirrels who planted hazelnut trees, and the crows who planted walnut trees. Mushrooms reappeared, ensuring us that the installment of the underground internet was in full progress. Of course, we humans also played an important role in regenerating the ecosystem by accelerating the soil recovery process and enriching the plant diversity. We planted fruit and nut trees, berry bushes, and beneficial herbs with special attention to put those species together that are naturally inclined to engage in reciprocal relationships with each other. This is called "guilding" in permaculture. We brought in flowers and bushes that are beneficial for bees and butterflies and which blossom at different periods so there is always food around. We dispersed seeds from plants collected in nature spots not far from the house to further promote biodiversity. The soil recovery and resulting dense, stacked cover of plants increased the water retaining capacity of the soil and so toads and frogs reappeared. In fact, wherever we introduced a small body of water, even a bucket, a toad or a frog would make it its home. Soil recovery also increased subsoil microbial life, which help to drawdown carbon from the atmosphere.

Since we are out to create a garden that is edible, we introduced several perennial vegetables like Jerusalem artichoke, wild leek, rhubarb, horseradish, sorrel, and plants that come back every year like purslane or rocket salad, all of which require very little or no maintenance. We have incorporated vegetable beds in which we grow squash, zucchini, pattypan squash, pumpkins, salads, chard, cabbages, and tomatoes. Beans and peas are grown in between the wildflowers. Most vegetables, apart from the tomatoes, grow very well on their own with very little to no help from us. In fact, we selected plant species that don't need a lot of attention and caring, because our busy lives prevent us from investing much work in the garden.

I estimate that we spend less than 25 hours working in our edible ecosystem over the course of a year, which encompasses preparing the vegetable beds, sowing the seeds in the spring, mowing a path, doing some mulching, and harvesting the produce. Yet the yield we get with such little effort is amazing. That is because we basically let nature do the work, we only create the conditions, so that she can grow into an edible ecosystem. Our philosophy thus brings together the disciplines of biologically inspired innovation, permaculture, rewilding, and regenerative design.

Of course, this also means that our garden looks very different from landscaped and kitchen gardens. It looks more like a wild nature spot because there are no straight rows and neat columns in our garden. However, we do mimic a specific part of a natural ecosystem: the forest edge. Forest edges are transition zones between the forest and another ecosystem like a meadow for instance. Such edges, where two communities meet and integrate, are called ecotones in biology. Edges between distinct ecosystems are often the places where both richness and innovation are boosted. An important ecotone for example is the estuary, where a freshwater river runs into the ocean. Here, the freshwater mixes with the salt water, creating a new type of water: brackish water. It is where ocean life and land life meet.

Ecotonal areas are often remarkably rich as they house a greater abundance and density of organisms and a greater number of species per standard unit of area than can be found in either flanking community. It also sparks innovation as organisms need new capabilities to fully take advantage of the new conditions created by this edge ecosystem. Trees growing in forest edges for instance, need to grow deeper and stronger roots as they are exposed to stronger winds than trees inside the forest. Bushes at the forest edge are also more frequently grazed upon by herbivores and are thus better equipped to renew themselves after pruning. Forest edges also produce more varied food sources because the plant community grows in a gradient, stacking different layers of plants for optimal use of space and sunlight.

And that is exactly what I set out to emulate in our garden. It is one of the basic principles of permaculture, to design according to at least seven different layers or dimensions: the overstory tree layer, the understory tree layer, the shrub layer, the herbaceous layer, the ground cover layer, the root layer, and the vine layer. So instead of the two dimensional organized "neatness" found in most gardens, our pattern is, like it is in nature, based on intelligently organized chaos to capture the maximum of sunlight and space while creating optimal robustness and resilience. A walnut and chestnut tree make up the overstory layer, together with the trees that were already present. A pear, an almond, a peach, a plum, a mulberry, and an apple tree make up the understory layer. Hazelnut shrubs, lilacs, blue berries and smaller fruit trees represent the shrub layer, and a wide variety of herbs and flowers make up the herbaceous layer. Purslane, dandelion and chickweed cover the ground along with several grasses and other weeds. Jerusalem artichokes, comfrey, and a variety of root vegetables make up the root layer, and grapes, peas and beans represent the vine layer.

Another important aspect in our garden experiment is also rewilding—giving nature free reign to do her thing—so when squirrels and crows started to co-design, we let them. And that works amazingly well, while the garden was a deteriorated, degraded, and lifeless monoculture when we moved into the house, six years later it is a hotspot for wildlife. Because of the dense soil cover and rich diversity in plants, it is a good habitat for insects. Bees, beetles, crickets, bumble bees, European hornets, hoverflies, grasshoppers, aphids, butterflies, dragonflies, wasps, woodlice, damselflies, and moths have all returned. So far, we have identified 15 different butterfly species in our garden, some which many of our friends have never seen before, like the old-world swallowtail or the hummingbird hawk-moth. And the insects attract the birds.

There are more than 20 different bird species that visit the garden. Regular visitors to the garden are robins, sparrows, Eurasian jays, thrushes, wrens, blackbirds, great tits, blue tits, coal tits, nuthatches, woodpeckers, crested tits, long-tailed tits, hawfinches, greenfinches, crows, wood pigeons and starlings. (While I am writing this, a falcon holding its prey in its claws flies over twice.) But also, mice, hedgehogs, squirrels, toads, frogs and bats are often seen in the garden. This, in turn, attracts predators like falcons, buzzards, sparrow hawks, herons, stone martens and weasels. And to our great delight, we have also observed several deer, barn owls, a goshawk, and a fox visiting the garden.

In and around the house, many songbird nests can be found in springtime, a time when the garden is especially buzzy with many birds foraging and feeding their offspring. Because some of these birds live so close to the house, it is also changing our relationship with them. Since we are part of this ecosystem and pose no threat, they come much closer, literally flying over our head when we are dining on the terrace, or perching on a branch that is only a meter away. In summer, the crickets greet us each night with their beautiful dusk chorus, which is, in my opinion, the best soundtrack to go to sleep. The garden is not only good for wildlife, it also rejuvenates us and helps us better tune in with the seasons. It gives peace and joy, so much so that we feel less inclined to take our holidays elsewhere. Spending the summer in the garden is a holiday in itself. I also consider the garden as a biodiversity bank, especially when all around us, nature is being replaced by asphalt, cement, or sterile lawns. The interest of our biodiversity bank is the offspring that the garden generates each year, which can disperse into new habitats. Today the biodiversity in the garden is striking—it is a home to more than 60 different animal species (and these are only the ones that have been observed)—particularly since our home is situated in the Flemish part of Belgium, the most densely populated and least forested area in Europe.

Of course, not all goes smoothly. Our redesign project is a process of trial and error and several mistakes have been made along the way. One I regret the most, I made early on. In the second year of redesign, we lost many sprouting vegetables like salads and chard to slugs. Blinded by this loss, I convinced myself it would be okay for a one time use of an eco-friendly product to kill off the slugs. The limited short-term gain was unfortunately offset by a longer-term disaster. I found several sickly and diseased hedgehogs, nature's answer to slug abundance, in and around the garden. Even though I knew they were also suffering because of the frequent use of pesticides on the corn field next to our land, I felt both guilty and stupid. I made the resolution to let nature fix the problems from now on. No chemicals will ever be used again in our plot.

In a sense, our garden project illustrates the different levels of the nature of innovation framework. The layered design of the garden is a way to *improve metabolic processes* and generate more (the operate level). Improving biodiversity and promoting installment of the Wood Wide Web is a way *to build resilience* so that the garden is better able to deal with changing conditions in the future (the maintain level). The abundance of food and safe shelters helps species to generate more offspring. Improved biodiversity above and below ground also enhances carbon drawdown and sequestration. These *create a positive impact* that benefits the wider ecosystem (the improve level).

And to get it up another level, to enable *the evolution of the wider system*, means that the garden project needs to spark cascading positive impacts elsewhere (the regeneration level). Achieving this is not easy and requires a whole other dimension of thought and development. Still, there is potential for it to grow regenerative impact. In the innovation sessions I organize for work, I regularly share our garden example, not only to illustrate how applying NI works in practice but also to share how we each can shift from a consumer role to one of stewardship. People often come to talk to me afterwards about what they can do in their own gardens. If they turn that idea into action and become a steward for their own garden regeneration project, then our local experiment has multiplied positive impacts elsewhere. If these in turn do the same, then our garden project has become an enabler of the evolution of the larger ecosystem towards a higher order of health, wealth, vitality and viability. It has become regenerative.

There are a few more lessons learned that are worthwhile to share. The truth is, it took me two years to become comfortable with the pattern of untidy chaos in the garden. Along with our garden, I also had to evolve. As humans, we like structure and tidiness. We like to "control" nature, especially in terms of which plants need to go where and which plants need to stay away. We furnish our gardens like we furnish our houses and apply the same cleanliness inside and outside. We adopt the same guidelines for designing our parks: they need to be efficient, clean, and sterile. That is not nature's way, yet we spend an incredible amount of time and resources to keep the weeds out of the lawn, the trees out of the flower beds, and the insects out of the vegetable beds. In fact, we have imprinted ourselves on the least efficient way to get things done by fighting natural development.

So, while I knew all of this, I underestimated how hard it is to let go of these deeply ingrained principles of structure, order, and cleanliness. For two whole years, I had to suppress the urge to create order in the garden and plant everything in neat rows or columns. I had to develop a new capability in myself to let go of the illusion of control and become more comfortable with organized chaos. I became pretty good at it, in fact so good that maybe I took it a bit too far. I adopted what Mark Shepard, a pioneer in sustainable agriculture and CEO of Forest Agriculture Enterprises LLC, calls the STUN (sheer, total, utter neglect) method. It is what the four words say: you leave the plants alone to fend for themselves. The philosophy is simple: if they can survive on their own, they belong here. If not, they will be replaced by plants that can.[13] That is how natural selection works and it is also the secret to very little work.

As a result, we did lose some young fruit trees in the beginning, but the ones that remained proved their worth. They have survived several storms and prolonged periods of drought. But after six years, our apple tree collapsed under its own weight of apples, teaching me that I have a role to play as well. In nature, trees seldomly collapse under the weight of their own fruit, because they have co-evolved with animals. Herbivores for instance, often prune the trees, eating the fresh new twigs, so the load-bearing branches can grow stronger. Unfortunately, our garden is not large enough to support an herbivore year-round and the visiting deer do not eat from the trees. Some pruning therefore, might need to be done by us.

Our garden ecosystem has become so successful in attracting birds that we are also attracting several birds of prey. In itself, it's a real delight to have a falcon fly over your head or a hawk sitting on a big tree looking down on the garden, but these raptors also like to eat our feathered employees. We had runner ducks that

---

[13] This applies to the perennials, trees and bushes. Annual vegetables do require a little water during a hot, dry summer season as do newly planted trees in their first 2-3 years.

recycle snails into eggs. Runner ducks are incredibly helpful employees because they do not disturb the groundcover like chickens. They are also friendly, sociable birds, and pretty funny too, following us around with flapping feet and nonstop quacking sounds. But to do their work, they need to be able to roam free in the garden, which gives both the local hawk and buzzard free reign, so it is hard to keep our feathered employees alive. When I looked for solutions, I learned that bird of prey attacks occur much less when there is a larger animal around, again highlighting the importance of diversity in an ecosystem.

I haven't figured out how to resolve that issue yet, but there is a popular saying in permaculture that states that the problem is the solution, which did turn out to be the case for the invasive black cherry trees in the garden. Instead of getting rid of them—as advised by many a naturalist in our neighborhood—we chose to view them not as pests but as biomass producers. So, we harness their ability of soil improvement by regular pruning. It is such a hardy tree that we can cut off all the branches, which are laid on the ground to improve the soil, and it will completely regrow again in no time. The thicker branches are used as fuel for our wood stove. And where the soil fertility has improved, the seeds of this weed tree no longer germinate. The work is done, and pioneers make room for the next stage of succession. So, the black cherry trees in our garden, proved to be incredibly valuable helpers in our quest to turn a poor degraded wasteland into a flourishing and edible ecosystem. The problem became the solution.

From reducing negative impact to creating positive impact —What can your company do?

One of the most impressive transformations in the business world is that of international carpet tile manufacturer, Interface. The listed multinational is active in more than 110 countries and has an annual turnover of $1.4 billion. In 1994, Ray Anderson, the founder of Interface, had an epiphany. He realized that the conventional way of producing things and doing business is destroying the planet, and instead of being a part of the problem, Ray wanted to become a part of the solution. Undeterred by the massive challenge and the initial skepticism in the business world, he set his company on a new mission: Mission Zero®, an initiative to eliminate all negative impact of the company on the environment by the year 2020. To achieve that goal, he and his team had to radically redesign the company, the products, and the way Interface did business.

The journey to climb "Mount Sustainability," as Ray calls it in his book *Confessions of a Radical Industrialist*, left the company better off in many ways. Profits went up, costs went down, and product quality, visibility, and customer and employee loyalty all improved. Historically, the production of carpet tiles was a highly polluting, water and petro-intensive process. To transform to a more benign model, they looked to nature for inspiration. So, Interface set up a collaboration with Karl-Henrik Robert from The Natural Step, and Janine Benyus from the Biomimicry Institute, and they invited Dayna Baumeister, business partner of Janine Benyus, to their offices in Atlanta for a workshop.

Dayna took them for a walk in the forest and asked the multidisciplinary team: "How does nature cover the floor?" After touring around a bit, they began to notice an emergent pattern on the forest floor. This pattern was entropy—or the chaotic disorder of leaves, sticks, pinecones and branches all dispersed at random on the ground. If one piece of the pattern was replaced it was nearly impossible to tell what had changed. They went back to the design studio and developed a new carpet tile line called Entropy®, inspired by the entropic pattern of the forest floor.

Compared to the traditional tile line series, this was a real innovation as colors were weaved in random patterns across the tiles, eliminating the conventional uniformity. Entropy carpet tiles, therefore, can be easily exchanged by any other entropy tiles, so clients do not need to store extra carpet tiles to ensure that dye lots are the same, or replace the entire carpet if a few tiles are damaged. This prolongs the life of the carpet and significantly reduces installation waste, and it became one of their best-sellers, representing more than 40% of their total sales. Yet that was not enough to achieve the Mission Zero goal, and so the next step they undertook was to explore how to shift from a linear take-make-waste model into a circular one, where old carpets can be recycled into new ones.

A problem the company encountered early on was the glue that fixed the tiles to the floor. Throughout its entire life cycle, glue causes problems. It is toxic, and it prevents disassembly of the tiles into reusable components. Again, Interface turned to nature for inspiration and asked: How does nature hold down the forest floor? The answer was gravity, and again the team set out to explore how they could leverage the power of nature. The innovation they came up with is called TacTiles®, a glue-free carpet installation system that uses small and square adhesive

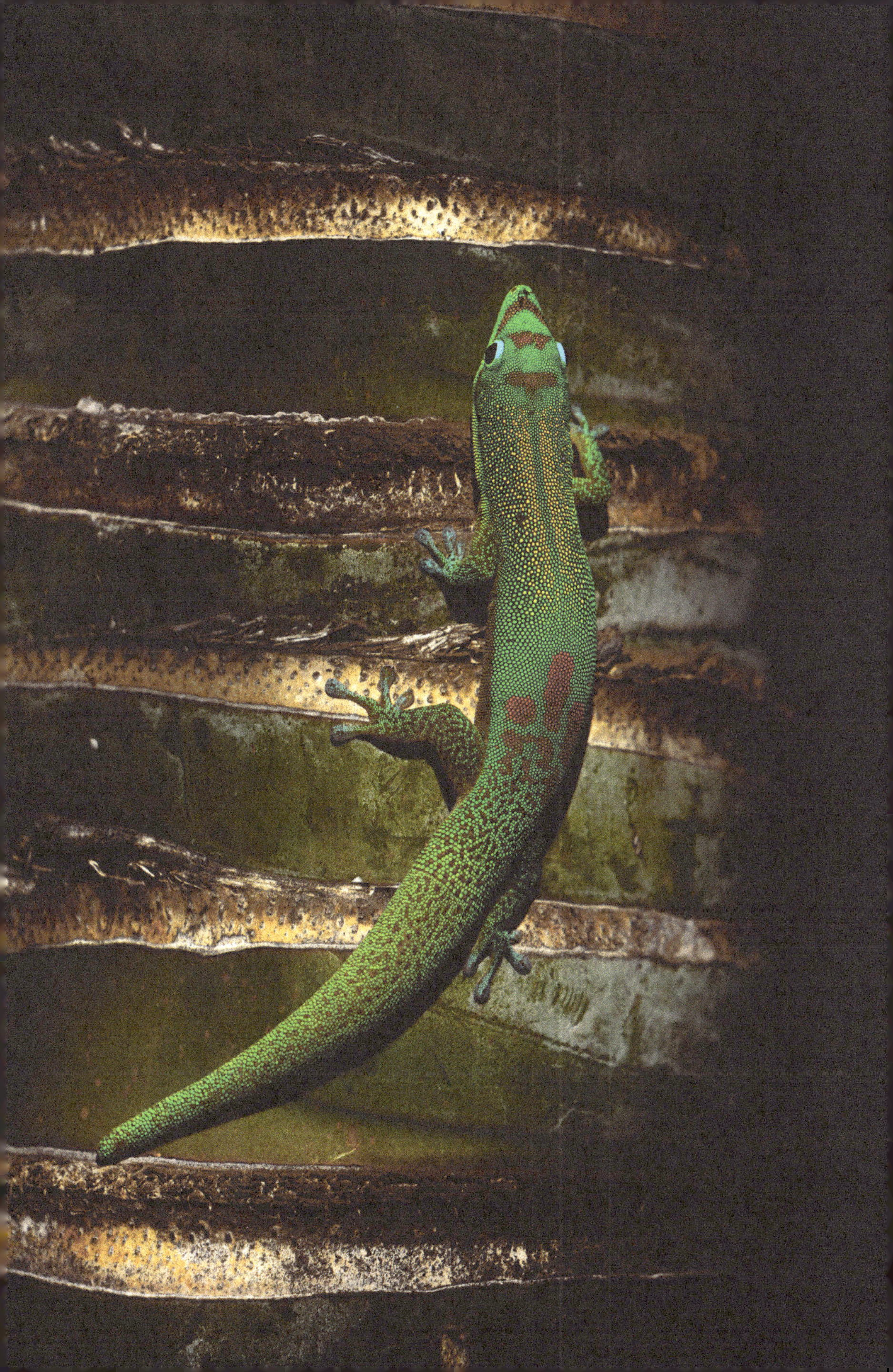

stickers to adhere carpet tiles together rather than to the floor. The collective weight of the carpet holds every tile in place and glue is thus no longer needed.

The interesting thing about this adhesive invention, is that it was inspired by an animal that can defy gravity—the gecko. A gecko is a small lizard that walks vertical surfaces with ease, crossing indoor ceilings without problems. Scientists credit this incredible ability to their toe pads, which are covered by millions of tiny hairs. Each hair induces a molecular attraction to the ceiling, called van der Waals force and millions of tiny forces build up into a superpower that defies gravity. The adhesive power of these hairs is so great that the gecko can stick to the ceiling with only one toe of one foot. The TacTiles technology of Interface was inspired by this toe pad technology, and the company has since installed over 60 million square meters of carpet without glue.

So, to harness the power of gravitation, Interface emulated a strategy from a reptilian superhero that learned to overcome gravity. Sometimes, the answer can be found in the opposite direction of what one is searching for. The TacTiles innovation is not only fast and easy to install, it eliminates toxic glues and makes replacements and recycling easier, leading to significantly less waste and costs. This fits the company's circular ambition to close its resource loops well. Interface's waste reduction efforts have resulted in a 91% decrease in total waste to landfills from their carpet factories since 1996, and almost 6 million kilograms of post-consumer carpet have been recycled through their ReEntry® program. Even more impressive is the fact that since 1996, the GHG (greenhouse gas) emissions intensity is down 96% and the total water intake intensity is down 89% at their manufacturing sites. In addition, 99% of the energy they use comes from renewable sources.

With the finish line of Mission Zero in sight, Interface re-envisioned its mission, and shifted from eliminating negative environmental impact to creating a positive one. Interface calls their new mission Climate take back™, and they commit to running their business in a way that creates a climate fit for life, while calling on others to do the same. Interface believes that reversing global warming is possible and the company focusses on four key areas:

1. Live Zero – Do business in ways that gives back whatever is taken from the Earth
2. Love Carbon – Stop seeing carbon as the enemy, and start using it as a resource

3 Let Nature Cool – Support our biosphere's ability to regulate the climate
4 Lead Industrial Re-revolution – Transform industry into a force for climate progress

In their process of creating positive impact, Interface teamed up with the biologists at Biomimicry3.8 to explore how they can create a factory that functions like a forest; A factory that just like a forest, enhances its environment because it produces ecosystem services like water storage, nutrient recycling, climate regulation, and soil formation via the use of ecological performance standards. Interface is now applying this approach to the redesign of their factories, beginning with a remodel near Atlanta, Georgia.

When the production of new carpets exceeded Interface's ability to gather recyclable carpets, the company started to look for new sources of nylon that they could recycle into carpet fibers. After some research, it turns out that a major waste source of nylon is the discarded fishing nets that pollute oceans and kill marine life. So, in collaboration with the London Zoological Society, Interface set up a pilot project in the Philippines where they paid local fisherman to fish up discarded fishing nets, which were then recycled into carpets. Part of the revenue was reinvested in the local community to restore the mangrove systems, so that in the future, the fisherman can fish for fish again. The pilot was so successful that Interface turned it into a self-sustaining project called Net-Works, and they are currently expanding into Africa. In 2017, Net-Works collected 224,000 kilograms of discarded fishing nets and turned them into carpets, thereby cleaning up the ocean and regenerating local fishing communities.

Interface continues to take its *Climate Take Back™* mission seriously, by exploring how to remove carbon from the atmosphere and replace the petroleum-based carbon in its products with bio-based carbon. One of the innovations in this regard is called CircuitBac Green, carpet backing based on bioplastics, and it effectively stores more carbon during its life cycle than it emits. This new innovation leverages photosynthesis—a process that naturally removes carbon from the atmosphere—but in this case, it stores carbon in carpet tiles instead of in plants. So, after the carpet is made there is less carbon in the atmosphere than before. Exactly what they want to achieve with their Climate Take Back mission—to innovate in a way that creates a climate fit for life.

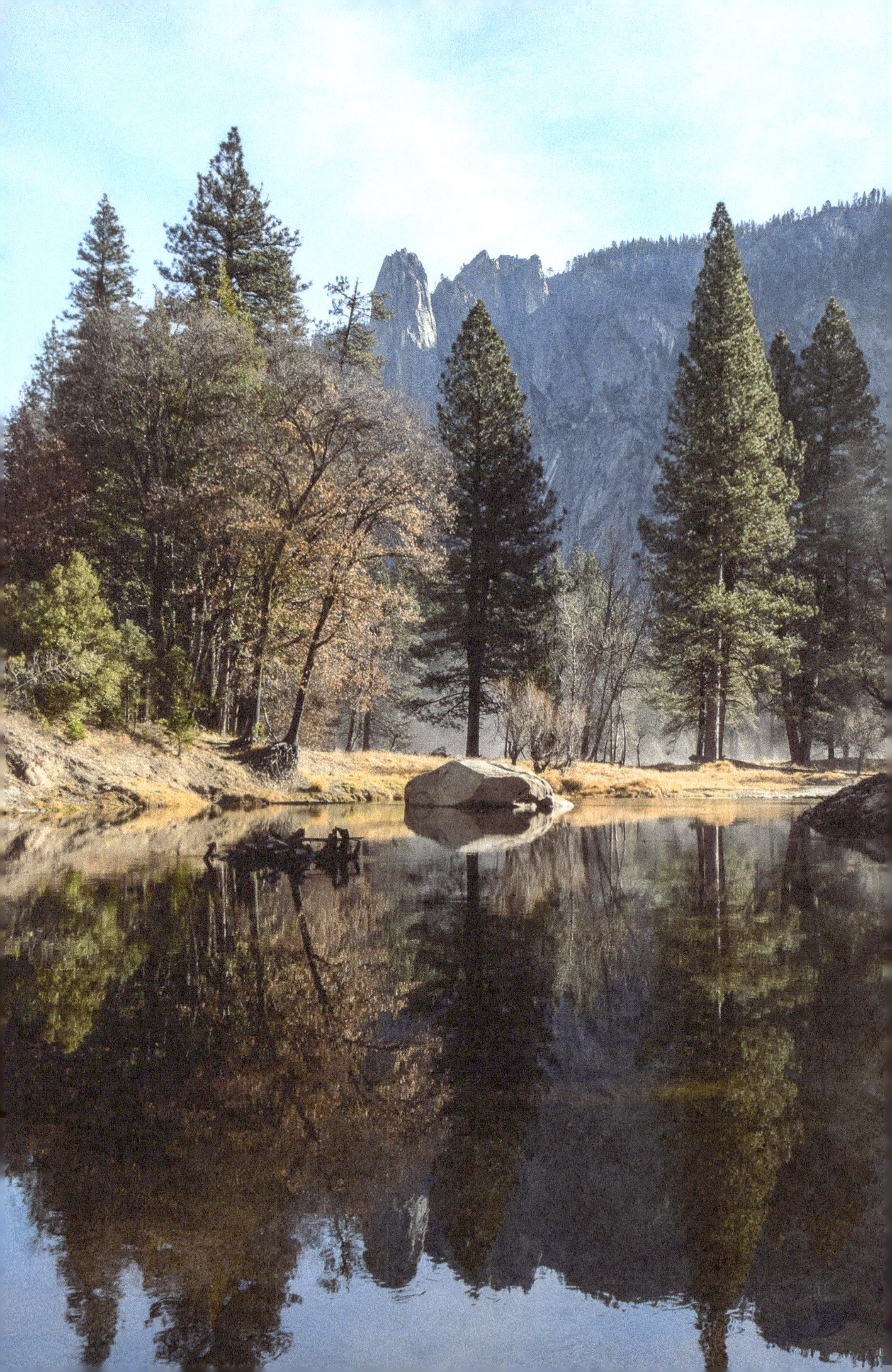

Doing well by doing good—the principle that guided Interface's transition process—has led to extraordinary results. This example also shows how having a bold and ambitious long-term mission can be a catalyst for multilevel innovation. Interface started off with product innovation (entropy carpet tile), then moved on to process innovation (tac-tiles), and then to system innovation (a factory like a forest). The Interface example also shows how they shifted from the *improve production processes* to the *sustainifying operations* innovation model where they aimed for zero negative impact. Now that this ambition is almost complete, the company has elevated their innovation strategy from sustainifying operations to *creating positive impact* that not only benefits them, but the wider biosphere as well. And in their quest to achieve that, they will undoubtedly have to evolve new capacities that enable the evolution of the wider system. Their new mission of "creating positive impact" will require a new business logic, one that enables regenerative value-creation.

From degenerative to regenerative value creation —What can the business world do?

The future doesn't need to be a repetition of the past. The Interface example shows us that even a highly polluting, water and petro-intensive carpet tile manufacturer can completely redesign its operations and DNA to move away from the degenerative model of value-creation. But to do so requires a radically new innovation culture. So how can the business world shift its logic from degenerative to regenerative, and more importantly, how can this transformation happen fast? In a world that is rapidly warming and deteriorating, where runaway degenerative change is spiraling out of control, we need everyone on board, because time and scale are of the essence. This means that we will have to learn to develop regenerative processes that can multiply regeneration exponentially, and for that to happen we will need to understand the difference between regeneration and degeneration. And technology can help us achieve just that.

Virtual reality can assist us in gaining a more systemic understanding of the foundations of life on Earth, which has been coined by the first astronauts as "the overview effect." If set up properly, a virtual trip to the moon can completely shift our view towards our home planet, seeing the fragility and miracle of a planet that can support life—just like it did for the astronauts that did travel into space.

Or, alternatively, VR can show us the devastating impact of plastic on ocean life as if we were swimming through it.

Augmented reality, if based on sound science, can help us see the relationships between things, the interdependence through which life evolves, and might help us better understand the chain of events that follow a specific behavior. AR can show us how the cheap mass-produced chicken lived and looked before it got slaughtered, how much child labor went into the production of that low-priced t-shirt, and how much pristine rainforest was destroyed to produce the palm oil for your shampoo. It can show us how our immune system is boosted after a trip to nature and how stress levels go up once you travel back into the city.

Blockchain technology is particularly interesting in order to change the logic of value-creation as transparent, decentralized, tamper-proof databases make it possible to both track and verify transactions and interactions without a centralized authority. Blockchains can significantly increase the transparency, accountability, and efficiency of supply chains from origin to shelf, to help prevent waste, inefficiency, fraud, and unethical practices. They can demonstrate the impact of the actions of people and companies. But most importantly, blockchain tech can help to incentivize regeneration instead of degeneration by changing the drivers of our economy from value extracting to value adding.

An impressive example of how these new technologies can be used for shifting from degenerative to regenerative value-creation is a blockchain based global network called Regen Network, developed by Regen Network Development, Inc. The network is comprised of developers, ecologists, scientists, and designers from all over the world who share the common purpose of planetary regeneration.

Regen network provides the tools that are needed to regenerate our planet, and the network's current focus is on realigning the economics of agriculture with ecological health, with an aim to develop a global market space that rewards regenerative farming practices by combining modern remote sensing technology with blockchain distributed ledgers. That way, food companies can track and verify their entire supply chain, while farmers can get paid for regenerative agricultural practices. A company that is currently exploring Regen's Blockchain tech is Lotus Foods, a certified B-Corp (Benefit Corporation) that sells organic and fair-trade specialty rice, which is grown on a family farm with respect for women, water, soil and community. The blockchain technology of the Regen

CHANGING THE LOGIC OF VALUE CREATION

Ledger works with the following three key elements for monitoring, verifying, and contracting or paying for ecological health outcomes:

1. Data verification, meaning that data provenance and quality can be tracked and authenticated by scientifically robust verification.
2. Smart contracts, meaning that contracts can be issued for ecological outcomes, such as carbon sequestration or water quality between users on the network.
3. Payments, meaning that users can pay for data and ecological health contracts.

With Regen tech, Lotus Food can get trusted and transparent verification of the impact that is related to their investment.

Another organization that works with Regen's blockchain tech, is the Rainforest Foundation. The Regen tool offers the foundation transparent verification that donations by investors go directly and 100% to the indigenous communities that are the guardians and stewards of the ecosystems, cutting out overhead costs that can amount to more than half of the donation. And these two companies are just the tip of the iceberg. There are so many more opportunities to use blockchain for regenerative value-creation.

One sector with huge potential according to Christian Shearer, co-founder and CEO of Regen Network, is the banking and insurance sector, especially when it comes to compliance and risk mitigation. Banks that do not want to be involved in financing deforestation, for instance, can use the blockchain technology to verify that the farmer or company is not involved in destroying forests. What is more, as banks often give mortgages for acquiring land, they can lower the interest rate when they have a way of assessing if the land is getting healthier and better over time, or set a higher interest rate when activities are lowering the health of the land through erosion, for example.

The tools developed by the Regen Network can thus help transition the investment sector from degenerative to regenerative value-creation. They show that it is not impossible to turn the deeply ingrained practice of degeneration around, and that technology, if aligned with NI, can spark a radically different innovation culture. One that leaves life on Earth healthier, wealthier, livelier, and more viable. The question is not whether it is possible, but rather what are we waiting for?

Because there is no return on investment if oxygen and clean water run out.

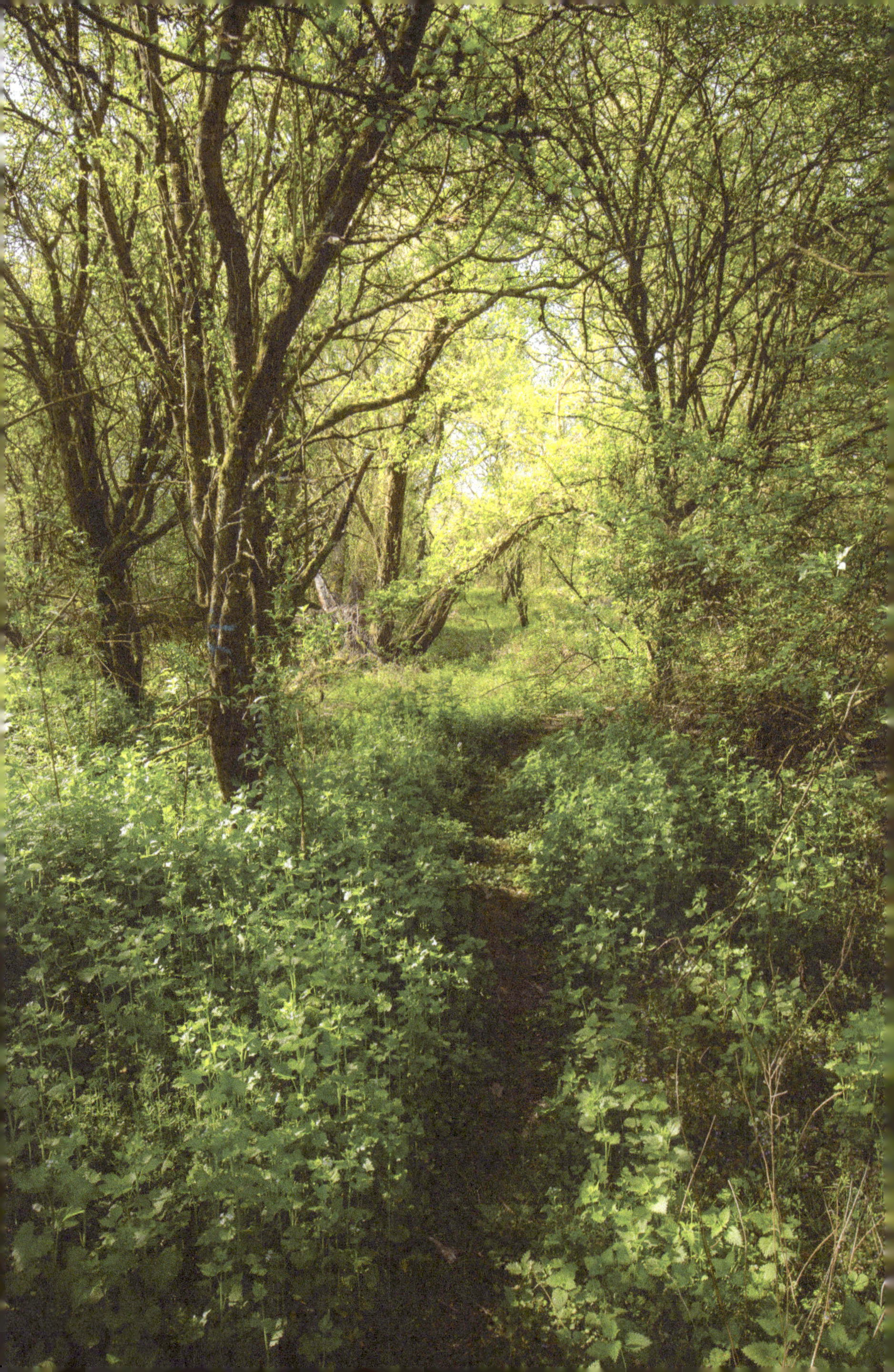

CHAPTER 7

CONCLUSION

We are alive. We are life. We are nature. Yet somewhere down the line we have alienated ourselves from the nature of life, from the environment in which we belong, and from our own nature. And while we have designed many of our institutions as machines, we are not automatons. We are built to evolve. Therefore, the quest before us is one of rediscovering essence, the essence of how life works and how we humans—just like whales, wolves, ants, fungi and other keystone species—can contribute to the continuation and regeneration of life. To move forward, we will need to learn how to become indigenous again, exploring how we can become locally attuned *and* globally aligned, so that we can rediscover our interdependency with our environment and with the web of life, where everything is connected to everything[14]. Only then will we realize that *the nature of the future and the future of nature are interdependent.*

If the past two centuries have taught us one thing, it is that it is better to work with nature instead of against her. Going against the ways in which life works is not only unwise, it is also inherently inefficient.[15] It costs energy, resources, health, and spirit. If we want to stay around in the long run, we will need to elevate current practice and process to the "regenerate" level of innovation. This requires us to reflect deeper and ask new questions. What needs to evolve first, our institutions, our businesses, our business models, or our mental models?

Now that we are beginning to understand the true nature of innovation in nature, we will realize that innovation requires life. And to stay alive, nature has come up with an ingenious strategy to influence the future. *Nature's blueprint for innovation is regeneration.* Leaving the wider system healthier, wealthier, more viable, and more vital than before is both life-affirming and life-enhancing. That is the essence of NI. Examples like Interface, Fungi Perfecti and New Forest Farm show what is possible when business innovation taps into the power of NI. Regeneration ensures continuous improvement of the value generating capacity of the system. It ensures that life can stay alive despite change and disruption.

---

[14] Finding our way home by "Becoming indigenous again" is a teaching shared by many indigenous leaders. Bob Randall, a Yankunytjatjara elder and traditional owner of Uluru (Ayer's Rock) in Australia explains that the land was here long before us. Therefore, we don't own the land. The land owns us.

[15] Remember the Harari quote: "Biology enables, culture forbids".

CONCLUSION

While the transition before us might appear massive and challenging, the first steps to shift from degenerative to regenerative value creation are actually quite simple. I agree with many visionaries who postulate that the future is better guided by values and principles than by data. Because if we build scenarios with data of the past, based on outdated models of reality, we are not predicting the future, we are repeating the past. Moreover, I believe that by adopting simple principles, we can cascade small changes into big change and do so quickly. And the *simple rules that govern how all life works* are a good start. Here are ten that can be drawn from the biological stories that were shared:

1. there is no taking without giving
2. it takes an ecosystem to sustain an ecosystem
3. interdependency rules; nothing occurs in isolation
4. the byproducts generated are as fundamental to evolution as the innovations themselves
5. diversity, decentralization, and redundancy build resilience; monocultures and monopolies build brittleness
6. keystone species create favorable conditions; conditions that enable regeneration from the bottom-up
7. it is the avoidance of competition that drives evolution
8. invest in the health of others to ensure your own
9. leave it better than you found it
10. never take all

Our garden, just like the Yellowstone example, shows how fast and profound restoration, and ultimately regeneration, can happen once *system evolution* is enabled. Imagine what would happen if we were to revive the authenticity and truthfulness of our words and actions by adhering to the principles: "Do what you say, say what you do," and "It is only an investment if it leaves the living world better off." Such small changes can lead to a massive effect, because principles are like fractals. What shows up in the individual, shows up in the collective. And when we can put principles before personalities, status, and power, like many of my mentors have shown, even the unimaginable can be achieved.

Our own history shows that there are two processes that lead to profound transformation: epiphanies or crises. I prefer change by design rather than by disaster. And epiphanies abound once we *renature human nature and rewild our innovation DNA*.

The NI to future-proof life is all around us. Are we ready to listen?

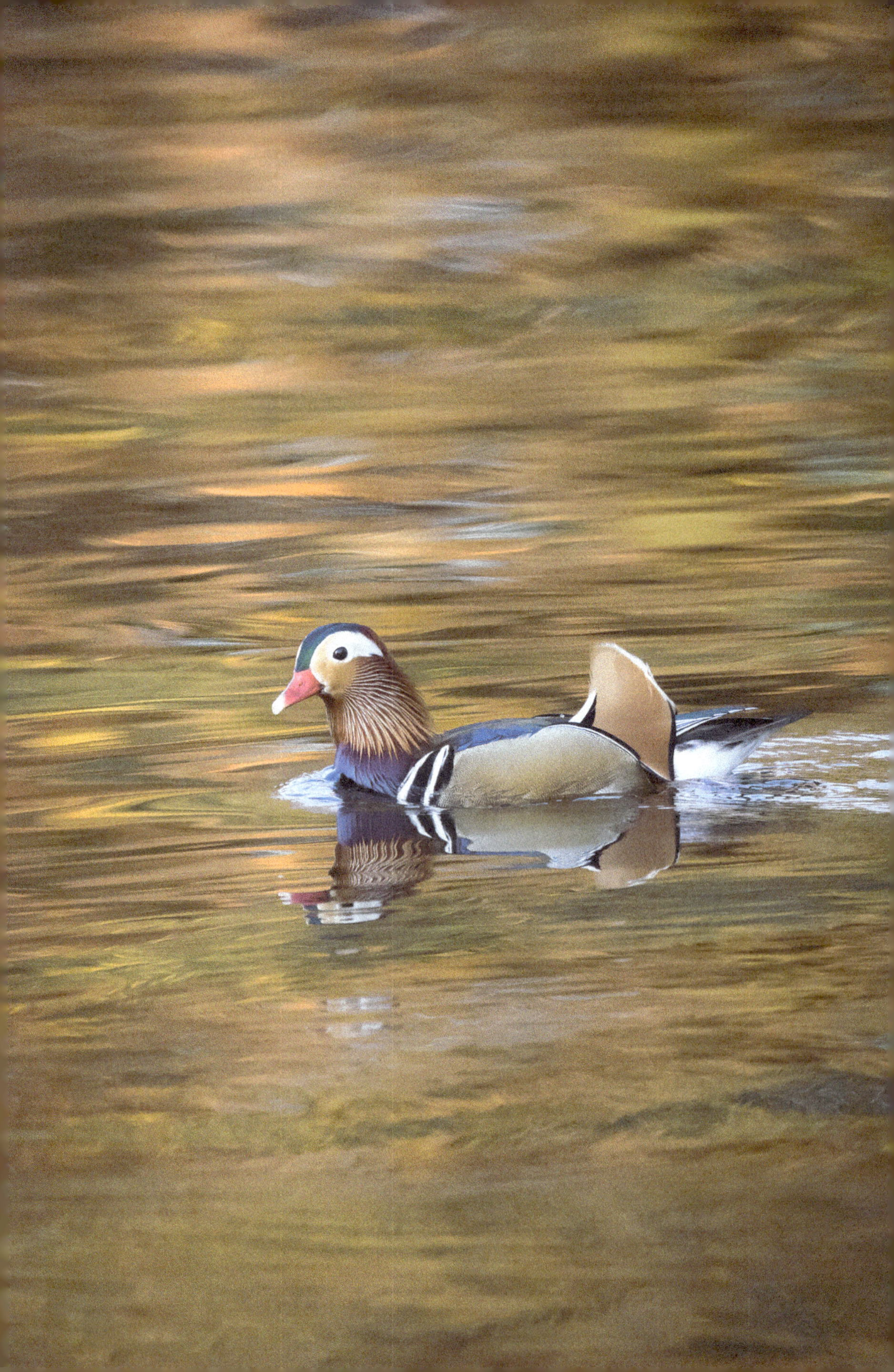

Epilogue

Now that my dogs understand that I know what it means when they sneeze, they are using the sneezing communication signal in other contexts. On hikes, our big dog often walks up to me, pushes my hand gently and looks straight into my eyes. When I ask, "Are you begging for a treat?" he sneezes, training me to give him a treat on command. This action never fails to put a smile on my face, and I am pretty sure he is smiling too (whatever the dog equivalent for smiling is). Even though this is just a personal example (I do not know if other dogs also use sneezing in decision-making processes), it illustrates how important it is to listen to the signals that are being shared. Because we all live in processes of co-evolutionary interdependence with the other organisms that share our world, and we depend on them to share their gifts too.

At the beginning of this book, I referred to two talented systems thinkers that inspired my thinking and it seems fitting to end with some of their insights too. In his book *One from many*, Dee Hock writes, "Those with the greatest power and wealth and the most prominent place in the old order of things have the most to lose. It is, therefore, understandable that so many of them close their minds to different possibilities and cling tenaciously to the old order of things. It is understandable that they engage in cosmetic change to palliate their discomfort and placate critics. It is understandable that they seek one another and merge the institutions they control to amass more and more power and wealth in order to perpetuate that to which they cling. It is understandable that they blind themselves to the fact that they are attempting to preserve the form of things long after form no longer serves function, a certain formula for failure… But what if those with the greatest power, wealth and position were to open their minds to new possibilities, loosen their tenacious grasp on the old order of things, abandon the palliative of cosmetic change, open their eyes to new forms of organization, seriously question and change their internal model of reality? What if they were to cage the four beasts that devour their keeper—ego, envy, greed, and ambition— and take the lead in a new order of things? What if they were to go before and show the way? Now there is a challenge worthy of both the best among them and the best within them. I know that they can. And I will never give up that belief, or hope, that in time, enough of them will."

Hock summarized the challenge to future-proof business so articulately that there was no point in reformulating it. And like Hock, I think there is a bigger role for business to lead this transition. Business has the resources, the brain power, the creativity, and the boldness to radically change innovation for the better. If we put our minds, hearts, and spirits together we can let go of business-as-usual and instead work towards new models that increase the viability, vitality, richness and health of this planet we call home. The question is, can we develop the will, the courage and determination to do things differently?

Tapping into the NI that stood the test of time, can help us navigate towards a future that is rich in more fulfilling ways than it is now. And, while science and technology will surely play an important part in discovering our pathway to the future, so will indigenous wisdom. I reserve the last word for Robin Wall Kimmerer. When she describes the ancient thanksgiving practice that embodies the Onondaga relationship to the world, she writes, "What would it be like to be raised on gratitude [for all of life], to speak to the natural world as a member of the democracy of species, to raise a pledge of interdependence? ... In the Thanksgiving Address, I hear respect toward all our nonhuman relatives, not one political entity, but to all of life. What happens to nationalism, to political boundaries, when allegiance lies with winds and waters that know no boundaries, that cannot be bought or sold?" As the stories shared in this book disclose, it is interdependence and interspecies reciprocity that builds bodies and ecosystems. Kimmerer illustrates this beautifully. "Plants give us food and breath. The breath of plants gives life to animals and the breath of animals gives life to plants". She concludes: "Science can give us knowing, but caring comes from someplace else."

Notes

Preface

1. Sneezing: Walker RH et al. 2017. Sneeze to leave: African wild dogs (Lycaon pictus) use variable quorum thresholds facilitated by sneezes in collective decisions. *Proc. R. Soc. B* 284 20170347; DOI: 10.1098/rspb.2017.0347.
2. De Waal F. 2016. *Are we smart enough to know how smart animals are?* W. W. Norton & Company Inc.
3. Kimmerer RW. 2013. *Braiding sweetgrass. Indigenous wisdom, scientific knowledge and the teachings of plants.* Milkweed editions.
4. Hock D. 2005. *One from many. VISA and the Rise of Chaordic Organization.* Berrett-Koehler Publishers, Inc.
5. On language: Kimmerer RH. 2017. "Speaking of Nature", *Orion Magazine*. https://orionmagazine.org/article/speaking-of-nature/
6. Governments that can't govern: this list was inspired by and adapted from Hock D. 2005. *One from many. VISA and the Rise of Chaordic Organization.* Berrett-Koehler Publishers, Inc.
7. Harari YN. 2015. *Sapiens. A brief history of humankind.* HarperCollins.

Introduction

8. Air pollution, impedes cognitive ability: Zhang X et al. 2018. The impact of exposure to air pollution on cognitive performance. PNAS 115 (37): 9193-9197. http://www.pnas.org/content/early/2018/08/21/1809474115. See also: Carrington D & Kuo L. 2018. See also "Air pollution causes 'huge' reduction in intelligence, study reveals", The Guardian. *https://www.theguardian.com/environment/2018/aug/27/air-pollution-causes-huge-reduction-in-intelligence-study-reveals*
9. Tap water polluted with microscopic plastic particles: Tyree C & Morrison D. 2020. "Invisibles. The plastic inside us. An Investigative Report", orb. https://orbmedia.org/stories/Invisibles_plastics
10. Chemicals in infants: Goodman S. 2009. "Tests Find More Than 200 Chemicals in Newborn Umbilical Cord Blood", Scientific American. https://www.scientificamerican.com/article/newborn-babies-chemicals-exposure-bpa/

11. Glyphosate use: Gillam C. 2017. Whitewash: The Story of a Weed Killer, Cancer, and the Corruption of Science. Island Press.
12. Chemical cocktail: Ghorani-Azam A et al. 2016. Effects of air pollution on human health and practical measures for prevention in Iran. Journal of Research in Medical Sciences : The Official Journal of Isfahan University of Medical Sciences 21, 65. http://doi.org/10.4103/1735-1995.189646
13. Deaths attributed to air pollution: Royal College of Physicians. 2016. "Every breath we take: the lifelong impact of air pollution". RCP Working party report. London.
14. Insectageddon: Monbiot G. 2017. "Insectageddon", The Guardian. https://www.theguardian.com/commentisfree/2017/oct/20/insectageddon-farming-catastrophe-climate-breakdown-insect-populations
15. The circularity gap report 2019: "The world is 9% circular. Our global engine is stuck in reverse", Circle Economy. https://www.legacy.circularity-gap.world/2019.
16. Only 1% of materials is still in use after six months: Leonard A. 2009. "The Story of Stuff." https://storyofstuff.org/wp-content/uploads/movies/scripts/Story%20of%20Stuff.pdf
17. Job motivation: Scott-Jackson W & Mayo A. 2017. Transforming Engagement, Happiness and Well-Being. Enthusing People, Teams and Nations. Springer International Publishing AG.
18. De Langhe R. 2017. "Mailverbod zal de burn-outcrisis niet oplossen. Integendeel", De Morgen 27/12/2017.
19. Woolley Barker T. 2017. Teeming. How superorganisms work to build infinite wealth in a finite world (and your company can too). While Cloud Press.
20. Super pests: Le Page M. 2019. "Superweeds are on the brink of becoming resistant to all weedkillers", NewScientist. https://www.newscientist.com/article/2206610-superweeds-are-on-the-brink-of-becoming-resistant-to-all-weedkillers/. A good example of how pesticides create super pests is illustrated in the interlude 'Spruce Budworms, Firs and Pesticides' in Meadows DH. 2009. Thinking in systems. A primer. Earthscan.
21. Super bugs: Harvard medical school. 2016. "The Evolution of Bacteria on a 'Mega-Plate' Petri Dish (Kishony Lab)", Youtube. https://www.youtube.com/watch?v=plVk4NVIUh8
22. Super cancer cells: Sun Y et al. 2012. Treatment-induced damage to the tumor microenvironment promotes prostate cancer therapy resistance through WNT16B. Nature Medicine 18: 1359–1368. A short description of this research can be read at https://www.natureasia.com/en/research/highlight/1822
23. Will AI spare us: Cellan-Jones R. 2016. "Stephen Hawking - will AI kill or save humankind?" BBC news. https://www.bbc.com/news/technology-37713629.
24. 99.9%: Slobodkin LB & Rapoport A. 1974. An optimal strategy of evolution. The quarterly review of biology, 49(3).
25. Porritt J. 2012. Capitalism as if the world matters. Taylor & Francis.
26. Benyus J. 1997. Biomimicry. Innovation inspired by nature. HarperCollins Publishers Inc.
27. Costanza R. 2009. Evolution is intelligent design. Trends in ecology & evolution, 24(8). https://doi.org/10.1016/j.tree.2009.05.001

NOTES

28. Intuition: Gigerenzer G. 2007. Gut Feelings: The Intelligence of the Unconscious. Viking Books.
29. Established businesses tapping into NI: Benyus J. 2018. "Designing Society through the Natural World", The Aspen Institute. https://www.aspeninstitute.org/blog-posts/designing-society-through-the-natural-world/ and https://biomimicry.net
30. Pioneering business enterprises: Many bio-inspired innovations are described on the asknature database developed by the Biomimimicry Institute. https://asknature.org
31. USGBC: Walker A. 2010. "Biomimicry Challenge: IDEO Taps Octopi and Flamingos to Reorganize the USGBC", Fastcompany. https://www.fastcompany.com/1643489/biomimicry-challenge-ideo-taps-octopi-and-flamingos-reorganize-usgbc
32. European Green Deal 2019: "Communication on The European Green Deal", European Commission. https://ec.europa.eu/commission/presscorner/detail/en/ip_19_6691
33. Three million permaculture practitioners: ECOLISE 2017 report. "A community-led transition in Europe – Local action towards a sustainable, resilient, low carbon future." https://www.ecolise.eu/wp-content/uploads/2017/06/ECOLISE-European-Day-of-Sustainable-Communities-booklet-Sept-2017.pdf
34. Sustainability is the by-product of regenerative value creation: Reformulated from Mang P & Haggard B. 2016. Regenerative design and development. A framework for evolving sustainability. Wiley & Sons Inc.
35. Holliday M. 2016. The age of thrivability. Vital perspectives and practices for a better world. Cambium.

New Insights in Biology Change the Way We Look at Things

36. Haskell DG. 2017. The songs of trees. Stories from nature's great connectors. Penguin, Random House LLC.
37. Hundreds of species in every leaf: Berg G et al. 2014. Unraveling the plant microbiome: looking back and future perspectives. Front. Microbiol. 5:148. doi: 10.3389/fmicb.2014.00148
38. Non-human cells outnumber human cells: Sender R et al. 2016. Revised Estimates for the Number of Human and Bacteria Cells in the Body. PLoS Biol 14(8): e1002533. https://doi.org/10.1371/journal.pbio.1002533
39. Fungi mine rocks: Jongmans A. G et al. 1997. Rock-eating fungi. Nature 389, no. 6652: 682-683. https://www.nature.com/articles/39493.
40. Fungi are probably the largest mining cooperative on Earth: Frazer J. 2015. "The World's Largest Mining Operation Is Run by Fungi", Scientific American. https://blogs.scientificamerican.com/artful-amoeba/the-world-s-largest-mining-operation-is-run-by-fungi/
41. Byproducts are fundamental to evolution: Livnat A. 2017. Simplification, innateness, and the absorption of meaning from context: How novelty arises from gradual network evolution. Evolutionary Biology 44: 145-189.
42. Interaction-based evolution: Livnat A. 2017. Simplification, innateness, and the absorption of meaning from context: How novelty arises from gradual network evolution. Evolutionary Biology 44: 145-189.

43. Carbon trading in trees: Klein T et al. 2016. Belowground carbon trade among tall trees in a temperate forest. Science 15 (352): 342-344. DOI: 10.1126/science.aad6188
44. Chemical signal: Amo L et al. 2013. Birds exploit herbivore-induced plant volatiles to locate herbivorous prey. Ecology Letters, doi: 10.1111/ele.12177.
45. Trees live longer and reproduce more in a healthy stable forest: Grant R. 2018. "Do Trees Talk to Each Other?" Smithsonian Magazine. https://www.smithsonianmag.com/science-nature/the-whispering-trees-180968084/
46. Wayne Weiseman et al. 2014. Integrated Forest Gardening: The Complete Guide to Polycultures and Plant Guilds in Permaculture Systems. Chelsea Green Publishing.
47. Darwin C. 1985. The origin of Species. Penguin Books.
48. Baumeister D. 2019. "The nature of competition." Synapse. https://synapse.bio/blog/the-nature-of-competition?
49. Nowak M. 2011. Supercooperators. Altruism, evolution and why we need each other to succeed. Free Press.
50. Parasites: For an overview of parasite-derived therapies for important autoimmune diseases see Wu Z et al. 2017. Parasite-Derived Proteins for the Treatment of Allergies and Autoimmune Diseases. Frontiers in Microbiology 8:2164. doi: 10.3389/fmicb.2017.02164
51. The harsher the conditions, the more organisms will try to cooperate: Klein R et al. 2009. Competition versus cooperation. Bio-inspired 7. http://biomimicry.typepad.com/files/bioinspired-v7.2c.pdf
52. Fractal which keeps our DNA from getting entangled: Mirny LA. 2011. The fractal globule as a model of chromatin architecture in the cell. Chromosome Research 19(1):37-51. doi:10.1007/s10577-010-9177-0.
53. Air pollution during pregnancy: Talbott et al. 2018. Air Toxics and the Risk of Autism Spectrum Disorder: The Results of a Population Based Case–control Study in Southwestern Pennsylvania. Environmental Health 14 (2015): 80. https://www.ncbi.nlm.nih.gov/pmc/articles/PMC4596286/
54. Spiraling dis-ease and disease in human populations: Prescott SL & Logan AC. 2017. The Secret Life of Your Microbiome: Why Nature and Biodiversity are Essential to Health and Happiness. New society Publishers.
55. Allergy and environmental biodiversity are interrelated: Hanski I et al. 2012. Environmental biodiversity, human microbiota, and allergy are interrelated. Proceedings of the National Academy of Sciences of the United States of America 109(21):8334-8339. doi:10.1073/pnas.1205624109.
56. The body's second brain: Sonnenburg J & Sonnenburg E. 2015. The Good Gut: Taking Control of Your Weight, Your Mood and Your Long-Term Health. Penguin Press.
57. Gut microbiome and brain: Foster JA. 2013. Gut Feelings: Bacteria and the Brain. Cerebrum 9. https://www.ncbi.nlm.nih.gov/pmc/articles/PMC3788166/
58. Microbiota and health: Smythies LE & Smythies JR. 2014. Microbiota, the immune system, black moods and the brain—melancholia updated. Frontiers in Human Neuroscience 8:720. doi:10.3389/fnhum.2014.00720.

NOTES

59. The western way of life decreases diversity in gut microbiota: For an overview of the latest science see Prescott SL & Logan AC. 2017. The secret life of your microbiome. Why nature and biodiversity are essential to health and happiness. New Society Publishers.
60. McDonough W & Braungart M. 2002. Cradle to Cradle. Remaking the way we make things. North Point Press.
61. Illusion that individually, we are too small to matter: Gorissen L & Meynaerts M. 2018. Change the world City by City. A change maker's guide to fast forward sustainability. LannooCampus.
62. One billion dogs: Atitwa SC. 2018. "How Many Dogs Are There In The World?" WorldAtlas. worldatlas.com/articles/how-many-dogs-are-there-in-the-world.html.
63. Wild wolves: Mech LD & Boitani L. 2003. Wolves: Behaviour, Ecology and Conservation. University of Chicago Press.
64. Wolves domesticated themselves: Hare B & Woods V. 2013. The genius of dogs. Discovering the unique intelligence of Man's Best Friend. Oneworld Publications.
65. Survival of the friendliest: Hare B. 2017. Survival of the Friendliest: Homo sapiens Evolved via Selection for Prosociality. Annual Review of Psychology 68:1, 155-186.
66. Antidepressant use: National Center for Health Statistics, United States, 2010. "Health, United States, 2010: With Special Feature on Death and Dying." Table 95. Hyattsville, MD.
67. Leaving well-paid jobs: Jones L. 2018. "Going solo: The rise of self-employment." BBC news. https://www.bbc.com/news/business-44887623
68. Enron: Turchin P. 2013. "Selfish Genes Made Me Do It!" The evolution institute, https://evolution-institute.org/blog/selfish-genes-made-me-do-it-part-i/
69. California calls out a power emergency: Egan T. 2005. "Tapes Show Enron Arranged Plant Shutdown". The New York Times. https://www.nytimes.com/2005/02/04/us/tapes-show-enron-arranged-plant-shutdown.html
70. Fraudulent black-outs: Borger J. 2005. "Tapes reveal Enron's secret role in California's power blackouts". The Guardian. https://www.theguardian.com/business/2005/feb/05/enron.usnews
71. Psychological definition of selfish motivation: Crocker J et al. 2017. Social Motivation: Costs and Benefits of Selfishness and Otherishness. Annual Review of Psychology 68:299-325.
72. Interview with Dawkins R. 2012. "Evolutie is eindeloze vooruitgang", De Morgen. https://www.demorgen.be/nieuws/evolutie-is-eindeloze-vooruitgang~bf46578e/
73. Thinking selfishness is ingrained in our DNA: Verhaeghe P. 2014. What about me? The struggle for identity in a market-based society. Scribe Publications.
74. Octopi build underwater cities: Scheel D et al. 2017. A second site occupied by Octopus tetricus at high densities, with notes on their ecology and behavior. Marine and Freshwater Behaviour and Physiology, 50(4): 285-291. DOI: 10.1080/10236244.2017.1369851
75. Sea Star Aquarium: "Otto the octopus wreaks havoc", 2008, the Telegraph. https://www.telegraph.co.uk/news/newstopics/howaboutthat/3328480/Otto-the-octopus-wrecks-havoc.html

76. Octopus intelligence: Simon M. 2015. "Absurd Creature of the Week: The Octopus That Does Incredible Impressions of Fish and Snakes", Wired. https://www.wired.com/2015/12/absurd-creature-of-the-week-the-octopus-that-does-incredible-impressions-of-fish-and-snakes/
77. Edit and redirect their own brain genes: Liscovitch-Brauer N et al. 2017. Trade-off between Transcriptome Plasticity and Genome Evolution in Cephalopods. Cell 169 (2): 191 - 202.e11. doi: 10.1016/j.cell.2017.03.025
78. Boquila shapeshifting: Mancuso S. 2017. The revolutionary genius of plants. A new understanding of plant intelligence and behavior. Atria Books.

Welcome to the Age of Bio-Logics

79. 50 million tons of spores: Elbert W et al. 2007. Contribution of fungi to primary biogenic aerosols in the atmosphere: wet and dry discharged spores, carbohydrates, and inorganic ions. Atmospheric Chemistry and Physics 7: 4569-4588. https://doi.org/10.5194/acp-7-4569-2007.
80. Moisture-loving mushrooms make rain: Hassett MO et al. 2015. Mushrooms as Rainmakers: How Spores Act as Nuclei for Raindrops. PLoS ONE 10(10): e0140407. doi:10.1371/journal.pone.0140407
81. Fungi may have colonized Mars: Rhawn GJ et al. 2019. Evidence of Life on Mars? Journal of Astrobiology and Space Science Reviews 1: 40-81.
82. Arctic foxes are ecosystem engineers: Gharajehdaghipour T et al. 2016. Arctic foxes as ecosystem engineers: increased soil nutrients lead to increased plant productivity on fox dens. Nature Scientific Reports 6, 24020. DOI: 10.1038/srep24020
83. Little green oases: Popescu A. 2016. "Arctic Foxes 'Grow' Their Own Gardens", National Geographic. https://news.nationalgeographic.com/2016/05/160520-arctic-foxes-animals-science-alaska/
84. Monbiot G. 2014. "Why whale poo matters", The Guardian. https://www.theguardian.com/environment/georgemonbiot/2014/dec/12/how-whale-poo-is-connected-to-climate-and-our-lives
85. Decline in fish stocks: See for example: Morissette L et al. 2010. Whales eat fish? Demystifying the myth in the Caribbean marine ecosystem. Fish Fish 11: 388–404; Morissette L et al. 2012. Marine mammal impacts in exploited ecosystems: would large scale culling benefit fisheries? PLoS ONE 7: e43966; Lavery T et al. 2014. Whales sustain fisheries: Blue whales stimulate primary production in the Southern Ocean. Marine Mammal Science 30. 10.1111/mms.12108.
86. Plankton: Roman et al. 2014. Whales as marine ecosystem engineers. Front Ecol Environ 12(7): 377-385. doi:10.1890/130220
87. Dimethyl sulfide: Savocaa MS & Nevitt GA. 2014. Evidence that dimethyl sulfide facilitates a tritrophic mutualism between marine primary producers and top predators. PNAS 111 (11) 4157-4161. www.pnas.org/cgi/doi/10.1073/pnas.1317120111
88. Killer whales: Estes, J. A. et al. 1998. Killer Whale Predation on Sea Otters Linking Oceanic and Nearshore Ecosystems. Science 282, (5388):473–476. JSTOR, www.jstor.org/stable/2897843.

NOTES

89. Sea otters: Wilmers CC et al. 2012. Do trophic cascades affect the storage and flux of atmospheric carbon? An analysis of sea otters and kelp forests. Frontiers in Ecology and the Environment 10: 409-415. doi:10.1890/110176.
90. Kelp forests: A really good short movie clip about sea otters as guardians of the kelp forests can be accessed on the website of the BBC: "Sea otters: Saving kelp forests and our climate", BBC. http://www.bbc.com/future/story/20140121-sea-otters-our-ocean-protectors
91. Sea urchin overgrazing: Terborg J & Estes J. 2010. Trophic Cascades. Predators, Prey, and the Changing Dynamics of Nature. Island Press.
92. Ecosystem engineers: Roman et al. 2014. Whales as marine ecosystem engineers. Front Ecol Environ 12(7): 377-385. doi:10.1890/130220
93. International Monetary Fund study: Chami R et al. 2019. "Nature's Solution to Climate Change." Finance & Development 56, no. 4. https://www.imf.org/external/pubs/ft/fandd/2019/12/natures-solution-to-climate-change-chami.htm
94. Between $205-408 million per year: Wilmers CC et al. 2012. Do trophic cascades affect the storage and flux of atmospheric carbon? An analysis of sea otters and kelp forests. Frontiers in Ecology and the Environment 10: 409-415. https://doi.org/10.1890/110176.
95. Wolf effect on elk: Creel et al. 2005. Elk alter habitat selection as an antipredator response to wolves. Ecology 86: 3387–3397. https://doi.org/10.1890/05-0032
96. Wolves changing rivers: Beschta RL & Ripple WJ. 2006. River channel dynamics following extirpation of wolves in northwestern Yellowstone National Park, USA. Earth Surface Processes and Landforms 31: 1525–1539.
97. Wolves changing rivers: Beschta RL & Ripple WJ. 2018. Can large carnivores change streams via a trophic cascade? Ecohydrology 12, e2048. https://doi.org/10.1002/eco.2048
98. Wolves changing rivers: Wolf et al. 2007. Hydrologic regime and herbivory stabilize an alternative state in Yellowstone national park. Ecological Applications 17: 1572–1587. doi:10.1890/06-2042.
99. Beaver as ecosystem engineer: Wright JP et al. 2002. An Ecosystem Engineer, the Beaver, Increases Species Richness at the Landscape Scale. Oecologia 132: pp. 96-101.
100. Ensure the success of their offspring: Woolley Barker T. 2017. Teeming. How superorganisms work to build infinite wealth in a finite world (and your company can too). While Cloud Press.
101. Biomimicry design lens: Dayna Baumeister. 2013. Biomimicry resource handbook. A seed bank of best practices. Biomimicry3.8.
102. Avert extinction cascades: Sanders D et al. 2018. Trophic redundancy reduces vulnerability to extinction cascades. PNAS 115 (10) 2419-2424; DOI:10.1073/pnas.1716825115
103. Prairie ecosystem: Helzer C. 2010. The ecology and management of prairies in the central united states. A Bur Oak Book, University of Iowa Press.
104. Prairie as a carbon sink: Dass P et al. 2018. Grasslands may be more reliable carbon sinks than forests in California. Environmental Research Letters 13, 074027.
105. Prairie as a carbon sink: Helzer C. 2010. The ecology and management of prairies in the central united states. A Bur Oak Book, University of Iowa Press.

106. Business monopolies and monocultures of thought and technology are just as brittle in the face of disruption as monocultures of weed in a farm field: Adjusted from Mang P & Haggard B. 2016. Regenerative development and design. A framework for evolving sustainability. Wiley & Sons Inc.
107. Species rich forests store twice as much carbon than single species plantations: Huang Y. 2018. Impacts of species richness on productivity in a large-scale subtropical forest experiment. Science 362 (6410): 80-83. DOI: 10.1126/science.aat6405
108. When it comes to the long-term health of the planet: Ulanowicz R. et al. 2009. Quantifying sustainability: Resilience, efficiency and the return of information theory. Ecological Complexity 6: 27-36. 10.1016/j.ecocom.2008.10.005.
109. Wilson EO. 2016. Half-Earth. Our planet's fight for life. Liveright Publishing Corporation.
110. The European Environment, state and outlook 2020 report: "Europe's state of the environment 2020: change of direction urgently needed to face climate change challenges, reverse degradation and ensure future prosperity", EEA. https://www.eea.europa.eu/highlights/soer2020-europes-environment-state-and-outlook-report
111. The root cause of our global crises: Hutchins G. 2014. The illusion of separation. Floris Books.
112. We are an ecology, and we are part of an ecology: Bateson N. 2016. Small arcs of larger circles. Framing through other patterns. Triarchy Press.
113. Nowak M. 2011. Supercooperators. Altruism, evolution and why we need each other to succeed. Free Press.
114. Earth-tech as breakthrough approaches in the fight against climate change: Chami R et al. 2019. Nature's Solution to Climate Change. Finance & Development 56, no. 4. https://www.imf.org/external/pubs/ft/fandd/2019/12/natures-solution-to-climate-change-chami.htm

Biology Is the Technology of the Future

115. Life's principles: Baumeister D. 2014. Biomimicry resource handbook. A seed bank of best practices. Biomimicry3.8. https://biomimicry.net/the-buzz/resources/designlens-lifes-principles/
116. Daily practice in the innovation labs of multinationals: Benyus J. 2018. "Designing Society through the Natural World", The Aspen Institute. https://www.aspeninstitute.org/blog-posts/designing-society-through-the-natural-world/ and https://biomimicry.net
117. Fortune: Harnish V. 2017. "5 Trends to Ride in 2017", Fortune. http://fortune.com/2017/03/17/trends-business-career-benefits/
118. We are here to make goods, not bads: Khalamayzer A. "Bill McDonough: We are here to make goods, not bads", GreenBiz. https://www.greenbiz.com/article/bill-mcdonough-we-are-here-make-goods-not-bads
119. Meaningfulness in jobs: Psychiatrist Edel Maex, head of the Stress Clinic in Antwerp states that people do not burn out from too much work but from pointless work, when they feel their work has no meaning. Interview by Debusschere B. 2019.

NOTES

"Als je jonge kinderen hebt en een baan, heb je eigenlijk twee fulltime jobs. En dat vinden we maar normaal", De Morgen. https://www.demorgen.be/nieuws/als-je-jonge-kinderen-hebt-en-een-baan-heb-je-eigenlijk-twee-fulltime-jobs-en-dat-vinden-we-maar-normaal~b4d66284/

120. Safe operating space of our planet: Steffen W et al. 2015. Planetary boundaries: Guiding human development on a changing planet. Science 347, 1259855. DOI: 10.1126/science.1259855
121. To become degreed chemists: Harman J. 2013. The Shark's Paintbrush. Biomimicry and how nature is inspiring innovation. Nicholas Brealey Publishing.
122. North American Jack pines: Wickens GE. 2001. Economic Botany. Principles and Practice. Kluwer Academic Publishers.
123. Hippo create their own sunscreen: Saikawa Y et al. 2004. The red sweat of the hippopotamus. Nature 429: 363.
124. Arctic wood frogs: Larson DJ. 2014. Wood frog adaptations to overwintering in Alaska: new limits to freezing tolerance. The Journal of Experimental Biology 217: 2193-2200 doi:10.1242/jeb.101931
125. Spider silk is stronger than Kevlar: Pawlyn M. 2016. Biomimicry in architecture. Second edition. RIBA publishing
126. Dorfman M. 2017. "Finally! Life friendly chemistry explained", Synapse. https://synapse.bio/blog//demystifying-life-friendly-chemistry
127. Nature uses only 28: "Nature's Unifying Patterns", Biomimicry toolbox. Biomimicry Institute. https://toolbox.biomimicry.org/core-concepts/natures-unifying-patterns/chemistry/
128. Billions of unique creatures that roam our planet: Larsen BB et al. 2017. Inordinate Fondness Multiplied and Redistributed: the Number of Species on Earth and the New Pie of Life. The Quarterly Review of Biology 92:3, 229-265. DOI: 10.1086/693564
129. They do not last, and they do not carry unintentional toxicities along with their primary function: Dorfman M. 2017. "Greening the red list: nature-inspired chemistry innovations for the building sector", Synapse. https://synapse.bio/blog/greening-the-red-list
130. Made from only proteins and polysaccharides: Vincent J. 2007. Is traditional engineering the right system with which to manipulate our world? Science in School 4: p 56-60.
131. Morpho butterfly color from structure: Butt H et al. 2016. Morpho Butterflies: Morpho Butterfly-Inspired Nanostructures. Advanced Optical Materials 4: 489-489. 10.1002/adom.201670018.
132. Less material, more design: Pawlyn M. 2016. Biomimicry in architecture. Second edition. RIBA publishing.
133. Termites outweigh humans ten to one: Margonelli L. 2018. Underbug. An obsessive tale of termites and technology. Oneworld Publications.
134. Anywhere between 100 and 10,000 trillion ants: Hölldobler B & Wilson EO. 1995. Journey to the Ants. A Story of Scientific Exploration. Harvard University Press.

135. Distributed leadership, collective intelligence, and collective decision-making: Woolley Barker T. 2017. Teeming. How superorganisms work to build infinite wealth in a finite world (and your company can too). While Cloud Press.
136. Livnat A. 2017. Simplification, innateness, and the absorption of meaning from context: How novelty arises from gradual network evolution. Evolutionary Biology 44: 145-189.
137. Octopi: Liscovitch-Brauer N et al. 2017. Trade-off between Transcriptome Plasticity and Genome Evolution in Cephalopods. Cell 169 (2): 191 - 202.e11.
138. Whitney Johnson. 2016. Disrupt Yourself: Putting the Power of Disruptive Innovation to Work. Taylor & Francis Group.
139. Mindfulness and meditation benefits: Walton AG. "7 Ways Meditation Can Actually Change The Brain", Forbes. https://www.forbes.com/sites/alicegwalton/2015/02/09/7-ways-meditation-can-actually-change-the-brain/#1acfd4c91465
140. Prone to view things pessimistically: ter Weijde R. 2015. Building positive organisations. A pragmatic guide to help people and organisations flourish. Warden Press.
141. Giving greater weight to criticism: Sikkink K. 2017. Evidence for hope. Making Human Rights Work in the 21st Century. Princeton University Press.
142. ter Weijde R. 2015. Building positive organisations. A pragmatic guide to help people and organisations flourish. Warden Press.
143. Regenesis: The Regenerative Practitioner Series. https://regenesisgroup.com/
144. Harness the power of collective intelligence and agility: Woolley Barker T. 2017. Teeming. How superorganisms work to build infinite wealth in a finite world (and your company can too). While Cloud Press.
145. Yale School of Forestry & Environmental Studies: Robbins J. 2020. "Ecopsychology: How Immersion in Nature Benefits Your Health", YaleEnvironment360. https://e360.yale.edu/features/ecopsychology-how-immersion-in-nature-benefits-your-health
146. Reduces blood pressure and heart rate: Mao GX et al. 2012. Effects of short-term forest bathing on human health in a broad-leaved evergreen forest in Zhejiang Province, China. Biomed Environ Sci 25(3):317-24. doi: 10.3967/0895-3988.2012.03.010.
147. Selhub EM & Logan AC. 2012. Your brain on nature. John Wiley & Sons.
148. Job satisfaction: Shin WS. 2007. The influence of forest view through a window on job satisfaction and job stress. Scandinavian Journal of Forest Research 22:3, 248-253, DOI: 10.1080/02827580701262733
149. Absenteeism: Elzeyadi I. 2011. Daylighting-Bias and Biophilia: Quantifying the Impacts of Daylight on Occupants Health. In: Thought and Leadership in Green Buildings Research. Greenbuild 2011 Proceedings. Washington, DC: USGBC Press.
150. Ability to focus and concentrate: Berman et al. 2008. The Cognitive Benefits of Interacting With Nature. Psychol Sci 19(12):1207-12. doi: 10.1111/j.1467-9280.2008.02225.x.
151. Creativity and problem-solving capacity: Atchley RA et al. 2012. Creativity in the Wild: Improving Creative Reasoning through Immersion in Natural Settings. PLoS ONE 7(12): e51474. doi:10.1371/journal.pone.0051474

152. In the presence of plants: Mancuso S. 2017. The revolutionary genius of plants. A new understanding of plant intelligence and behavior. Atria Books.
153. Immune system: Li Q. 2010. Effect of forest bathing trips on human immune function. Environ Health Prev Med 15(1): 9–17.
154. Number of killer T-cells: Li Q et al. 2008. A forest bathing trip increases human natural killer activity and expression of anti-cancer proteins in female subjects. J Biol Regul Homeost Agents 22(1):45-55.
155. Looking at nature footage: "Watching nature programmes makes you happier new research reveals", BBC. https://www.bbc.co.uk/mediacentre/worldwide/2017/rhp
156. Higher levels of nervousness and feelings of depression: Preuß M et al. 2019. Low Childhood Nature Exposure is Associated with Worse Mental Health in Adulthood. International Journal of Environmental and Public Health 16(10): 1809. https://doi.org/10.3390/ijerph16101809
157. Sick building syndrome: Norbäck D. 2009. An update on sick building syndrome. Current Opinion in Allergy and Clinical Immunology 9(1):55-59. 0.1097/ACI.0b013e32831f8f08
158. Disconnection from nature: Arvay CG. 2018. The Biophilia Effect: A Scientific and Spiritual Exploration of the Healing Bond Between Humans and Nature. Sounds True.
159. Space and plants: Mancuso S. 2017. The revolutionary genius of plants. A new understanding of plant intelligence and behavior. Atria Books.

Improving Business and the World Through NI

160. Shark's skin structure: Oeffner J & Lauder GV. 2012. The hydrodynamic function of shark skin and two biomimetic applications. Journal of Experimental Biology 215: 785-795; doi: 10.1242/jeb.063040. See also Smirnoff D. 2017. "Scales manipulate flow", Asknature. https://asknature.org/strategy/scales-manipulate-flow/#.WsM1QGaB2b8
161. Distinct diamond pattern with tiny riblets: Asknature team. 2016. "Sharklet surface texture", Asknature. https://asknature.org/idea/sharklet-surface-texture/#.WsNA5WaB2b8
162. Sharklet Technologies Inc: Company website. https://www.sharklet.com
163. Mosquito syringe system: Asknature Team. 2016. "Mosquito inspired microneedle", Asknature. https://asknature.org/idea/mosquito-inspired-microneedle/#.W3facC-B3-Y
164. Fascicle: Kong X. Q. and Wu C. W. 2010. Mosquito proboscis: An elegant biomicroelectromechanical system. Physical Review E 82, https://doi.org/10.1103/PhysRevE.82.011910
165. Japanese engineers: Izumi H et al. 2011. Realistic imitation of mosquito's proboscis: Electrochemically etched sharp and jagged needles and their cooperative inserting motion. Sensors and Actuators A 165: 115–123. 10.1016/j.sna.2010.02.010
166. Slug Snot Could Be a Valuable Medical Tool: Thompson A. 2017. "Slug Snot Could Be a Valuable Medical Tool", Popular Mechanics. https://www.popularmechanics.com/science/health/news/a27513/glue-out-of-slug-snot/

167. Next-generation tissue adhesives: Li J et al. 2017. Tough adhesives for diverse wet surfaces. Science 357 (6349): 378-381. DOI: 10.1126/science.aah6362
168. Tissium. Company website. https://tissium.com
169. Asknature team. 2016. "BioMimics 3D stent technology", Asknature. https://asknature.org/idea/biomimics-3d-stent-technology/
170. Veryan Medical. Company website. https://www.veryanmed.com/uk/
171. Enhanced medicinal benefits: Stamets P & Zwickey H. 2014. Medicinal Mushrooms: Ancient Remedies Meet Modern Science. Integrative Medicine, a clinician's journal (Encinitas) 13(1): 46–47. https://www.ncbi.nlm.nih.gov/pmc/articles/PMC4684114/
172. Mycelium: Stamets P. 2005. Mycelium running. How mushrooms can help save the world. Ten Speed Press.
173. 130 medicinal functions: Wasser SP. 2014. Medicinal Mushroom Science: Current Perspectives, Advances, Evidences, and Challenges. Biomedical Journal 37:345-356.
174. Economics and IP rights: Paterson RR & Lima N. 2014. Biomedical effects of mushrooms with emphasis on pure compounds. Biomedical Journal 37(6): 357-68. http://biomedj.cgu.edu.tw/pdfs/2014/37/6/images/BiomedJ_2014_37_6_357_143502.pdf
175. Stamets P. 2005. Mycelium running. How mushrooms can help save the world. Ten Speed Press.
176. Fungi Perfecti. Company website. https://fungi.com
177. Mycelia Reduce Viruses in Honey Bees: Stamets et al. 2018. Extracts of Polypore Mushroom Mycelia Reduce Viruses in HoneyBees. Nature Scientific Reports 8:13936. DOI:10.1038/s41598-018-32194-8
178. Microalgae: Tamara S. et al. 2019. A Colorful Pallet of B-Phycoerythrin Proteoforms Exposed by a Multimodal Mass Spectrometry Approach. Chem 5 (5): 1302. DOI: 10.1016/j.chempr.2019.03.006
179. Microalgae: Nield D. 2019. "Scientists Get Closer Look at Weird Algae That Are More Efficient Than Solar Panels", Nature. https://www.sciencealert.com/tiny-fluorescent-microalgae-could-inspire-the-next-generation-of-solar-panels
180. Pax Scientific. Company website. http://paxscientific.com.
181. Doubled its sales every year since: Harman J. 2013. The Shark's Paintbrush. Biomimicry and how nature is inspiring innovation. Nicholas Brealey Publishing.
182. Turbulent. Company website. https://www.turbulent.be/pricing
183. A production line in Belgium: Vanhoutte I. 2017. "Turbulent, in de vortex van de wereldwijde energierevolutie", Mo. https://www.mo.be/zeronaut/turbulent
184. Firefly: Bay A et al. 2012. Search for an optimal light-extracting surface derived from the morphology of a firefly lantern. Optical Engineering 52. 028001. 10.1117/1.OE.52.2.028001.
185. Firefly: Bay A et al. 2013. Optimal overlayer inspired by Photuris firefly improves light-extraction efficiency of existing light-emitting diodes. Optics Express 21, A179-A189
186. Commercialize the firefly technology: Jones A. 2019. "Firefly-inspired surfaces improve efficiency of LED lightbulbs", Penn State News. https://news.psu.edu/story/559722/2019/02/18/research/firefly-inspired-surfaces-improve-efficiency-led-lightbulbs

NOTES

187. Tardigrades: Boothby TC et al. 2017. Tardigrades Use Intrinsically Disordered Proteins to Survive Desiccation. Molecular Cell 65: 975-984. https://doi.org/10.1016/j.molcel.2017.02.018
188. Tardigrades: Asknature team. 2017. "Biomatrica SampleMatrix", Asknature. https://asknature.org/idea/biomatrica-samplematrix/#.W3gHxC-B3-Y
189. Thereby eliminating the need for refrigeration: Asknature team. 2017. "VitRIS and HydRIS vaccine stabilization technologies", Asknature. https://asknature.org/idea/vitris-and-hydris-vaccine-stabilization-technologies/
190. Reduce refrigeration costs: Asknature team. 2017. "Biomatrica SampleMatrix", Asknature. https://asknature.org/idea/biomatrica-samplematrix/#.W3gHxC-B3-Y
191. The most significant global solution for cutting greenhouse gas emissions: In terms of estimated atmospheric CO2-equivalent reductions. See: Hawken P. 2017. Drawdown. The most comprehensive plan ever proposed to reverse global warming. Penguin Books.
192. Only 60 harvests left on Earth: Arsenault C. 2014. "Only 60 Years of Farming Left If Soil Degradation Continues", Scientific American. https://www.scientificamerican.com/article/only-60-years-of-farming-left-if-soil-degradation-continues/
193. IPBES report: "Nature's Dangerous Decline 'Unprecedented', Species Extinction Rates 'Accelerating'", IPBES Media release. https://www.ipbes.net/news/Media-Release-Global-Assessment
194. Citizen science project in Belgium: Heylen K & Huyghebaert P. 2019. "In bijna alle mezennesten zitten pesticiden, ook het verboden DDT: Frappant en zorgwekkend", VRT. https://www.vrt.be/vrtnws/nl/2019/09/12/zorgwekkend-hoog-aantal-pesticiden-veroorzaakt-grote-mezensterft.app/?fbclid=IwAR0Vb5kFqDuIiu4SBGTv5xJEYfUdgu_JsKbWgiSAibHcfqdb_0lz-JsbHbk
195. Polyculture agroforestry: Maezumi SY et al. 2018. The legacy of 4,500 years of polyculture agroforestry in the eastern Amazon. Nature Plants 4: 540–547.
196. Amazonian soil: Quintero-Vallejo E et al. 2015. Amazonian Dark Earth shapes the understory plant community in a Bolivian Amazonian Forest. Biotropica 47, 152 - 161.
197. Agroforestry can increase yield and improve food security at the same time: Waldron A et al. 2017. Agroforestry can enhance food security while meeting other sustainable development goals. Tropical Conservation Science 10:1–6.
198. Millions of permaculture practitioners: ECOLISE 2017 report. "A community-led transition in Europe – Local action towards a sustainable, resilient, low carbon future." https://www.ecolise.eu/wp-content/uploads/2017/06/ECOLISE-European-Day-of-Sustainable-Communities-booklet-Sept-2017.pdf.
199. New Forest Farm: Shepard M. 2013. Restoration Agriculture: Real World Permaculture for Farmers. Acres U.S.A., Inc.
200. Polyface Farm. Company website. http://www.polyfacefarms.com/our-story/
201. Increases the nutritional qualities of the meat: Salatin J. 1995. Salad Bar Beef. Polyface Inc.
202. Polyface Farm services: http://www.polyfacefarms.com/salad-bar-beef/
203. Food forest Ketelbroek: Tegenlicht reportage 2019. "Plattelandspioniers", VPRO. https://www.vpro.nl/programmas/tegenlicht/kijk/afleveringen/2019-2020/plattelandspioniers.html

204. Personal communication with several food forest experts at the 2020 Permaculture Winter Conference on Food Forests at Heerdeberg in Cadier en Keer, the Netherlands.
205. Silvopasture: In Hawken P. 2017. Drawdown. The most comprehensive plan ever proposed to reverse global warming. Penguin Books.
206. Silvopasture: Toensmeier, Eric. The Carbon Farming Solution. White River Junction, VT: Chelsea Green Publishing, 2016.
207. Climate win-win: Hawken P. 2017. Drawdown. The most comprehensive plan ever proposed to reverse global warming. Penguin Books.
208. Dehesas: Gaspar P et al. 2009. Sustainability in Spanish Extensive Farms (Dehesas): An Economic and Management Indicator-Based Evaluation. Rangeland Ecology and Management 62(2), 153-162. https://doi.org/10.2111/07-135.1
209. Dehesas: "Finca Casablanca Dehesa farm developing a sustainable model", High Nature Value Farming Link Network. A H2020 project funded by the European Union. http://www.hnvlink.eu/download/Spain_FincaCasablancaDehesafarmdevelopingasustainablemodel.pdf
210. Realize financial gains of $699 billion globally: In Hawken P. 2017. Drawdown. The most comprehensive plan ever proposed to reverse global warming. Penguin Books. See also https://www.drawdown.org/solutions/food/silvopasture
211. Land Institute. Organization website. https://landinstitute.org/our-work/ecological-intensification/
212. Kernza wheat: Biomimicry Solutions Carbon 2019 Report. "Nature inspired solutions to combat climate change", Biomimicry3.8.
213. Kernza wheat: https://landinstitute.org/our-work/perennial-crops/kernza/
214. Carbon Action project: Baltic Sea Action Group. 2019. "Carbon Action". https://carbonaction.org/front-page/
215. Cement production: Asknature team. 2019. "Calera MAP cement-making process", Asknature. https://asknature.org/idea/calera-map-cement-making-process/#.W2gh9S-B3-Y
216. Release a ton of carbon dioxide into the atmosphere: Harman J. 2013. The shark's paintbrush. Biomimicry and how nature is inspiring innovation. Nicholas Brealey Publishing.
217. We produce about 15 billion tons of cement every year: Pawlyn M. 2016. Biomimicry in architecture. Second edition. RIBA publishing
218. Third largest emitter of carbon dioxide emissions: Chatham house report 2018. "Making Concrete Change: Innovation in Low-carbon Cement and Concrete". https://reader.chathamhouse.org/making-concrete-change-innovation-low-carbon-cement-and-concrete#
219. Blue planet. Company website. http://www.blueplanet-ltd.com
220. Similar mineralization processes as marine ecosystems: Biomimicry Solutions Carbon 2019 Report. "Nature inspired solutions to combat climate change", Biomimicry3.8.
221. San Francisco International Airport: http://www.blueplanet-ltd.com/#services
222. Calera: Asknature team. 2019; "Calera MAP cement-making process", Asknature. https://asknature.org/idea/calera-map-cement-making-process/

NOTES

223. Calera. Company website. http://www.calera.com
224. Biorock: https://en.wikipedia.org/wiki/Biorock
225. Hundreds of Biorock projects: Goreau TJ. 2012. Marine Electrolysis for Building Materials and Environmental Restoration. IntechOpen. DOI: 10.5772/48783. https://www.intechopen.com/books/electrolysis/marine-electrolysis-for-building-materials-and-environmental-restoration
226. Biorock Pavilion: Pawlyn M. 2016. Biomimicry in architecture. Second edition. RIBA publishing.
227. Biorock Pavilion: https://vimeo.com/86747640
228. Termites, labeled the greatest insect builders by Guinness World Records: http://www.guinnessworldrecords.com/world-records/greatest-insect-builder
229. Termite mounds: McCarthy TS et al. 1998. The role of biota in the initiation and growth of islands on the floodplain of the Okavango alluvial fan, Botswana. Earth surface processes and landforms 23 (4): 291-316.
230. Termite mounds: Pringle RM et al. 2010. Spatial Pattern Enhances Ecosystem Functioning in an African Savanna. PLoS Biology 8(5): e1000377. doi:10.1371/journal.pbio.1000377
231. Drylands with termite mounds: Bonachela JA et al. 2015. Termite mounds can increase the robustness of dryland ecosystems to climatic change. Science 347: 651-655. DOI: 10.1126/science.1261487
232. Australian compass termites: Pawlyn M. 2016. Biomimicry in architecture. Second edition. RIBA publishing
233. Termite mound climate: Pawlyn M. 2016. Biomimicry in architecture. Second edition. RIBA publishing
234. Termite cooling system: "What Termites can teach us about cooling our buildings", The New York Times. https://www.nytimes.com/2019/03/26/science/termite-nest-ventilation.html
235. Eastgate office and shopping Centre: Asknature team. 2016. "Eastgate Centre", Asknature. https://asknature.org/idea/eastgate-centre/#.W2lQ6y-B2CQ
236. Powered by the sun: Singh K et al. 2019. The architectural design of smart ventilation and drainage systems in termite nests. Science Advances 22 (5), eaat8520. DOI: 10.1126/sciadv.aat8520
237. The mound functions like an external lung: Ocko SA et al. 2017. Solar-powered ventilation of African termite mounds. Journal of Experimental Biology 220: 3260-3269. doi: 10.1242/jeb.160895
238. Crystal Palace: In Mancuso S. 2017. The revolutionary genius of plants. A new understanding of plant intelligence and behavior. Atria Books.
239. Pavilions at the Bundesgartenschau horticultural show: Aouf RS. 2019. "University of Stuttgart creates biomimetic pavilions based on sea urchins and beetle wings", dezeen. https://www.dezeen.com/2019/05/08/university-stuttgart-biomimetic-pavilion-bundesgartenschau-horticultural-show/
240. Refrigeration management: Hawken P. 2017. Drawdown. The most comprehensive plan ever proposed to reverse global warming. Penguin Books.
241. Cacti: Tributsch H. 1985. How Life Learned to Live: Adaptation in Nature. MIT Press.

242. Cacti spines: Kiwoong K et al. 2017. Hydraulic Strategy of Cactus Trichome for Absorption and Storage of Water under Arid Environment. Frontiers in Plant Science 8:1777.
243. University of Arizona Health Sciences Education Building: Marani M. 2019. "This Arizona medical school blends into the desert with a folded copper façade", The Architect's Newspaper. https://archpaper.com/2019/03/bspb-phoenix-facade/#gallery-0-slide-0
244. Triodos Headquarters: https://triodosopreehorst.nl/nieuw-kantoor-van-triodos-bank-bereikt-het-hoogste-punt/
245. Madaster: https://www.madaster.com/nl/over-ons
246. Söderlund S & Newman P. 2015. Biophilic architecture: a review of the rationale and outcomes. AIMS Environmental Science 2: 950-969. DOI: 10.3934/environsci.2015.4.950
247. Children's Psychiatric Center: http://www.kpc-genk.be/kpc-bouwt
248. Weaved the inside and outside together: van Synghel K. 2015. "Een blik op de school van morgen", De Standaard. https://www.standaard.be/cnt/dmf20151005_01904233
249. Integrate a mini farm in its gardens: KPC Jaarverslag 2016. http://www.kpc-genk.be/sites/default/files/uploads/kpc_jaarverslag_2016_0.pdf
250. Renature cities: Shishegar N. 2014. The Impact of Green Areas on Mitigating Urban Heat Island Effect: A Review. The International Journal of Environmental Sustainability 9:119-130
251. Nature-based solutions: "Nature-Based Solutions", European Commission. https://ec.europa.eu/research/environment/index.cfm?pg=nbs
252. Benyus J. 1998. Biomimicry. Innovation inspired by nature. HarperCollins Publishers Inc.
253. Pioneering how chemistry can be done differently: In Harman J. 2013. The shark's paintbrush. Biomimicry and how nature is inspiring innovation. Nicholas Brealey Publishing.
254. Warner Babcock Institute for Green Chemistry. Company website. https://www.warnerbabcock.com/green-chemistry/about-green-chemistry/
255. To "ask" a molecule what their role should be by studying its fundamental structure: In Harman J. 2013. The shark's paintbrush. Biomimicry and how nature is inspiring innovation. Nicholas Brealey Publishing.
256. Volatile and particulate chemicals in households: Baron J. 2019. "Bringing Attention To Indoor Air Pollution", Forbes. https://www.forbes.com/sites/jessicabaron/2019/02/19/bringing-attention-to-indoor-air-pollution/#7cd5e1138b3c
257. Columbia Forest Products. Company website. https://www.columbiaforestproducts.com/product/purebond-classic-core/
258. A plant-based alternative that can achieve the same performance as the mussel glue: Asknature team 2016. "PureBond technology", Asknature. https://asknature.org/idea/purebond-technology/
259. Humans have made 8.3 billion tons of plastic: Cagle S. 2019. "Humans have made 8.3bn tons of plastic since 1950. This is the illustrated story of where it's gone", The guardian. https://www.theguardian.com/us-news/2019/jun/23/all-the-plastic-ever-made-study-comic?fbclid=IwAR3GyLU-8NOs49YRSKR8yllTYxyfXdlyYozlU2FWZKIBTV4xT-yJyOy6Ujo

NOTES

260. The petrochemical industry produces about 300 million tons of plastic per year: "Shrilk: Biodegradable Plastic", Wyss Institute for Biologically Inspired Engineering. https://wyss.harvard.edu/technology/chitosan-bioplastic/
261. Bioplastics accounted for only 0.2% of the global polymer market: Künkel et al. 2016. Polymers, Biodegradable. In: Ullmann's Encyclopedia of Industrial Chemistry. Weinheim: Wiley-VCH.
262. Shrilk: "Shrilk: Biodegradable Plastic", Wyss Institute for Biologically Inspired Engineering. https://wyss.harvard.edu/technology/chitosan-bioplastic/
263. Ready for licensing: "Inspired by Insect Cuticle, Wyss Researchers Develop Low-Cost Material with Exceptional Strength and Toughness", Wyss Institute for Biologically Inspired Engineering. https://wyss.harvard.edu/inspired-by-insect-cuticle-wyss-researchers-develop-low-cost-material-with-exceptional-strength-and-toughness/
264. Another bio-inspired chemical for next generation materials: GaleWyrick S. 2019. "Biomimetic products enable a circular economy", Synapse. https://synapse.bio/blog/biomimicrydesignjam-gmfxa
265. Newlight Technologies Inc. Company website. https://www.newlight.com
266. Abalone shell: In Pawlyn M. 2016. Biomimicry in architecture. Second edition. RIBA publishing.
267. Abalone shell: In Janine Benyus. 1997. Biomimicry. Innovation inspired by nature. HarperCollins Publishers Inc.
268. Abalone shell self-healing: Dastjerdi AK et al. 2013. The weak interfaces within tough natural composites: Experiments on three types of nacre. Journal of the Mechanical Behavior of Biomedical Materials 19, 50-60. https://doi.org/10.1016/j.jmbbm.2012.09.004
269. Weak interfaces make materials tough: Asknature team. 2017. "Weak interfaces make material tough", Asknature. https://asknature.org/strategy/weak-interfaces-make-material-tough/#.W3p9jS-B3-Y
270. Glass that is 200 times tougher: Mirkhalaf M et al. 2014. Overcoming the brittleness of glass through bio-inspiration and micro-architecture. Nature Communications 5: 3166.
271. 8.7 million different species that roam the Earth today: Sweetlove L. 2011. Number of species on Earth tagged at 8.7 million. Nature News. https://www.nature.com/news/2011/110823/full/news.2011.498.html
272. Far exceed the performance of their modern engineering analogs: Frølich S et al. 2017. Uncovering Nature's Design Strategies through Parametric Modeling, Multi-Material 3D Printing, and Mechanical Testing. Advanced Engineering Materials 19 (6): e201600848 https://onlinelibrary.wiley.com/doi/full/10.1002/adem.201600848
273. Waterproof floating rafts: Mlot NJ et al. 2012. Dynamics and shape of large fire ant rafts. Communicative & Integrative Biology 5(6): 590–597. http://doi.org/10.4161/cib.21421
274. http://uk.businessinsider.com/hurricane-harvey-fire-ant-colonies-form-floating-rafts-2017-8?r=US&IR=T
275. Solar powered ventilation: Ocko SA et al. 2017. Solar-powered ventilation of African termite mounds. Journal of Experimental Biology 220: 3260-3269; doi: 10.1242/jeb.160895

276. Collective decision-making processes: See for instance this movie clip where Cornell Professor Thomas Seeley explains how honeybees use swarm intelligence to select a new nest site: https://www.youtube.com/watch?v=sX8B135Ypq8&app=desktop
277. Simple rules: Oldroyd BP and Pratt SC. 2015. Comb Architecture of the Eusocial Bees Arises from Simple Rules Used During Cell Building. Advances in Insect Physiology 49: 101-121.
278. Quorum voting systems: Fewell J.H. 2015. Social Biomimicry: what do ants and bees tell us about organization in the natural world? J Bioecon 17: 207. https://doi.org/10.1007/s10818-015-9207-2
279. One of the greatest management challenges of our time: Brinker S. 2016. "Martec's Law: the greatest management challenge of the 21st century", Chiefmartec.com. https://chiefmartec.com/2016/11/martecs-law-great-management-challenge-21st-century/
280. In pyramid models: See Laloux F. 2016. Reinventing organisations. Nelson Parker.
281. Nayar V. 2010. Employee first, customer second. Harvard Business Review Press
282. He himself answered hundreds of questions a week: In Woolley Barker T. 2017. Teeming. How superorganisms work to build infinite wealth in a finite world (and your company can too). While Cloud Press.
283. After the global recession in 2009: In Woolley Barker T. 2017. Teeming. How superorganisms work to build infinite wealth in a finite world (and your company can too). While Cloud Press.
284. Holds a 50% market share for its product: In Laloux F. 2016. Reinventing Organizations: An Illustrated Invitation to Join the Conversation on Next-Stage Organizations. Nelson Parker.
285. Buurtzorg. Company website. https://www.buurtzorg.com
286. Buurtzorg had lower overhead costs than other home-care providers: For a recent overview see: https://www.commonwealthfund.org/publications/case-study/2015/may/home-care-self-governing-nursing-teams-netherlands-buurtzorg-model
287. Waggl. Company website. https://www.waggl.com/about-us/
288. It is a much more rewarding system that allows employees to flourish: In Laloux F. 2016. Reinventing Organizations: An Illustrated Invitation to Join the Conversation on Next-Stage Organizations. Nelson Parker.
289. Was intrigued by the thin line between chaos and order: Mead T. 2018. Bioinspiration in business and management. Innovation for sustainability. Business expert press.
290. VISA principles: Hock D. 2005. One from many. VISA and the Rise of Chaordic Organization. Berrett-Koehler Publishers, Inc.
291. From 1969 to 2004: Hock D. 2005. One from many. VISA and the Rise of Chaordic Organization. Berrett-Koehler Publishers, Inc
292. By 2019: VISA Inc. Annual Report 2019. https://s24.q4cdn.com/307498497/files/doc_downloads/Visa_Inc_Fiscal_2019_Annual_Report.pdf
293. Paradox and conflict are inherent characteristics of chaordic organization. Hock D. "The nature and creation of chaordic organizations", the Systems Thinker. https://thesystemsthinker.com/the-nature-and-creation-of-chaordic-organizations/
294. De kringwinkel Okazi: https://www.dekringwinkel.be/centrum/16/page/Zelfsturende-organisatie.html

NOTES

295. De kringwinkel Okazi: "Werkboek voor teamleiders", Springplank vzw.
296. Playa Viva: Mang P & Haggard B. 2016. Regenerative development and design. A framework for evolving sustainability. Wiley & Sons Inc

Changing the Logic of Value Creation

297. Charles Krone: See Mang P & Haggard B. 2016. Regenerative development and design. A framework for evolving sustainability. Wiley & Sons Inc.
298. Buffalo saliva: Liu, J et al. 2012. Plants can benefit from herbivory: stimulatory effects of sheep saliva on growth of Leymus chinensis. PloS one 7 (1): e29259. doi:10.1371/journal.pone.0029259; McNaughton SJ. 1976. Serengeti migratory wildebeest: Facilitation of energy flow by grazing. Science:191:92–94; Owen DF & Wiegert RG. 1976. Do consumers maximize plant fitness? Oikos: 27:488–492.
299. Prolongs the growing season of plants: Geremi C et al. 2019. Migrating bison engineer the green wave. PNAS 116 (51): 25707-25713. DOI: 10.1073/pnas.1913783116; see also Yong E. 2019. "What America Lost When It Lost the Bison", the Atlantic. https://www.theatlantic.com/science/archive/2019/11/how-bison-create-spring/602176/?fbclid=IwAR00qXIKpwtRZpQ87Bup3Jn1bgZMEn2pKilhtQCZhrH85IZ6Ts1rdANnEHo
300. "Never take all" principle in indigenous cultures: see Kimmerer RW. 2013. Braiding sweetgrass. Indigenous wisdom, scientific knowledge and the teachings of plants. Milkweed editions.
301. Unlocking the potential to become more and do more: See Sanford C. 2017. The Regenerative Business. Redesign work, cultivate human potential, achieve extraordinary outcomes. Nicholas Brealey Publishing.
302. Theory on regenerative development and design: Mang P & Haggard B. 2016. Regenerative development and design. A framework for evolving sustainability. Wiley.
303. Insights from transition science: see for instance Gorissen L et al. 2016. Transition Thinking and Business Model Innovation–Towards a Transformative Business Model and New Role for the Reuse Centers of Limburg, Belgium. Sustainability 8, 112. https://doi.org/10.3390/su8020112.
304. Regenerative practitioner: see Regenesis Institute for Regenerative Practice. https://regenesisgroup.com
305. If you have ever slept with a mosquito in your room then you know that no one is too small to matter: Reworked from a quote that has been attributed to the Dalai Lama.
306. Samenland: http://www.samenland.be/?lnts100
307. Ants: Kovář, P et al. 2013. Ants as Ecosystem Engineers in Natural Restoration of Human Made Habitats. Journal of Landscape Ecology 6 (1): 1805-4196. 10.2478/v10285-012-0061-9
308. Ecotone: "Ecotone, Edge effect", Encyclopaedia Britannica. https://www.britannica.com/science/ecotone#ref277755
309. Interface annual turnover: Marsman J. 2019. "Deze Interface verbindt alles en iedereen voor een duurzame toekomst – purpose professionals", MaatschappijWij. https://maatschapwij.nu/purpose-professionals/geanne-van-arkel-interface/

310. Mission Zero: "Our Sustainability Journey", Interface. https://www.interface.com/EU/en-GB/about/index/Mission-Zero-en_GB
311. Anderson R. 2009. Confessions of a radical industrialist. How interface proved that you can build a successful business without destroying the planet. Random house business books.
312. A walk in the forest: Mead T. 2018. Bioinspiration in business and management. Innovation for sustainability. Business Expert Press.
313. Representing more than 40% of their total sales: Mead T. 2018. Bioinspiration in business and management. Innovation for sustainability. Business Expert Press and https://www.interface.com/US/en-US/about/modular-system/Biomimicry
314. TacTiles : Tactiles Brochure. Interface. https://www.interface.com/EU/en-GB/about/modular-system/TacTiles-en_GB
315. Gecko: Shouse B. 2002. "How Geckos Stick on der Waals", Sciencemag. https://www.sciencemag.org/news/2002/08/how-geckos-stick-der-waals
316. Interface. Company website. https://www.interface.com/US/en-US/about/modular-system/Biomimicry
317. Mission Zero accomplishments: "Lessons for the future. The Interface guide to changing your business to change the world", Interface. 2018. http://interfaceinc.scene7.com/is/content/InterfaceInc/Interface/Americas/WebsiteContentAssets/Documents/Sustainability%2025yr%20Report/25yr%20Report%20Booklet%20Interface%5FMissionZeroCel.pdf
318. Shifted from eliminating negative environmental impact to creating a positive one: Marsman J. 2019. "Deze Interface verbindt alles en iedereen voor een duurzame toekomst – purpose professionals", MaatschappijWij. https://maatschapwij.nu/purpose-professionals/geanne-van-arkel-interface/
319. Climate take back: Interface. Company website. https://www.interface.com/US/en-US/campaign/climate-take-back/Climate-Take-Back
320. Four key areas: Interface. Company website. https://www.interface.com/US/en-US/campaign/climate-take-back/Four-Pillars-en_US
321. A factory that just like a forest: Mead T. 2018. Bioinspiration in business and management. Innovation for sustainability. Business Expert Press and https://www.interface.com/US/en-US/about/modular-system/Biomimicry
322. Net-Works. Company website. https://net-works.com/lang/nl/
323. Expanding into Africa: Mead T. 2018. Bioinspiration in business and management. Innovation for sustainability. Business Expert Press and https://www.interface.com/US/en-US/about/modular-system/Biomimicry
324. Net-Works. Company website. https://net-works.com
325. CircuitBac Green: Interface. Company website. https://www.interface.com/EU/en-GB/about/modular-system/circuitbac-green-en_GB
326. Effectively stores more carbon during its life cycle than it emits: Interface. Company website. https://www.interface.com/US/en-US/campaign/climate-take-back/carbon-storing-carpet-en_US

NOTES

327. The overview effect: Sample I. 2019. "Scientists attempt to recreate 'Overview effect' from Earth", The Guardian. https://www.theguardian.com/science/2019/dec/26/scientists-attempt-to-recreate-overview-effect-from-earth?fbclid=IwAR0mSX52vKmtRNVkt3bggY-mNbaQdoSS8w4giHvzHfZA9n_2ro1yiuStaIU
328. Regen Network Development, Inc. Company website. https://www.regen.network
329. Lotus Foods. Company website. https://www.lotusfoods.com
330. A company that is currently exploring Regen's Blockchain tech is Lotus Foods: Based on a personal interview with Christian Shearer, co-founder and CEO of Regen Network.

Conclusion

331. Becoming indigenous again: see for instance Bob Randall. 2009. "Another Way Of Seeing: We Don't Own the Land. The Land Owns Us", Films for Action. Global Oneness project. https://www.filmsforaction.org/watch/the-land-owns-us/
332. Values and principles rather than data: Two fields that explicitly start from principles to inspire innovation are permaculture (12 design principles) and biomimicry (Life's Principles). For permaculture a good reference is: Holmgren D. 2002. Permaculture: Principles and Pathways beyond Sustainability. Holmgren Design Services. For biomimicry, a good reference is: Baumeister D. 2014. Biomimicry resource handbook. A seed bank of best practices. Biomimicry3.8.
333. Principles are like fractals: one of the insights shared through the "Regenerative Practitioner Series" organized by Regenesis Institute for Regenerative Practice. https://regenerat.es/the-regenerative-practitioner-series/

Photograph Credits

A huge thank you to all photographers who capture the beauty of nature on camera and for sharing these pictures with the general public.

xii	African wild dogs by Cameron Oxley on Unsplash	68	Flock of birds by Ray Hennessy on Unsplash
xiv	Great bittern by Raf Gorissen	71	Hiking in nature by Raf Gorissen
xx	Hallerbos by Raf Gorissen	74	Water by Raf Gorissen
9	Mountain goat by Raf Gorissen	77	Reef shark by Ali Abdul Rahman on Unsplash
10	Turaco by Leen Gorissen	82	Sea Anemone closeup by NOAA on Unsplash
13	Leaf by Clay Banks on Unsplash	87	Amazon rainforest by David Geere on Unsplash
16	Tree by Raf Gorissen	92	Sea turtle by David Troeger on Unsplash
25	Wolf by ML on Unsplash	100	Mussles by Peter Secan on Unsplash
30	Octopus by Vlad Tchompalov on Unsplash	107	Bee by Raf Gorissen
34	Whales by Guille Pozzi on Unsplash	114	Falcon by Raf Gorissen
37	Mushroom by Raf Gorissen	117	Tree by Raf Gorissen
46	Kingfisher by Raf Gorissen	124	Ladybug by Raf Gorissen
54	Ants by Matheus Queiroz on Unsplash	133	Gecko by Patrick Hendry on Unsplash
57	Feathers closeup by David Clode on Unsplash	136	Landscape by Nina Luong on Unsplash
58	Arctic fox by Bryan Walker on Unsplash	140	Nature trail by Raf Gorissen
61	Tree frog by Raf Gorissen	144	Mandarin duck by Raf Gorissen
62	Abalone shell by Raf Gorissen	170	Canyon by Raf Gorissen
65	Sun bear by Raf Gorissen		

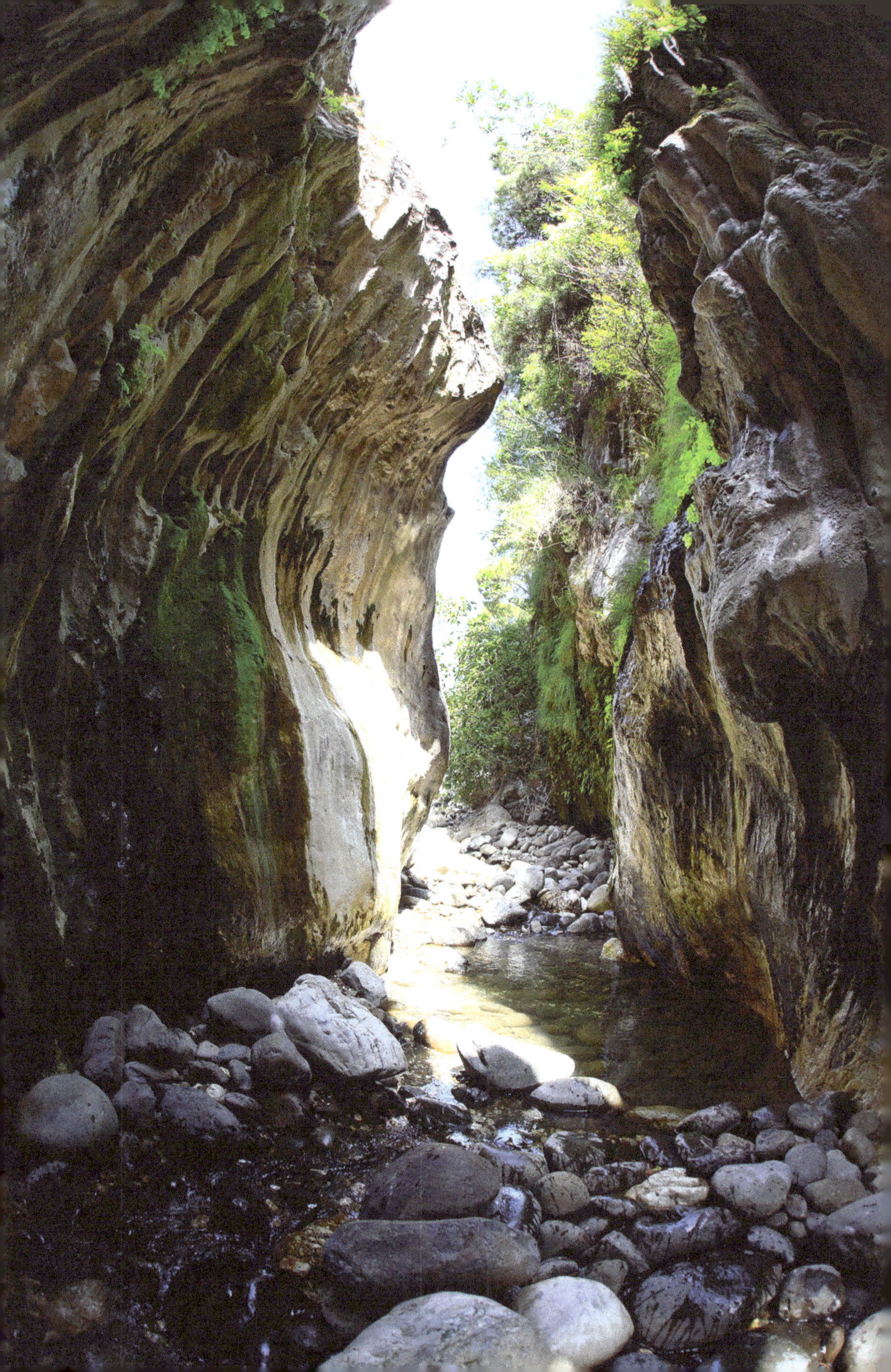

Acknowledgements

The work presented in this book builds on the work, understanding and wisdom of many great thinkers, curious minds and explorative souls that inspired me. To name them all is nearly impossible! There are, however, a few that had a profound impact on my thinking for which I am incredibly grateful. They are: Pamela Mang and Ben Haggard for helping me gain a deeper understanding of regenerative development, for showing me how it is brought into practice and for help with the development of the nature of innovation framework; Dayna Baumeister, Janine Benyus and the biomimics at Biomimicry3.8 and the Biomimicry Institute for the insightful immersion workshops, the generation of the Life's Principles Design tool, the asknature database and all the pioneering work that they do; Toby Herzlich for sharing and showing the leadership dimension of this work; Tamsin Woolley-Barker for her deep dive into the organizational relevance of how life works, her quirky humor and contagious enthusiasm, Saskia van den Muijsenberg for our fun collaborations in bringing biomimicry and regenerative thinking into the world, Taco Blom for his action-research inspired approach to permaculture and for being such a gifted student and master in bio-inspired landscape design; Professors Robin Wall Kimmerer and David George Haskell for their beautiful stories on nature, indigenous wisdom and science; David Attenborough and the BBC film crews for showing us the beauty of the natural world and the devasting impacts of current Industrial Intelligence; Dee Hock from VISA for his inquisitive mind and enormously innovative and courageous business approach; Jay Harman from Pax Scientific and Paul Stamets from Fungi Perfecti for being visionaries and role models for a new kind of entrepreneurship; Michael Pawlin for showing how nature can inspire a new course for architecture and Giles Hutchins and Laura Storm for exploring what regenerative leadership entails.

Not to forget the many biologists that have dedicated their life's work to understanding the way life works and all colleagues, friends and entrepreneurs that are bringing nature-inspired innovation into the world. I am deeply grateful for the richness you all bring to my life.

Special thanks to PJ Perquy, Hans Van Dyck, Willem Van Aelten and Peter Schollaert for advice on earlier versions of the book, to Janna Hockenjos for the line editing and Emily Witthohn for the proofreading. Also, a big thank you to my parents for ignoring what was at the time a well-meant advice of one of my schoolteachers, who told them that letting me study biology was the biggest mistake of their lives. I am still so very grateful that you believed in my potential and were not blinded by expert opinions or my grades. Kuddos to my brother, who captures nature's beauty so eloquently in photographs—some of which are included in this book—and who is the best brother one could wish for. I am very grateful for having a learning buddy in Yeshua Adonai who continuously challenges and elevates my thinking and who is the walking proof of the transformational power that resides inside of us. I learned so much through our shared journey!

To all my friends, old and new: thank you for being there, for our shared passion for nature and for keeping the fire alive! Infinite thanks to my partner Robby Oblonsek for his ongoing support, for the many lively dialogues during our nature walks, for advice on earlier versions of the book, and most of all, for being such a fun and beautiful human being. Couldn't have done this without you! And finally, a tremendous thank you to nature for the miracle of life, the countless gifts and epiphanies she keeps sharing and for being such a powerful source of health, wellbeing and inspiration. I hope humanity will learn to come home soon.

Glossary

Abiotic: not associated with or derived from living organisms

Adaptation: process by which a species becomes fitted to its environment

Biodiversity: the diversity of life including the variety of living organisms, the genetic diversity among them, the communities and ecosystems

Biome: a major ecological community of organisms adapted to a particular climatic or environmental condition on a large geographic area in which they occur. For instance, terrestrial biomes include tundra, grasslands, savannas, deserts, tropical forests, etc.

Biotic: associated with or derived from living organisms

Co-evolution: a process that occurs when two or more species reciprocally affect each other's evolution

Context: the setting and conditions in which something exists

Degenerative: tending to or characterized by action which leads to decline and deterioration

Design: the total of all adaptations that allows an organism to appropriately respond to the dynamics of change

Ecosystem: a community of organisms embedded in their physical environment

Ecosystem services: benefits provided by natural ecosystems on which life depends

Ecosystem engineer: organisms that play a key role in modifying, maintaining and/or creating habitat

Emulate: to mimic deep principles or patterns instead of copying them

Evolution: the cumulative genetic process in a population of organisms from generation to generation

Genotype: the genetic makeup of an individual

Green chemistry: the way life does chemistry which is inherently safe to life

Habitat: the natural environment or place where an organism, population or species lives

Keystone species: an organism that is critical for the overall structure and function of an ecosystem because they influence the survival of the other species in the system. It can be a huge predator or an unassuming plant, but without them the ecosystem may not survive

Life: nature, all things living

Life-enhancing: that which supports and promotes life

Life-friendly: that which is friendly to life in terms of being non-toxic, non-hazardous and non-degenerative

Life's principles: a set of patterns exhibited by life that contributes to life's ability to survive and thrive

Life's principles design lessons from nature: a design tool developed by a team of biologists from Biomimicry3.8 that summarizes the deep principles for survival and thrivability found in nature to guide human innovation processes

Metabolize: the process of chemical reactions that take place within each cell of a living organism and that provide energy for vital processes and for synthesizing new organic material

Natural: conforming to the order, laws, or actual facts, of nature

Nature: life, all things living including humans

GLOSSARY

Natural intelligence: the intelligence deeply embedded in all life forms that stood the test of time; the success factors that allowed life to endure despite major upheaval and millions of years of change and disruption

Natural selection: the process by which only the organisms best adapted to their environment succeed

Phenotype: the physical or chemical expression of an organism's genes

Regenerate: a process of renewal that leads to a higher order of health, wealth, vitality and viability

Regenerative: tending to or characterized by action which leads to a better, higher or more worthy state than the existing one